Modern Game Testing

Learn how to test games like a pro, optimize testing effort, and skyrocket your QA career

Nikolina Finska

BIRMINGHAM—MUMBAI

Modern Game Testing

Group Product Manager: Rohit Rajkumar

Publishing Product Manager: Vaideeshwari Muralikrishnan

Senior Content Development Editor: Feza Shaikh

Technical Editor: Joseph Aloocaran

Copy Editor: Safis Editing

Project Coordinator: Aishwarya Mohan

Proofreader: Safis Editing

Indexer: Pratik Shirodkar

Production Designer: Vijay Kamble

Marketing Coordinator: Anamika Singh, Namita Velgekar, and Nivedita Pandey

First published: July 2023

Production reference: 1220623

Published by Packt Publishing Ltd.

Livery Place

35 Livery Street

Birmingham

B3 2PB, UK.

ISBN 978-1-80324-440-2

www.packtpub.com

Contributors

About the author

Nikolina Finska is a gaming industry veteran and QA guru, with over 10 years of expertise in the game sector and another 10 in the software industry. She was nominated for the Tester of the Year award by the Finnish Testing Association for her contributions to QA methods.

Nikolina worked on over 20 games and oversaw QA on various *Angry Birds* franchise games. She has done practically every type of QA in the past, from localization to live OPS, on a variety of platforms, including massive databases, the web, and every imaginable gaming platform. Nikolina is a popular guest lecturer on QA and games production at Finnish universities. Besides QA, Nikolina teaches game production, entrepreneurship, and general leadership.

I want to thank my spouse, Jorma, for his support, advice, and encouragement while writing this book. Big thanks go to my late dogs, Kara and Tron, who were always by my side and made long writing hours easier to bear.

About the reviewer

Juha Pomppu is a process and software quality professional with so many hats – QA lead, auditor, trainer, coach, mentor, community builder, conference manager, and team leader.

He started his IT life with home computers, coding low-level demos with the MOS 6510 and Motorola 680x0 assembly languages. He doesn't code anymore, but this hobby gave him a deep understanding of how computers work.

Today, his professional passion is in quality management systems, modern software development processes, and software quality assurance – and, of course, people and teams, because together we can create systems with high quality.

Table of Contents

3

A Deeper Look – Types of Testing in Games   37

4

Deeper Look – Testing on Various Gaming Platforms – Mobile, PC, and Console   55

5

It Must Be Hardware: Testing Hardware in Modern Game QA   69

Part 2: Test Strategy and Execution

6

Friend or Foe – Test Cases   79

7

It Works on My Machine: Bug Flow   91

8

I Thought I Fixed That: How to Write Efficient Bug Reports   105

12

Beyond Testing – Introduction to Test Management   171

13

There Are No BUGS Without U – QA and the Game Team   185

Preface

It is surprising how difficult it is to find relevant information about how modern game testing works. While we can find lots of information about how to test more traditional, premium games, somehow, more detailed guidelines into modern games QA, especially on mobile and in live ops, are almost impossible to find. My goal in writing this book was to give you a deep insight not only into how modern games are tested today, but also into how to work efficiently with agile methodologies, flat team organization, and the unique challenges of free-to-play games. We will go into great detail about the best QA practices that will ensure your games are high quality, on budget, and released on time. While we will briefly discuss automation testing, please note that the focus of this book is primarily on manual testing. *Modern Games Testing* was written with the intent to provide plenty of practical examples, rooted in personal experience, helping you get an inside look at the fascinating world of games QA.

Who this book is for

This book is aimed primarily at game testers but also game producers, game developers, testing managers, and other QA professionals who want to learn more about modern approaches to game QA and use them to build more efficient and cost-effective QA teams and products. It is desirable that you have prior professional testing experience, either in software or games testing, and/or experience working in the gaming industry. Basic familiarity with agile working practices such as scrum is needed to fully understand all concepts explained in the book. A basic understanding of the gaming industry ecosystem will help you understand the covered topics in more depth.

What this book covers

Chapter 1, *Setting the Stage – Introduction to QA for Modern Games*, discusses the importance of QA and the main differences between games and software QA.

Chapter 2, *All Engines Go – The Basics of Game QA*, examines what we test in games and the main challenges of games QA.

Chapter 3, *A Deeper Look – Types of Testing in Games*, explores the different types of testing in games and how to execute them.

Chapter 4, *Deeper Look – Testing on Various Gaming Platforms – Mobile, PC, and Console*, delves into the specifics of QA on different gaming platforms.

Chapter 5, It Must Be Hardware: Testing Hardware in Modern Games QA, covers the importance of hardware and how to create optimal test sets.

Chapter 6, Friend or Foe – Test Cases, discusses how to write great test cases and their alternatives.

Chapter 7, It Works on My Machine: Bug Flow, explores how to set up efficient bug flow and statuses.

Chapter 8, I Thought I Fixed That: How to Write Efficient Bug Reports, examines in detail how to write great bug reports.

Chapter 9, It Works, but It Hasn't Been Tested: Testing Approach, delves into agile methodology and its approach to testing.

Chapter 10, Eat, Sleep, Test, Repeat: Test Methodology, covers the most commonly used QA methodologies with practical examples.

Chapter 11, Are You on the Right Version? Live Ops and QA, examines the details of how QA works in live ops.

Chapter 12, Beyond Testing – Introduction to Test Management, explores in detail how to make a test plan and efficient testing estimation.

Chapter 13, There Are No BUGS without U – QA and the Game Team, gets you familiar with a career in QA and explores the future of QA.

To get the most out of this book

Please get yourself familiar with the basics of agile methodology. Familiarity with games business models and genres will help you understand the material in more depth.

Download the color images

We also provide a PDF file that has color images of the screenshots and diagrams used in this book. You can download it here: `https://packt.link/LG6tq`.

Conventions used

`Code in text`: Indicates code words in text, database table names, folder names, filenames, file extensions, pathnames, dummy URLs, user input, and Twitter handles.

There are a number of text conventions used throughout this book.

Bold: Indicates a new term, an important word, or words that you see on screen. For instance, words in menus or dialog boxes appear in **bold**. Here is an example: "We can also see that the bug has a **Repro rate** value of 10/10. That affected the **Priority** value, which is set to **Highest**.".

> **Tips or important notes**
> Appear like this.

Get in touch

Feedback from our readers is always welcome.

General feedback: If you have questions about any aspect of this book, email us at `customercare@packtpub.com` and mention the book title in the subject of your message.

Errata: Although we have taken every care to ensure the accuracy of our content, mistakes do happen. If you have found a mistake in this book, we would be grateful if you would report this to us. Please visit `www.packtpub.com/support/errata` and fill in the form.

Piracy: If you come across any illegal copies of our works in any form on the internet, we would be grateful if you would provide us with the location address or website name. Please contact us at `copyright@packt.com` with a link to the material.

If you are interested in becoming an author: If there is a topic that you have expertise in and you are interested in either writing or contributing to a book, please visit `authors.packtpub.com`.

Share Your Thoughts

Once you've read *Modern Game Testing*, we'd love to hear your thoughts! Scan the QR code below to go straight to the Amazon review page for this book and share your feedback.

`https://packt.link/r/1803244402`

Your review is important to us and the tech community and will help us make sure we're delivering excellent quality content.

Download a free PDF copy of this book

Thanks for purchasing this book!

Do you like to read on the go but are unable to carry your print books everywhere?

Is your eBook purchase not compatible with the device of your choice?

Don't worry, now with every Packt book you get a DRM-free PDF version of that book at no cost.

Read anywhere, any place, on any device. Search, copy, and paste code from your favorite technical books directly into your application.

The perks don't stop there, you can get exclusive access to discounts, newsletters, and great free content in your inbox daily

Follow these simple steps to get the benefits:

1. Scan the QR code or visit the link below

https://packt.link/free-ebook/9781803244402

2. Submit your proof of purchase

3. That's it! We'll send your free PDF and other benefits to your email directly

Part 1:
Game Testing Foundation

In this part of the book, we will get familiar with the basics of games QA, including the different types of testing, working with gaming platforms, and how to utilize hardware in game testing.

This part has the following chapters:

- Chapter 1, *Setting the Stage – Introduction to QA for Modern Games*
- Chapter 2, *All Engines Go – The Basics of Game QA*
- Chapter 3, *A Deeper Look – Types of Testing in Games*
- Chapter 4, *Deeper Look – Testing on Various Gaming Platforms – Mobile, PC, and Console*
- Chapter 5, *It Must Be Hardware: Testing Hardware in Modern Games QA*

1

Setting the Stage – Introduction to QA for Modern Games

At its core, **quality assurance (QA)** in game development isn't much different from QA in other types of software. However, there are some QA testing aspects that are specific to games.

But, let's first start by introducing *how* QA is done in modern games, *when*, and *by whom*? How is it organized in this extremely fast-paced industry? These are some of the questions we are going to answer in this chapter.

In this chapter, we will first discover the main differences between the testing of games and the testing of other types of software. Then, the reader will learn more about the importance of QA. Finally, we will go through a couple of real-world scenarios that showcase what can happen when testing goes wrong in the gaming industry.

By the end of this chapter, you will have good insights into the basics of game QA and its importance.

In this chapter, we will cover the following topics:

- Understanding the evolution of modern game testing
- Exploring the differences between software and game testing
- Why is QA important for games, especially within the agile process?
- When and how should QA testing for games be performed?

Understanding the evolution of modern game testing

Today, QA is one of the key components of any modern software development process. It is unimaginable to release software to users without testing it first. Users now have so many choices with regard to apps, games, and digital tools, and if you release software that does not work properly or has usability issues, you risk losing many of your users. Even worse, you risk your reputation as a developer if players discover something in your game that doesn't work and publish this information online on game forums and social media.

Therefore, QA is an important component of the development process.

QA and testing are *interchangeable* terms. Throughout history, humans have striven to provide quality of execution in their work – from the ancient pyramids through medieval fortresses to modern software. At its core, modern QA has its roots in medieval professional guilds, such as those for tailors, merchants, and smiths. To ensure that the quality of their products met the required quality standards, guilds implemented strict peer control that in many ways is similar to testing today. They set quality standards that guild members had to meet in order to become part of and stay in the guild. These parameters ensured that guild members everywhere provided a high level of service and in return, drove more business to them.

Modern testing is not too far from that: we test software to ensure that it meets the required quality standards and includes all implemented and approved features. Of course, these days, we have replaced the quality standards set by guilds with ones set by product owners and end users.

Modern game testing has developed along with the growth of the gaming industry. Games became widely popular in the 1980s, and they kept on evolving to various new platforms: first consoles, then home PCs, and, in the 21st century, mobile and other handheld devices. It doesn't look like the industry is going to slow down anytime soon either. The gaming industry in 2021 was globally worth more than 180 billion USD, more than the music, TV, and film industries put together (`https://www.thc-pod.com/episode/the-gaming-industry-is-now-bigger-than-movies-and-music-combined`). The biggest money makers are mobile and **free-to-play** (**F2P**) games, and the top earners among them bring in over a billion USD per year (`https://newzoo.com/key-numbers;https://www.statista.com/statistics/263988/top-grossing-mobile-ios-gaming-apps-ranked-by-daily-revenue/`).

Games are a big business today and quality is more important than ever. With that said, there are no common standards for game QA across the industry. Every gaming studio is different and even within the same company, different teams follow different QA practices. The differences are even more significant when testing for different gaming platforms – while testing on consoles hasn't changed too much since the beginning of game development, mobile game testing is embracing the latest trends in QA to be able to support more fast-paced development.

The terminology used in game testing is not unified (a particular term may mean completely different things in different studios), and even QA jobs might have different levels of responsibilities or completely different job descriptions from studio to studio. Taking into account all those differences, certain things remain the same. Testers generally spend months testing games repeatedly, using different approaches and shifting focus to different parts and characteristics of the game.

What would we consider to be QA today? There are many different definitions out there, but at its core, game QA is a set of testing activities, including test execution, exploration, and verification, that aims to ensure that games meet design specifications, technical quality, platform regulations, and player expectations. As we can see just from the definition, QA in gaming entails a lot of responsibilities and requires a whole range of skills. A **game tester** is a person who must fully understand the product's vision, is familiar with technical risks and dependencies, can juggle conflicting priorities, knows the game better than anybody, and represents the players' interests.

Now that you have a basic understanding of the prerequisites and best practices of QA for games, let us try and understand what makes game QA different from normal software testing. Knowledge of these differences, especially in terms of the unique aspects we test for in game development, is essential for us to master QA testing and meet the end user's expectations within the gaming industry.

Exploring the differences between software and game testing

Regardless of whether our software is used in medical devices, spaceships, or the games we play, the testing methodology, if not the same, is remarkably similar. But, even if testing medical software might *seem* more demanding, it doesn't mean that testing games is going to be any easier. It's challenging to adequately perform QA on time and within budget. Usually, if development encounters problems and misses milestones, QA testing, which generally occurs toward the end of the development cycle, will also be postponed. Unfortunately, software release dates are rarely moved forward. Hence, the more delayed development is, the shorter the time span allowed for QA checks. However, the scope for testing stays the same or even grows wider. That's why the profession of game testing is somewhat notorious for its long working hours and high stress levels.

As per their definition, games also comprise software, just like the app you use on your phone to track your steps, the software that assists pilots to fly planes more efficiently, and even the software you use to read this book! All these digital products have their differences – in terms of complexity, the programming language they use, the target audience, user experience, and so on. However, they also have lots of similarities.

Software that is used in airplanes, medical devices, and military applications is considered **life-critical**. That means that if such software fails for any reason, it can lead to the loss of human life. When we compare this to game software, the worst consequences of bugs in game systems are a loss of progress or, in the case of F2P games, a loss of money. While unpleasant for users, failures in game software are much less impactful.

Looking at the difference through the lens of QA, life-critical software testing is usually more rigid, takes longer, and has strict, well-defined requirements. When we talk about non-life-critical software, testing practices will very much depend on the internal company processes and software development methodology in use. Although some aspects of software testing are company- or industry-specific, the following aspects are common:

- Stability
- Scalability
- Functionality of features
- **User interface** (**UI**) look and function
- User flow and **usability** (**UX**)
- Performance under stress
- First-time user experience (FTUE)
- Localization

When testing games, in addition to the aforementioned aspects, we also test for certain specific aspects that are generally not tested in any other category of software development. These include the following:

- Fun factor
- **Artificial intelligence** (**AI**) in games
- Game physics
- Evaluation of game rules
- Level progression
- Game difficulty balancing
- Multiplayer functions
- Playthrough
- Realism
- Consistency
- Game levels
- Achievements
- Sound and music
- Voice-overs

We can see from the preceding list that although there are many crossover areas in testing, gaming software has its own specific requirements that require mastering. In this book, we will cover in detail the methodologies and practices that will help you do that.

Now that you know what makes game QA unique, let us understand why testing these unique factors is necessary to launch and maintain a successful game in the market.

Why is QA important for games, especially within the agile process?

By now, it's obvious that QA is an *essential* part of ensuring the quality of a product. But, just *how* important is it? What will happen if QA is not done, or if it hasn't been done well? There are quite a few examples of software failures that have had a big impact on end users and caused significant damage and even loss of human life.

One of the more well-known examples is the case of Stanislav Petrov, an air defense officer in the USSR, who potentially managed to avert a third world war. On September 26, 1983, while on duty, Officer Petrov received a notification from the nuclear early warning system, showing that the US had launched its nuclear missiles, attacking the USSR. Officer Petrov realized in time that the system was malfunctioning and that the alarm was false.

Gaming examples are less scary, but one that really showcases how bad game bugs can get is the case of the *World of Warcraft Hakkar* bug. The final boss in the *Zul'Gurub* raid, the *Blood God Hakkar*, was designed to spray *Corrupted Blood* when killed on enemies close to him, potentially killing weaker heroes. Unfortunately, that caused pets in the game to become *poisoned* and they quickly managed to spread the *plague* and *kill* thousands of players. Of course, all those deaths were digital and *Blizzard*, the game's developer, reacted fast and released a patch that revived most of the slain characters. To learn more about the Hakkar bug and the impact it had on the game and the players, see `https://en.wikipedia.org/wiki/Corrupted_Blood_incident`.

From these couple of examples, we can already see how important role QA plays in software testing. Without skilled, efficient, and timely QA, we can lose users, revenue, and even human lives. But modern QA is important for other reasons as well. With the rise of the **free-to-play (F2P)** business model and the huge importance of **live operations (live ops)**, game development had to change its methodology to accommodate fast-paced, iterative development. Most of the game development industry has now switched from the waterfall model to *agile methodology*.

For QA testers in gaming, that was a significant change in terms of when and how testing was executed. Instead of being done at the end of the development, QA now plays a more active part in development teams, with testers representing the players' perspective and working closely with designers and coders as part of the team. QA testers verify issues that are highlighted by the player support team, do early tests of new features, and learn about technical risks from developers. From being purely quality gatekeepers and critics, in modern game development, QA testers are part of a team that has an accurate understanding of how users will really interact with the game.

While having QA functions embedded into the team will not replace proper playtests, it does give developers early insights into how a player will perceive certain features or changes in the game. This can make product development more efficient and help avoid making expensive design and balancing mistakes that can cause lots of harm to the end product. And while not all agile teams will have embedded QA, the ones that do usually make sure that they take full advantage of the intimate player knowledge that the QA specialists hold, as well as their deep insight into game strengths and weaknesses. This reliance on QA specialists or teams not only makes QA important to prevent games going live with bugs such as *Hakkar* but also helps make for more fun, engaging, and at the end of the day, more profitable games.

When and how should QA testing for games be performed?

There are lots of discussions about *when QA is executed*. Traditionally, QA was always done toward the end of development. This was especially true when using a *waterfall system*. Following the waterfall development rules, QA testing is performed only after development has concluded and the finished software is handed over to the testing team. The following figure shows how the waterfall model follows specific steps in a particular order:

Figure 1.1 – Waterfall system

In a waterfall system, testing is done only when development is finalized. However, with the rise of agile methodology, gaming studios have gradually started to adopt this method of development as well. Furthermore, with the explosion of mobile gaming and F2P games, it became obvious that agile development was necessary for efficient live ops. This required that we change the way we test games. Handing the product to the testing team when *"done"* became impossible, because modern F2P games never end, and hence development is never finished.

When should QA for games be performed?

Game development has evolved into an iterative model, where we develop smaller chunks of code that are tested as they are developed. As we can see in the following figure, agile development is iterative – small, usable pieces of code are frequently released and tested:

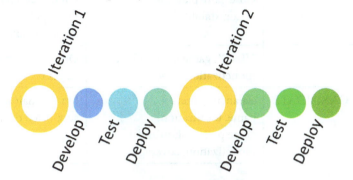

Figure 1.2 – Iterative development

The aim of agile methodology is to develop **minimum viable features** that can be continuously improved in future iterations.

There are several unique aspects of testing in an agile environment:

- Testing is continuous: a QA tester still holds the position of *gatekeeper* and has the responsibility of validating whether a feature or the whole build is of good-enough-quality to be released to the target audience. However, besides that, QA testers also test early features, validate usability flow, develop test cases based on use case scenarios, and perform many other tasks. If your game is live, the QA team will additionally handle live testing and verification of bugs coming from player support, forums, and your game's social media channels.

- To be able to support continuous testing, QA is part of the agile team, rather than a separate unit. It is impossible to get full insight into agile development if QA is not part of the team. In modern game development, we still often use outsourced testers for the *QA-heavy* stages: first-time releases, major updates, or significant changes such as the introduction of multiplayer. However, very often we have situations where we have one full-time QA team member and a scalable external QA partner.

- Testers must adapt their approach to testing based on the development stage and feature readiness. It doesn't help to report minor bugs while testing the first version of a major feature. This can be particularly challenging for QA testers. These professionals need to have experience, skills, and great collaboration with the rest of the team to fully understand the product priorities and focus their testing effort on the right thing at the right time. In the following table, you can find a high-level overview of what the testing focus should be in each stage of game development.

MILESTONE	TESTING FOCUS	HOW TO TEST
PRE-PRODUCTION	User stories, scalability, game design flow	Document reviews, decision tables
ALPHA	Core gameplay, fun factor, stability	On the selected principal device, emulators
BETA	UI, UX, game flow, FTUE, monetization, coverage	On a wide range of target devices
RELEASE CANDIDATE	Balancing, meta game, localization, game polish, shop and monetization, coverage	On the main supported devices

Table 1.1 – Testing focus per development phase

- Testers represent the player in the team. It's their job not only to test the code, but also to collaborate in the development process, putting themselves in the players' shoes. This approach requires testers to have an in-depth understanding of the target audience, its preferences, its likes and dislikes, and a solid knowledge of competitors' games. Most of the time, the QA specialist closely collaborates and communicates with player support; testers can consequently gain precious insights into players' gaming patterns, game preferences, and the things they find most frustrating.

Based on everything we have discussed up to here, we can freely conclude that optimally, QA testing should start as soon as we start development. Many studios still hold on to old ways of working and test only at the end of the development cycle, as it's perceived to be cheaper. This type of testing is usually very stressful as there is rarely enough time to ensure adequate testing coverage and many serious bugs can easily creep into the live game. By having QA performed in a more iterative way, we decrease that risk. This approach is potentially much cheaper than having to fix the damage of a failed product launch.

By now, we have a better understanding of when games should be tested. But, how should the testing be undertaken?

How should QA testing for games be performed?

When we start thinking about testing, it's important to have some kind of understanding of what the desired outcome of our test is. That will allow us to compare the actual result of the test with the desired outcome. For some tests, this might be obvious – for example, the test case *open settings and mute the sound* has the obvious desired outcome that the game is muted.

For other scenarios, however, it's not so simple. If we investigate a test case such as *check whether game loads*, it might seem deceivingly obvious: of course, the game should load! But, how long should the loading process take? Should there be any sort of loading indicator? Will the audio be on or off while loading? As we can see, it's not necessarily that simple to determine what the desired outcome is. This test case is something my team and I had to experience ourselves to find the answer to. It took our team almost a week, while also researching competitors, to finally agree on what the expected outcome of that particular test case should be. The desired outcome of a test case is also sometimes called the **test oracle**.

More often than not, we also use **test cases** for testing. Even if they are not a mandatory part of game testing, they are very frequently used across various gaming studios. We will study test cases in depth later in the book, but for now, it's sufficient to become familiar with their general definition. Test cases are written instructions that list specific steps for how testing should be performed.

Besides test cases, testers can execute tests using different types of documentation. Many teams create their own product **test plans**, which are detailed, carefully planned documents describing all aspects of testing that will be undertaken for a specific game. Test plans usually don't contain test cases themselves, but they specify test case tools, who created them, how, when, and based on what. The plan might also contain links to the test case repository.

If your team has fully embraced agile development practices, you might also use **test charters**. Test charters are less formal documents compared to test cases. They generally contain information about what the testing goal is and some ideas and approaches regarding how to reach it.

Lastly, let's talk about who is doing the testing. By now, you have probably realized that we are using *tester* and *QA specialist/tester* as interchangeable terms. There are really no differences between the two, but, as we don't have a unified industry terminology, there might be some differences between the two, depending on how a particular studio interprets testing tasks. However, besides professional QA personnel, there are other people who perform testing as well:

- Developers
- Members of your development team apart from developers (designers, artists, etc.)
- The marketing team
- Product managers
- Players

It's part of the developer's job to do testing as well, although they use a very different methodology from testers. Developer testing focuses on what is called *white-box testing*. This implies testing mostly focused on unit tests and code reviews. While these tests are exceptionally useful, they have slightly different purposes compared to the tests performed by QA teams.

In modern agile teams, most of the team performs at least some type of testing. Designers review the logic and validity of their designs. Artists check how their work looks and feels in the game. UX designers review any changes in the user flow. The producer will have an overall look at all the components, trying to assess the level of completion and early build quality. All of these help the QA team to get a better picture of where the specific risks are and focus their efforts in the right place at the right time.

When we talk about marketing, we primarily talk about player support. It is wise to keep the player support team informed well in advance about any game developments and provide them with design documents and access to early builds. That will help them understand the game better and address customer comments and complaints properly. As they are the people spending the most time with the players, very often, you get valuable feedback from those early play sessions.

Lastly, players themselves are also testers, whether we like it or not. They will play the game in all the possible ways they see fit and report bugs through player support, forums, or social media. You might ask, if they test it themselves, why would we bother paying specialists to do it? This is because, usually, when a player notices bugs in the game, it's already too late, especially if the bug is a serious one. We might already have lost part of our players or a significant amount of revenue.

However, there are ways of utilizing players' testing in a more formal way. We do that through **beta testing** or playtests. In these types of tests, we allow smaller, often specifically selected groups of players to play early builds of the game. The primary goal of these tests is to get an idea of how players will receive the game and their likes and dislikes, but they also very often yield useful bugs.

Summary

In this chapter, we learned about some of the basics of modern game testing. This will help you to easily transition into modern, fast-paced game teams and adapt more quickly to agile teams. You also learned about the main differences between testing software and games, which lays the foundation for what comes next: practical QA steps and the challenges that come with it.

2

All Engines Go – The Basics of Game QA

In this chapter, we are going to dive deep into the core of game QA and examine in detail the elements that should be tested in games. We will learn how QA works in practice and what the main challenges of game QA are. At the end, we will touch upon modern agile practices and how game QA fits within these practices.

The goal of this chapter is to provide you with practical information on modern game testing that will allow you and your team to optimize their efforts and focus on the most important elements. You will also learn more about how game QA functions within the modern agile development framework.

By the end of this chapter, you will have a good understanding of the following:

- What is tested in games?
- What is the most important element to test?
- How to prioritize in QA
- The basics of QA in practice
- Where QA fits in the modern agile methodology

What is tested in games?

By now, we already know that there are lots of similarities between general software and games. In practice, this means that games must go through the same vigorous testing as any other software. We have also established that games have their own unique characteristics. Looking at games as a whole, they lie at the intersection of technology, art, and business. This makes them a unique type of software that requires us to consider a broader picture when talking about testing games.

The gaming industry is notorious for its lack of documentation, and very often testers need to figure out themselves what to test and how. It's advisable to get any *design documents* or use cases to help you determine the scope of testing and the expected results. In general terms, we are testing the following:

- **Stability**
- **First-time user experience** (FTUE)
- **Core game loops**
- **Level progression**
- **Game physics** (if the game has physics)
- **Game logic**
- **AI behavior**
- **Usability flow** (UX)

We will go through each of these aspects in the following subsections.

Stability

Stability is the core element of any application and forms the foundation for all other QA efforts.

So, the primary aspect that we want to test in a game is its stability, which is an indicator of whether the following have been achieved:

- The game can be installed on a target platform
- The game's installation process is not too long
- The game runs on the target platform
- The game runs on multiple versions of an operating system
- The game runs at appropriate framerate and doesn't have delays or glitches
- The game is stable and doesn't crash
- The game doesn't freeze
- The game doesn't kick a player out of the game

As we can see from this list, there are quite a few aspects of stability that we need to consider. Another thing we need to pay attention to is that some of these requirements are *ambiguous*. When we say *the installation process is not too long*, what does that mean? Is there a standard *optimal time* for this? The answer is not straightforward. Some complex games can have long loading times; this is something that would not be acceptable for casual games. Ultimately, the right answer is determined by the actual players. Will players accept this long installation process? If the answer is *no*, then the installation takes too long. Another more practical way to set specific values for this requirement is to check the loading times of similar games that can be considered your competition. You probably want to stay in the same range as your competitors, or do better.

Of course, when we talk about *premium* PC games, this particular requirement is not that important. Players already paid for the game, and they are committed to waiting until the game is loaded. They might not be too happy about it, but this will not affect your game sales. On the other hand, if we talk about a free-to-play mobile game, this same problem can spell disaster for your game. Players have low levels of commitment as they didn't spend money on it in advance and there are many competitors offering a similar gaming experience, also for free. If it takes too long for your game to load, they might just abandon it and move on to the next best thing. Even worse, they might give you a one-star review in the store and say that the *game doesn't work*, which will discourage other players from downloading your game.

In the example above, we can see how the specifics of the platform and business model directly affect the importance of QA.

Another reason why it is important to test game stability first is the fact that this is a *precondition* for all other tests you will run. You will struggle with testing progression or game logic if the game is unstable, and you won't be able to test anything if the game doesn't load. These tests are always part of **Basic Acceptance Testing** (**BAT**) and are usually run first.

After stability, the next thing we want to test is whether the game does what it is supposed to do.

First-time user experience (FTUE)

FTUE is similar to a *tutorial*. We test how the player is onboarded to the game: is the gameplay explained well enough? Is it paced properly? Does the player have enough chances to practice what they are taught? Is it too long? Is it correct? Is it misguiding? Asking these types of questions gives us practical guidance on how to test the FTUE. We do have to keep in mind though that these answers will vary from game to game. As with many other things, often, the answers depend on the specific game genre and the target audience. While **role-playing games** (**RPGs**) and many strategy games are known for their steep learning curves, most casual and puzzle games have more detailed explanations on how to play the game and don't become too challenging early on.

Core game loops

Core game loops are the main game design mechanics. These are the main actions that the player carries out in a game; these actions strongly depend on the game genre. For example, in *match-three* games, the player will be taken to a level where they need to match three or more elements to create strings. Matching the elements clears the board and the player is rewarded with a specific number of points for each match. When the player reaches a certain number of points, the player will *win* the level and be able to move on to the next level. This is the core game loop of a match-three game; we can see many items that we can test here:

- Can you start a level?

- Does each level start at zero points?

- Can you do the matching as intended?

- Does each match give you the appropriate number of points?

- Does the physics of matching work (do matching items disappear, explode, etc.)?

- Are matched elements removed from the board?

- Does a level really end when the target is reached?

- Can you move to the next level when the current level is *won*?

- Do points reset with each new level?

There are many more things we can test on each *level* but asking these questions will tell us if the core game loop works as intended.

> **Note on testing more complex games**
>
> More testing is required for more complex games, such as strategy games, where a player needs to get currency to build a building (generator) that generates goods that are used to build an army, and an army in turn is needed to conquer more territory, as more territory brings more currency. As we can see, these game loops are much more complex with more co-dependencies, and as such, will take more time to test fully.

Level progression

We already mentioned level progression when we spoke about core game loops. Many games have **levels** – sequential stages of the game that showcase that a player's skills and fortunes are growing with the time they spend in the game. They act as a motivator for the player and are one of the reasons why they keep playing the game. Levels can be obvious and part of the gameplay: they may be displayed on a map or similar and numbered. But they can also be incorporated more deeply into the gameplay and shown as the player's skill level, settlement level, or similar. We can find great examples of embedded levels by looking at games in the 4X genre such as *State of Survival*. Regardless of how levels are displayed, we need to test the following:

- Can you start the level?

- Does it start with appropriate resources/counters?

- Can you finish the level when the targets are met?

- Can you pass the level?

- Can you start the following level?

- Are leveling-up rules clearly visible?

Besides the technicalities of moving to the next level, here we also need to pay attention to the *difficulty* of the level. This is one of the parts of testing that is very specific to the gaming industry. How can we determine whether a level is too difficult or too easy? Usually, with free-to-play games, we can adjust the degree of difficulty relatively easy. But, with premium and boxed games, it's often impossible or exceptionally hard. One of the best ways to decide what is too hard/too easy is to try to put yourself in the player's shoes. Who is playing your games? What level of gameplay difficulty will they expect? As a tester, it's always recommended to play similar games yourself, to get a sense of how difficulty is balanced. It is also advisable to have discussions with level designers and get a better understanding of the desired balance.

Game physics

Some of the most successful games out there are **physics** based. *Angry Birds*, *Goat Simulator*, *Portal*, and *Half Life* are all examples of games that rely heavily on the physics gameplay element. By physics, we mean mimicking the behavior of objects in real life: for example, heavy objects will fall faster, or if you hit a ball with more force, it will fly further. Of course, games are supposed to be fun, and sometimes the laws of physics are bent or even broken. In *GTA*, your car has a *flying car* mode; in some games, you can jump really high; or, for example, in *Madden* you can get an acceleration boost that allows you to run extremely (unnaturally) fast.

> **Note on testing physics in games**
>
> When testing physics in a game, it is very important to understand how objects in the game are *supposed* to behave: are physics in the game a copy of the real world or does the game design allow for certain freedom? After we are clear on that, we should focus on testing physics consistency: that flying car mode should really enable us to fly the car, or tapping the character twice should allow him to jump extra high every single time when physics apply in the game.

Game logic

Game logic is somewhat like game physics, but not all games utilize physics for their main gameplay. Game logic means a game is behaving in the expected manner. For example, if you are testing a story-driven game, you need to make sure that the dialogue makes sense and that the story is progressing in an understandable and logical way.

AI behavior

In many games, especially ones with slightly more complex gameplay, we encounter **non-playable characters (NPCs)**. Their role might be to guide us through the game, assist us, or, more often, act as our nemesis that needs to be defeated. The behavioral patterns of these characters can range from very simple to more complex. Some of them are so complex that it's hard to tell if they are a real player or **AI**!

For example, let's take a soccer game. Before you start to play against a real-world opponent (multiplayer mode), you might get a couple of practice rounds against an AI team to build up your team and earn some experience. If the AI is designed well, the opponent's team will act as if it is managed by a real player; it will play following the rules and respond to your team's actions. A tester's job is to make sure that all programmed behavior is as realistic as possible and responsive to the player's actions.

Usability flow (UX)

Usability is one of the most important parts of any software. It's the same with games – it is very important that a player's journey through a game is fluid, logical, and easy to understand. If not, players will leave the game fast. But how do we test UX in games?

UX testing is a discipline on its own and it's usually done by representatives of the players. As a part of generic game testing at a high level, we need to test the game flow. To do this, we can ask the following questions:

- Is the game flow easy to follow?
- Are transitions logical from the players' perspective?
- Can players easily transition from one screen to another?
- Are there any dead ends in the game?
- Is there anything frustrating or unnecessarily complicated?

Of course, there are plenty of other things we need to test in games. Many of them will depend on the game genre, platform, and even business model. We will go through many of them in detail in the following chapters, but let's go through them briefly here:

- **Platform compatibility**
- **Purchasing**
- **Visuals**
- **Audio**
- **Multiplayer**
- **Playthrough**
- **Third-party integrations**

- **Achievements**
- **Consistency**
- **Compliance and legal requirements**
- **Game world rules**
- **Fun factor**
- **Hardware compatibility**

Platform compatibility

We will touch upon platform compatibility testing in *Chapter 4, Deeper Look - Testing on Various Gaming Platforms – Mobile, PC, and Console*. Depending on the platform, this can be a very important part of testing. Regardless of which platform we publish our game on, it's always a tester's job to make sure that all platform requirements are met in the game.

Purchasing

Purchasing is another exceptionally important thing to test in the games. If your game is **free-to-play (F2P)**, which has been the predominant business model in the gaming industry for the last decade, you want to make sure that players' purchasing experiences are smooth and glitch-free. When testing purchases, we should investigate the following things:

- Can I access the in-game shop?
- Does the shop display the correct amounts, visuals, and names of items for sale?
- Can I execute the purchasing action without any interruptions?
- Do I get items that I purchased?
- Am I charged the correct amount?
- If the supply is unlimited, can I repeat the purchase?

Visuals

Every game has its own visual identity. When we test visuals, we want to make sure that the game looks good and that there are no visual glitches or obvious mistakes. We also check the following:

- Do animations play correctly?
- Are any of the visuals missing?
- Are any of the visuals misplaced?
- Are any of the visuals significantly distorted?

- Is the **user interface** (UI) clearly visible?
- Can interactive visual elements (such as buttons) be tapped, and do they do what they are supposed to do?

Audio

Audio is also a very important component of the gaming experience, particularly when we look into deeply immersive games on PCs and gaming consoles, games that include actors dialogue, have music as a part of the core gameplay, and where the game's atmosphere is important for the overall experience. Can you imagine a battle scene without the sounds of weapons clashing? Or investigating a dark alley at night for clues, without eerie music following your journey? To make sure that the audio works as intended, these are following things we need to pay attention to:

- Does the audio actually play?
- Is the sound clear, without any interruptions or distortions?
- Can the audio be switched off?
- Does the audio play in a timely manner, without delays, and in correspondence to the actions that a player does on the screen?

Multiplayer

Multiplayer is one of the most complex and time-consuming things to test in games. First, let's answer the question of what multiplayer is. We consider multiplayer any action that involves other players in the game; it could be one other player or many. Multiplayer can be collaborative – several players join a group (most often called a *guild*) and work together toward common goals and the betterment of the whole guild. Equally, multiplayer is also competitive – competing for resources, territory, or skills with another player or group of players. As we see, just by its nature, it's impossible to properly test multiplayer with only one tester. Moreover, lots of collaborative or competitive actions in the guild happen over a specific period of time.

> **Leaderboards example**
>
> For example, let's look into a simple multiplayer feature: the leaderboard. Leaderboards are always time-determined: they can be daily, weekly, monthly, or all time. Also, they can be determined by an event in the game – if your game has special events that last for a certain period, that particular event might have its own leaderboard. Even if it's a feature that seems relatively simple, once we scratch the surface, we can see that there are plenty of parameters we need to check to be able to confirm that this feature works well.

Figure 2.1 – Competitive versus collaborative multiplayer

Some of the high-level tests that we want to run when testing multiplayer are as follows:

- Can multiple players join the common activity?

- Do all players have the same playing experience (no delays, glitches, freezes etc.)?

- Does multiplayer activity follow set rules (for example, a guild can have up to 20 members, or players can only fight 3v3)?

- Are players matched correctly in PvP?

- Do you have a chat in the game? If yes, does it follow the specified rules (local, global, security, etc.)?

Playthrough

While playthrough was traditionally the *bread and butter* of game QA, in modern games, this is not the case. Full playthroughs are rarely done in mobile F2P games because it would take far too much time with little benefit. By their core design, F2P games never end and players are supposed to be able to play them continuously for years to come. Performing complete playthroughs on games like these is practically impossible. On the other hand, it's still a very important part of testing premium games, especially ones that are released in physical format. Those games are a finite product, with a specific number of hours they can be played, and we want to make sure that these games work as intended from beginning to end.

Third-party integrations

In modern games, especially mobile ones, third-party integrations have become the norm. There is rarely a game that doesn't have some sort of analytics in it. If your game shows ads, it will come with an ad platform included and potentially mediation platforms as well. While we don't test those additions ourselves, we want to make sure that they are correctly installed and do what they are supposed to do.

For example, if our game contains ads, we want to make sure that they work as intended: they can be seen without issues, and if players are rewarded for watching ads, we should check that they receive the correct reward for watching them.

Achievements

Achievements testing is a huge and very important task for console games and can take a long time. Some of these achievements are purposely created to require a player to play the game for a long time or on an exceptionally difficult setting. Very often, there is a *specialized* group of testers who test achievements, as it requires testers to also be skillful gamers. While most of the time, we can rely on the help of *cheat menus* that are created specifically for testing purposes, we still need to make sure that achievements are attainable, and therefore, it is advisable to try to obtain them without cheat menus when possible. In mobile games, achievements can also be important depending on how they were implemented in the game design; however, testing achievements doesn't usually require such an intensive effort, as they are not a prerequisite for passing game *submissions*. We will learn more about submissions in *Chapter 11, Are You on the Right Version? Live Ops and QA*.

Consistency

Consistency testing is especially important when we work with large games that have a rich metagame and plenty of content. In these cases, you might have a large game development team working on the game or even several ones. It can easily happen that terminology, parts of a narrative, or even how something in the game looks or sounds get mixed up. In consistency testing, we make sure that text, names, looks, behavior, and sounds are consistent throughout the game.

Compliance and legal requirements

Compliance testing is its own discipline within testing, especially with consoles. We will examine it more in *Chapter 4, Deeper Look - Testing on Various Gaming Platforms – Mobile, PC, and Console*. Legal requirements testing is somewhat related to this. While nobody expects testers to be legal experts and it's not really a QA job to make sure that all legal issues are covered in a game, it is good to keep an eye out for something that might raise a possible copyright issue and that credits are listed as agreed. For example, while I was testing achievements for one of the console games I worked on, I noticed that one of the achievements was called NASA. I thought it was worth checking if copyrights are needed for such usage. It turned out that we couldn't just simply use the name without explicit permission, and it was a valid legal issue.

Game world rules

When we create game settings, we create different environments that very often are worlds with their own rules. Every game you play, even the tiniest mobile game, has its own setting. Worlds will have maps or just general environments in which players move, perform actions, match items, battle with cards, merge, flip, fight, collect, and do thousands more different things. Each of these worlds, even if it's trying to emulate real-world scenarios, has its own rules. They are defined by the game design and game mechanics. A big part of testing is validating that these game rules work as intended.

Fun factor

The fun factor of a game cannot be quantified or measured; as a result, there's a lot of subjectivity involved when testing for the fun factor. Without it, games will not really be successful with players. But how do we define fun for each game? The fun factor is very hard to quantify, and testers often have to rely on their own experiences and familiarity with the given genre to make sure that the game is fun to play. A good rule of thumb here is to play several other successful games of a similar genre. You will get a good idea of what feels like fun for the player. It is also important to understand who your game's target audience is. Players who enjoy first-person shooters might not necessarily enjoy match-three games and vice versa. In testing the fun factor, the most important quality a tester can bring to the table is to be able to put themselves in the players' shoes. Being able to understand what the target audience expects and desires to see in these types of games will help a tester be more objective.

Hardware compatibility

Lastly, we will touch upon hardware compatibility. This is another major part of testing that requires thorough preparation and planning. While it's not so much of an issue for console games or even PC games (although PCs do come with thousands of different specifications), it is very important for mobiles, especially when considering the Android platform. There are over 10,000 Android phones on the market, made by different manufacturers. Making sure that the game works well on most of them is no small task. We will discuss this in more depth in the chapters that follow.

We have now covered in detail the wide range of elements to be tested in games. With so many different aspects available to test, next we will focus on how to figure out what the most important thing to test is at any given time.

What is the most important thing to test?

There is no simple, straightforward answer to this question. There are many dependencies that will affect what the most important thing to test is:

- Timelines: when are we doing the testing?

- Platform: different platforms have different rules

- Target audience: who is your player and how do they behave in the game?

- Business model: is our game an open or closed ecosystem (F2P versus premium)?

- Build readiness: what is ready to be tested?

- Target market: different markets bring different challenges

- Business requirements: do we have a partnership or stakeholder that requires us to focus on something specific?

- Technical changes

These are by no means all the possible dependencies. The gaming business is a very fast-paced industry and constantly changes and evolves. This also affects QA as one of the crucial parts of game development. How we do determine the most important thing to test? Let's look at the **timeline priorities** first. Based on where you are in game development, your testing focus will shift. There is no need to test detailed content, for example, when we are in early game development and still developing the architecture. Game testing always follows game development, and we focus on testing what is in development at the current milestone (see *Figure 1.2* in *Chapter 1, Setting the Stage - Introduction to QA for Modern Games*).

We can see that there is a significant shift in focus as we pass different game development milestones. Not only do we shift focus on what is tested, but also how it is tested. As a game develops, we slowly expand the range of testing performed. In this way, testers contribute in the best possible way to the overall development effort and we get optimal execution overall.

We also want to make sure that we *find the most complex and hardest-to-fix bugs* early on. If we find a bug that affects game architecture or exposes significant game design flaw late in development, this bug will be much more expensive to fix than if we were to find it early on. This is due to the fact that development in the early phases is very much focused on building the architecture, while the design is still relatively fluid without too many co-dependencies. When the **game release** date is still far off in the future, there is plenty of time to fix bugs without requiring extra resources, long working hours, or timeline pressures. By contrast, finding such bugs just before the game is released causes lots of problems and increases costs. Most of the game content is already locked – fixing issues in the foundation of the game will possibly affect lots of co-dependencies with other elements in the game, potentially causing other bugs or instabilities in other parts of the game. Due to tight release deadlines, these issues must be fixed before a certain date, which leads to working overtime and even pulling in extra resources. This type of situation is one (among many) of the reasons why traditional game QA is not the best way to test games. Handing over the *finished* product for testing means that all bugs, big and small, will be found at the same time, which can cause lots of stress and increased costs for development teams.

We already discussed that some features of the game, by nature, just take longer to test. If a game has *multiplayer* or *achievements* functionalities, for example, we need to make sure that there is sufficient time to test them. The closer we get to the release date, the more important these types of tests become.

One thing that is important to mention is that game QA never really ends. The only point when QA is really finished is when the game is not supported anymore or is removed from the store. When a game goes live, we enter live operations or the *live ops* phase, which comes with its own set of QA challenges.

In the live ops phase, priorities change even more frequently, and player input becomes a significant factor in determining the most important thing to test. For example, if we get lots of complaints through player support or social media about a particular issue or feature of the game, this issue will quickly become a priority to test.

Sometimes, even the **game genre** can dictate what aspect of the game should be prioritized for testing.

Let's take audio, for example. Most players play games on mobile phones with the audio turned off. This is due to the nature of the platform: mobile games are played in public transport, waiting rooms, and even school classes and work meetings. It makes sense that many players decide to turn the sound off on their mobile device. On the other hand, there are many successful games out there that are based on music and sound. There are rhythm-catching games, such as *Piano Tiles*, where it's important for the player to hear the sounds as part of the core gameplay experience. So, while in many mobile games, audio might not be the most important thing to test, it is very important for games that have sound and music at their core.

Business requirements are another important reason that can heavily affect testing priorities. For example, in one of the companies I worked for, the board of directors intervened and wanted a particular issue to be fixed immediately, and the bug fix to be verified. Needless to say, our team reshuffled priorities and made the board request a priority. A similar thing can happen when, for example, you are aiming to get featured by a mobile platform. The platform might give you a list of things that they want your game to have in order to be featured. Usually, those requests take priority in development and thus in QA as well.

In all of the preceding examples, we can notice a common string: QA follows development efforts. In modern game testing, it is important that the QA specialist is a member of the game team, working closely with developers. A QA specialist can act quickly, adjust testing plans to meet the real needs of the project, and spend their time in the most efficient manner. In more traditional QA, plans would be solid, and QA staff would very often be the last ones to find out about any last-minute changes. When they did, it was usually already too late to shift the testing focus. This resulted in many testing hours being wasted, as well as long working hours and lots of pressure to accommodate last-minute changes. With mobile games being constantly worked on and developed, it's nearly impossible to have traditional QA and expect to get good results. While traditional QA is still frequently practiced in console and PC environments, QA has significantly evolved in the mobile gaming context, picking up development best practices.

Game QA in practice

How does game QA look in practice? We already went through several examples of how QA works in the gaming industry. One important distinction we can make is to split QA into two major game life cycle phases:

Figure 2.2 – Game life cycle phases

In the **pre-launch phase**, as we have seen in the previous sections, QA works together with the development team on pre-determined, long-term production timelines. Very often, QA will be added to the team only much later in game development, and early testing efforts will be done by the development team. There is the single pressure point of the release date, and that is generally an equally important and stressful day for QA regardless of which platform, business model, or genre they are dealing with. The release or launch date is the first time your game will go live to a wide audience, and it involves significant marketing efforts and costs to attract players to the game. This is particularly important for premium games, where most of the revenue is generated within the first 30 days after launch.

In the **post-launch phase**, or **live ops**, QA is very different. Development times are much quicker and plans are changed more often, and game **key performance indicators** (**KPIs**) as well as player opinions very often re-shape production schedules. Most mobile games in the live ops phase have a cadence of content updates that recurs every two weeks or so. Furthermore, owing to the constant development of technology and the release of new phone models on the market, QA must keep an eye on the latest industry developments and make sure that game is still compliant with new versions of operating systems, works well on new mobile devices, and successfully meets the other challenges of a live product. So, how do we perform QA in practice?

QA usually works in following way:

Figure 2.3 – Testing cycle

The preceding figure shows the standard **testing cycle**:

1. QA gets a working build for testing. It's only distributed internally to the testing team and is not available for the general public yet. This build is deployed in a test environment. Testers usually receive a change log or release notes, which list the changes made in this build. This helps QA to focus their testing efforts and develop additional test cases if needed.

2. Testers execute testing. This is the core of our work. We use the knowledge we have about the platform, the game itself, what to test in games in general and in this particular build, along with any documentation we got from the dev team, and apply a testing methodology and approach that is the most appropriate for the testing we are doing. Testers usually use a set of test cases as a script for their testing efforts.

3. The output of our work is bugs. Most of the time, QA will find at least some bugs in the software that is being tested. They may be major or minor bugs, and together with the producer or product manager, it will be decided which bugs must be fixed. Bugs are reported in a common repository (bugs database).

4. The bugs are then fixed by developers and committed to QA to test. We need to make sure that bugs found previously are truly fixed and confirm that those fixes didn't cause any other issues. When validating bug fixes, it's important to use the same parameters we had when we originally reported the bug.

5. After all the relevant bugs are fixed and validated as such by QA, the development team deploys the build in a live environment – it is released to the public gaming audience.

6. It is always advisable that QA also tests the build that is released. While the test environment should always closely copy the production environment, there are still some differences. Testing a live build immediately upon launch helps us find any significant issues with the game in a live environment and helps us minimize the damage that such issues would otherwise have on the players.

In **live ops**, when we finish with one release, we very often already need to prepare for or even start testing the next one.

In game development, QA very often acts as a sort of **gatekeeper** – a green light or QA confirmation is required before a game or game update can be released. In small studios, this is generally a simple process, and the discussion to send the game for QA might happen only via an informal meeting or email. But in larger studios, this process can be very heavy and involve multiple steps. It often involves detailed testing reports and large meetings where findings are discussed and final decisions are made as to whether the game should go live or not. While this detailed process ensures that there is team alignment and the product is mature enough for launch, it can easily be way too time consuming for *live ops*. A heavy release process can become cumbersome and disrupt update cadence, which, in turn, can push players away from the game. If there is no fresh content to play, players might turn to competitors' games and never come back. Unfortunately, even if QA has general ownership of *greenlighting* the release, it rarely has ownership of the process or the final word.

Now that we know more about how to determine what to test and how game QA works in practice, we will next learn more about the main challenges in game QA.

Game QA challenges

We can already see that there are many challenges in QA. We will list some of them and offer practical advice on how to handle them.

Frequent changes in technology

It is a fact that technology is advancing and constantly changing. Since we're working in a digital environment, we need to stay aware of what is going on not only in the gaming industry but also in technology in general. We need to consider how these changes will impact the games we are working on. Do we need to upgrade our engine version? How will we test the impact of that? How will our game perform on a 5G network? Will the game run on the latest model of iPhone? While many testers are also passionate gamers, to be excellent in QA, we need to keep up with advancements in technology as well, as they will affect how our games are made and how they are updated. With an awareness of advancements in technology, we will be able to develop new and relevant test cases that will ensure that our game will work great with all new technology upgrades.

Changes in platform guidelines and regulations

Every platform has its own set of rules and regulations. Some of them are stricter than others, but they all change every now and then. Sometimes, those changes will make our job easier but more often than not, they throw us a curve ball that we might struggle to catch on time. Furthermore, platforms don't necessarily inform developers when they change their requirements or guidelines; we have to learn about them the hard way, when our submissions fail. If your studio is big enough to have a submissions team, make sure to check in with them regularly and see if platforms still have the same requirements. If you are working in a smaller team, it is recommended to have someone in QA responsible for keeping an eye on platforms and making sure that all compliance tests are frequently updated. Remember that platforms set their own rules, so there is no point in arguing or ignoring them. It's in our interest for the game to be published on time, and having a complete understanding of the platform requirements in advance is one of the key components in achieving that.

Conflicting priorities

If there is one skill that would be considered crucial for QA, it is prioritization. We already know that QA has a lot to test, even in what we would consider *small games*. It is important to understand what we need to test and when. When in doubt, it can be helpful to talk to your product manager and producer to get a clear picture of the game release pipeline and product requirements. And that brings us to the following item.

Limited time for QA

There is never enough time for QA. We can always find something else to test. Unfortunately, very often during the pre-release game development, the team decides to make major changes in game design or even in architecture, but it doesn't necessarily push forward release dates. That puts QA in a very unenviable position: there is more work, but the timeline is shorter. In situations like this, prioritization is key. But, besides that, it's important to state clearly to other stakeholders and the game management team that there might not be enough time to test everything as planned. By doing that, everyone in the studio will be aware of the risks of limited QA, and if it's considered a really high risk, there might be some additional QA time or resources added to the project to minimize the probability of critical bugs slipping through.

Considered an entry-level role but with lots of requirements

Another unfortunate thing with QA is that is generally considered an entry-level role in the gaming industry. When you start in QA, there is not much structured training to take advantage of and it takes time before someone really grows into a good QA. But due to the entry-level positioning of QA in development, many great QA people decide to switch to other disciplines such as game design and production when they become experienced enough. This can cause lots of challenges in doing QA professionally and efficiently. Here we can find an example of how things can go very wrong when QA for a highly anticipated game was done by a team that was too junior for the task: `https://www.thegamer.com/cyberpunk-2077-quantic-lab-cd-projekt/`.

Working with the development team

Working with the development team can be an excellent experience, and it generally makes the QA job more rewarding and even easier. You can ask questions directly to team members, understand planned features better, participate in game development, and give early input. But it can also be very challenging. Some teams are not used to working closely with QA or they consider the QA team the enemy of the development team. During my time in QA, I even once heard a comment to *stop putting bugs in the game*. I assure you that QA doesn't put bugs in a game, but we do find them – that's our job! The key to working with the dev team is clear communication and mutual respect. As long as we report relevant bugs that are useful to the team and work in a collaborative manner, with clear communication, most of these challenges can be resolved.

Of course, QA doesn't work only with the development team. We work also with marketing, analytics, player support, and other departments. It can often happen that QA will receive a request from another department to do testing for them. While it's great to help other teams, it's QA's duty to make sure that they fulfill their tasks first. Once I worked in a team where our QA lead spent most of his time verifying issues that were reported through player support. While that was worthy help, he didn't manage to keep up with the testing of regular updates and the number of live bugs just kept increasing. We resolved that issue by training player support in basic QA practices and assigned a player support agent to the game team to have better insight into how development worked, when bugs will be fixed, and to be able to do basic verification of the bugs reported by players.

Live bugs

Bugs that come from a live environment are generally considered more severe than the ones found in production. This is because it's the players that experience them and very often they are reported by players themselves, writing angry emails to customer support, posting negative comments on game forums and social media, and giving one-star reviews in the Google Play/App Store. The damage is already done. Unfortunately, it is generally perceived that live bugs are the fault of the QA team. In reality, live bugs mostly occur because QA didn't have enough time to perform thorough testing. Live bugs are challenging not only because of the effect they have on players, but also because they come from reports outside of the game teams. This means we often don't have all the parameters regarding where and how a bug appears. If we don't have a good communication pipeline between player support and the production team, we might not even hear about this bug for a long time. Ultimately, we have to find time to fix this bug or even make a decision on rolling our update back to a previous version. This can be very complicated and sometimes risky.

Another challenge when dealing with live bugs is distinguishing real issues from non-issues or identifying issues that are happening to only a very small portion of the players. It's human nature that we immediately react to someone who is loud about the bug they found or who threatens to leave the game. While happy players are of utmost importance to the success of any game, it is also important to have a look at the overall picture. Is this issue affecting only one player? Is it escalating quickly? What is the effect on players – are they losing progress, money, or can they even run the game? Even if a player is very loud, an issue that affects thousands of players should take priority over addressing an issue that is an edge-case scenario for one or a handful of players.

Gaming studios develop different processes for handling live bugs and escalating the issues that players are facing. While there is no universally-accepted, perfect solution, if we have processes in place that work and are efficient enough to resolve these types of issues quickly, we will be ready to face the challenges of working with live games.

In the previous section, we learned how testing works in practice and what things we need to pay attention to. In the following section, we will learn more about where QA fits in modern agile practices.

Agile practices and game QA

Before we dive into agile practices, we should revisit agile's predecessor, **waterfall**. The waterfall methodology was used in software development until the early 2000s, when the transition to agile methodology started. The gaming industry heavily relied on waterfall and still does to some degree, but the need for fast-paced live ops (or, as it's sometimes called, **games as a service**) couldn't be properly met by following the rigid waterfall system. How does the waterfall methodology work in the games industry?

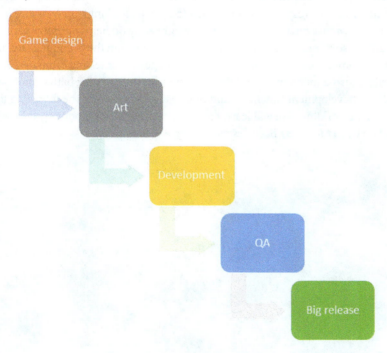

Figure 2.4 – Waterfall methodology

We can see that in game development, a project is *handed* over from one team to another when it's considered done. This process is linear and visually looks like a cascading waterfall, hence the name. When we start working on a game using the waterfall methodology, designers first create the overall game design, then an artist develops all the required art, which is then handed over to developers who code the game features based on the game design and bring the art to life in the game. At the end of the cycle, QA is passed a build that is considered done to test it in time for the big release date.

While this system has its advantages, it is a lengthy process, and it usually takes years to create a game following this methodology. It is also a rigid system, where it's very difficult to get any feedback early in development. For example, certain designs might be exceptionally difficult to implement with a given technology, but we will not be able to address this issue until the game is handed over to the development team. With emerging new technologies, the changing preferences of players, and the need for fast content updates in free-to-play games, this model doesn't serve game development anymore.

With the growth of the free-to-play business model in the early 2010s, the agile methodology saw increased adoption in gaming studios and consequently in QA as well. Today, free-to-play is the dominant business model in the industry and agile practices are dominant in mobile gaming studios.

The change to agile methodology was not only about how development takes place. It also changed the role of QA in the development team. In agile, QA represents the player and is *embedded* in the development team. It participates in feature development and provides valuable input. QA does think a little bit differently from the rest of the team. While the dev team thinks *"how can we build it?"*, QA often focuses on *"how can we break it?"* Having this insight early on helps optimize game design and allows for more robust solutions. Being involved in development from the beginning also allows QA to have a deeper understanding of the game we are testing, to get better testing estimates, and prioritize work better. Agile is also a much more *collaborative* system: it allows for better understandings of different disciplines, development timelines, and business requirements. The following figure shows the agile development workflow. We will learn more about the agile methodology applied to gaming in *Chapter 9, It Works, but It Hasn't Been Tested: Testing Approach*.

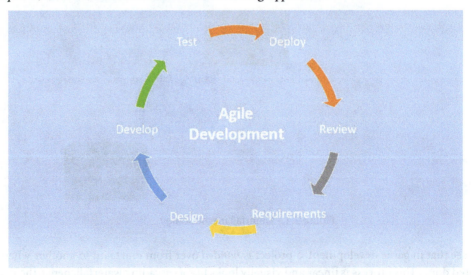

Figure 2.5 – Agile development

Another major difference in the agile methodology is that it is, by nature, *iterative*. The goal of agile teams is to produce a workable piece of software as soon as possible. Very often, big features will be broken down into smaller pieces so they can be worked on in an iterative manner. Making features small means that all team members work on the same feature almost at the same time. Testing these small pieces of working software enables us to avoid long, exhausting QA rounds at the end of the development cycle.

Not all agile methodologies are the same. There are several main agile methodologies used in modern games development:

- **Scrum**
- **Kanban**
- **Lean development**
- **Crystal**
- **Combinations (such as Scrumban)**

Any methodology can be called agile as long as it fits into the four core pillars of agile: individuals and interactions over processes and tools, working software over comprehensive documentation, customer collaboration over contract negotiations, and responding to change over following the plan. You can learn more about agile methodologies by reading the Agile Manifesto at `https://agilemanifesto.org/`.

In the gaming industry, we mostly use Scrum, Kanban, or a variation of these two. Let's now look into them more closely.

Scrum

Scrum is by far the most popular and widely used agile methodology. It is represented in the following diagram.

Figure 2.6 – Scrum methodology

While the methodology is simple, the biggest shift in agile development is the mindset change. Scrum is based on five values (source: `https://scrumguides.org/scrum-guide.html#scrum-values`):

- *Courage* – to do the right thing and handle tough challenges
- *Focus* – everyone is focused on sprint goals and tasks
- *Commitment* – team members commit to achieving the sprint goals
- *Respect* – team members respect others and trust their competence and character
- *Openness* – the Scrum team agrees to be open about all the work and challenges in performing the work

Most of the time, the hardest transition is the adoption of these values and mentally changing how we do the work. How do these values affect QA in Scrum?

In many ways, they make the QA job easier. QA is often a bearer of bad news: something is broken or not working as intended; there is not enough time to test; a bug fix doesn't really work. Having *openness* and *courage* as the core values of Scrum development makes it easier for the rest of the team to appreciate this QA point of view, and furthermore to see the full value it provides. Working so closely with other team members also allows QA to make fast checks of smaller pieces of software and catch potentially severe issues early in the development process. In Scrum, QA also has a voice: it participates in *Sprint planning* as well as in *retrospective meetings*. Open communication helps resolve any issues that might arise in the team or the testing process.

> **Sprint**
>
> During a sprint planning meeting, items are chosen from the product backlog, assigned a specific weight, and added to the sprint backlog. The *sprint backlog* is a list of items that teams commit to execute during the sprint. *Scrum teams* are usually small, a maximum of 15 people and ideally even smaller. *Sprints* last between 1 and 2 weeks, and at the end of the sprint, the team ships a workable piece of software: a feature, new content, bug fixes, or any combination of them. At the end of the sprint, teams hold a retrospective meeting where they discuss what went well and what went wrong.

Kanban

Kanban is another very popular agile methodology that is frequently used in the gaming industry. Kanban was invented in Japan for *Toyota*. You can learn more about the history and practice of Kanban at `https://kanban.university/kanban-guide/`.

Kanban focuses on managing the flow of tasks and limiting the workload. One of the simplest, but also most innovative features of Kanban is to focus on *finishing*, not on *starting*. As humans, we can only focus on one task at a time. Rather than having multiple tasks open, in Kanban we put emphasis on finishing what we started. Another great thing about Kanban is that it's a system that doesn't necessarily require change for the sake of change. Every Kanban methodology implementation starts with reviewing what are we currently doing and what works well. There is no need to reject elements of *Scrum* or even the *waterfall* methodology if they work for the team. As we focus on the flow in Kanban, it's important to be able to visualize it. Very often teams use physical boards, as well as digital ones, to display the tickets. While there is no ultimate right or wrong Kanban board, they usually look something like this:

Figure 2.7 – Kanban board example

We can see that every task is represented by a separate *ticket*. QA has its own column, where we can see what testing tasks are currently being addressed. Work distribution is based on *pulling* – team members pull the ticket from the previous column when they have time to work on it.

Kanban is an amazing system that allows for very fluid collaboration and gives an instant overview of where the team is in executing the planned work. Of course, like every other methodology, it does have its own set of challenges. It relies heavily on people being experienced enough and having the confidence to decide what task to pull into their own column. It also relies on people's ability to limit the tasks that they are working on. Very often, digital versions of the Kanban board will even have a technically imposed limit on **work in progress** (**WIP**), meaning it will restrict the number of tasks you can have in your column. This prevents tasks from piling up. Kanban has been proven to work exceptionally well in live ops, where teams need to move fast and iterate quickly. Kanban is also very often used with some kind of *time-boxing* method. Often, those are sprints that work the same as they would in Scrum, or involve *releases*, where the work of the team matches the timeline of planned releases. Kanban allows the QA team the same level of participation in the game development process as in Scrum, but additionally gives more clarity on the status of each task. Most importantly, the usage of *WIP limits* in Kanban prevents QA from being overloaded with tasks. It is an ideal process for resolving bottlenecks and helps improve QA efficiency, decreases confusion, and minimizes risk.

Summary

In this chapter, we learned in detail what is tested in games and the basics of how to do it. This information is crucial for any test planning and prioritization. We also learned at a high level how modern game testing works in the agile framework and how this is differentiated from the traditional waterfall model.

In the next chapter, we will dive deeper into the types of testing in games. We will learn how functional testing works, explain the importance and practice of localization testing, and provide practical tools for executing the other types of testing we encounter in the gaming industry, including regression, acceptance, and stress testing, among others.

3

A Deeper Look – Types of Testing in Games

In this chapter, we begin by taking an in-depth look at the most common type of testing in games – **functional testing**. Then, we will dig into **compliance testing**, followed by **localization testing** and **regression testing**.

These are by no means all the types of game testing; in the final chapter, we will touch upon other types of testing that are necessary for modern game QA. We will learn about the basic differences when testing on different platforms and where these tests fit in the game development process.

What you'll learn here is exceptionally important, as it will provide the foundation for all that you'll subsequently learn. By mastering these topics, you will get a solid grasp on how testing is organized for different platforms and all the important aspects that need to be taken into account when planning and estimating testing efforts.

In this chapter, we'll be taking a look at the following topics:

- Functional testing
- Compliance testing
- Localization QA
- Regression testing
- Other types of testing – stress testing, acceptance testing, and more

Functional testing

What is *functional testing*? As the name suggests, functional testing is a type of testing where we verify whether a game or part of the game functions as designed. Besides game features, usability and stability testing also fall under the functional testing umbrella. Functional testing literally means that we are testing whether the game and its components are working as they should. This part of testing makes up the bulk of a tester's job, and it's considered the main part of testing.

Functional testing is not a specialized discipline, and as such, it's expected that every tester can execute functional tests, even those at a junior level. While everyone in QA is expected to be able to do functional testing, it often happens that testers, with time, specialize or just become much better at testing specific features of games – for example, testers can specialize in testing achievements, multiplayer games, late gameplay, and so on.

With functional testing being such a large category, it's important also to mention what is *not* considered functional testing. If we follow the definition, things such as the fun factor, scalability, security, performance, and production quality are not part of functional testing. We will talk more about those later in this chapter.

Now that we know what it is (and what it is not), we will look into how it is executed.

How do we carry out functional testing?

Firstly, we need to understand what the feature being tested is supposed to do. Sometimes, it is obvious. Let's presume that you are testing the gameplay in the game *Candy Crush*. You can quickly see that you are supposed to match elements on the screen to empty the play area. It is easy to figure out what we would consider a pass and what we would consider a fail.

With games growing more and more complex, especially with long-lasting F2P games, new features can be quite complex. They might be targeted only at players who play the game for a very long time, have co-dependencies with already existing features, or reuse items that were already in the game.

Understanding these types of features would require that the tester themselves play a game for some time and/or maintain very detailed documentation, describing how a feature fits within the existing game ecosystem. In such cases, it is always advisable to combine functional testing with *regression testing* to obtain optimal coverage and avoid unpleasant surprises.

During game development, before a game is live, functional testing is the main testing activity.

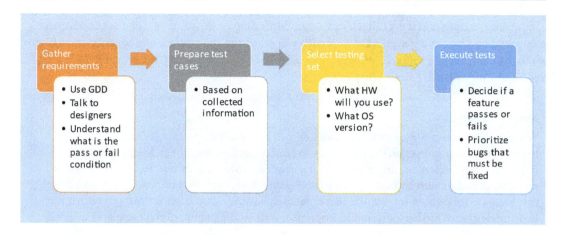

Figure 3.1 – Functional testing

In functional testing, it is important that the tester has a good understanding of what is considered to be a pass and a fail. While this might seem obvious, it's not always the case. For example, a feature may sometimes work – a player can play the game and it's stable, but the in-game character may seem overbearingly strong. The tester won't necessarily know what the right amount of strength is for that character to show unless they have access to the **game design document** (**GDD**) where this is determined, or the designer didn't explain the intended impact of the character in the game.

We generally use **test cases** when we run functional testing. Since it's presumed that a function or feature is new, we might have to create new test cases. If we don't use test cases at all, it's wise to at least keep testing notes that can be used as the base for regression tests later. We will talk in more detail about regression testing later in this chapter.

It is very important that we execute functional tests in the right **testing environment**. Primarily, we should check with game developers in which environment they deployed new code. As a standard, functional testing is usually done in QA or an environment that resembles the live environment. Testers should also ensure that they have a **cheat mode** available in a game. It might be very cumbersome, if not impossible, to properly execute functional tests if testers can't use a cheat mode, especially if the game is already far into development. Depending on our target platform, we want to have the right set of hardware and operating system. This is not an issue for console games, but when we talk about mobile games, it's an important step in preparing for testing. We will talk more about hardware in *Chapter 5, It Must Be Hardware: Testing Hardware in Modern Game QA*.

Lastly, we execute tests and report all relevant bugs. Depending on the phase of game development and the impact a bug has on a player, a QA specialist will select the appropriate **bug severity** and assign bugs to the developer to be fixed. We will learn more about bug reporting in *Chapter 8, I Thought I Fixed That: How to Write Efficient Bug Reports*

Note – bug severity

When we do game testing, not all bugs we find will be equally important. While some of them have a very minor impact on the player (for example, misalignment of an icon), some of them can impact players very harshly. Let's say that a player downloads your **free-to-play** (**F2P**) game, and after they have purchased an item in the in-game store, they don't receive an item that they just bought. This would impact the player severely (as they would get nothing in return for their money) and, furthermore, could jeopardize your studio's reputation if the player decides to share their bad experience on game forums and social media. Setting up appropriate bug severity when a bug is found is extremely important and one of the most important skills game testers should have.

We can approach functional testing in two different ways – positive and negative testing.

In **positive testing**, we follow an optimal player's route and the use case of how a player is supposed to use the feature being tested. We test whether that function works as intended.

In **negative testing**, testers check whether a game or feature works as intended, even when a player follows a less-than-optimal path. In practice, that would mean that we explore what happens when a player *plays the game wrong*.

For example, let's take a car racing game. You are testing a specific, newly added racetrack. You start the race in the car you selected, but instead of following the track like other players, you start to drive backward. What happens?

Finally, we will investigate what type of issues we can find during functional testing. When functional tests are usually run for the first time, we can find the following:

- Incomplete or conflicting documentation
- Missing functionalities
- Broken functionalities
- Visual bugs
- Audio bugs
- Broken UX flow
- Broken UI functionality
- Broken links

These are not all the types of issues we will find, but these will give you a good idea of the importance of functional testing.

We now have an understanding of how functional testing works and why is it so important when testing games. Next, we will learn about compliance testing.

Compliance testing

In game QA, we would consider *compliance testing* to be any type of QA that is testing the compliance of a game with the target platform and/or operating system. All digital platforms for game distribution have some sort of requirements that games need to meet in order to be published on them. Those regulations are non-negotiable; failing to meet them will result in the game not being published on the platform. All games targeted for any platform are required to go through a submission process, and generally, compliance readiness will be assessed during that process. We will talk more about the submission process in *Chapter 11, Are You on the Right Version? Live Ops and QA*.

The following are things we need to keep in mind when we talk about compliance testing:

- There are significant differences in compliance requirements between platforms
- Platforms occasionally change their requirements
- Compliance testing can be potentially extremely demanding and difficult to do without prior experience
- There are different consequences for failing compliance tests, and they can potentially be very serious for the game we are working on

Let's take a deeper look into the specifics of compliance testing.

Mobile (iOS and Google Play)

Compliance testing for the *Google Play* store and *App Store* (iOS) is generally not too demanding. Both platforms have publicly available guidelines at `https://play.google.com/console/about/guides/releasewithconfidence/` and `https://developer.apple.com/app-store/review/guidelines/` respectively.

This makes it easy for developers to implement the guidelines and for testers to follow them. Both platforms are prone to frequent changes in compliance requirements though, and it's important that testers regularly follow up for any changes. App Store requirements are generally considered to be slightly more demanding, and Apple does more rigorous internal testing.

> **Note – testing on other mobile platforms**
>
> There are other stores on the Android platform besides Google Play (which is the largest). Most mobile phone manufacturers also have their own stores (Samsung, Xiaomi, Huawei, etc.), and they might have slightly different compliance rules than Google Play. It is always important to check directly with the store about what kind of compliance requirements they have. While Amazon also runs on a version of Android, it has its own devices, its own ecosystem, and its own store, with different requirements. Just like with other mobile-based marketplaces, compliance testing is relatively straightforward but, nonetheless, important to do right.

Gaming consoles (PlayStation, Nintendo, and Xbox)

Compliance testing is exceptionally important for gaming consoles, and it is considered to be a demanding testing task. In many large gaming studios, which produce multiple console games, there are specialized departments that focus only on compliance testing, or there are team members who are specialized in it. Many QA companies also have specialized console compliance testing teams.

We should also keep in mind that compliance testing for a console differs quite a bit from platform to platform. They all have their unique requirements lists that need to be adhered to. For **Sony PlayStation**, there is TRC; for **Xbox** (**Microsoft**), TCR and XR; and for **Nintendo**, there is Lot Check. And while Xbox and Nintendo compliance documentation are relatively easy to follow, PlayStation's TRC can be challenging to fully understand and apply.

Console compliance is not necessarily only about how a game is supposed to work. The documentation also provides detailed instructions on specific technologies that need to be used, language that the game needs to display when performing specific system actions, and even branding that a gaming studio is required to use.

Another important aspect of testing compliance for consoles is that we can't test it on any store-bought console. In order to do QA for console games that are not commercially published yet, QA would need to use a specific console *test set* that can be only obtained directly from the console manufacturer. We will talk more about hardware testing and requirements in *Chapter 5, It Must Be Hardware: Testing Hardware in Modern Games QA*.

PC and Mac

The PC doesn't have a default store for games. Players can purchase and download games from one of the many popular online stores, such as *Steam*, *GOG*, or *Epic Games*, but they can also download them directly from the developer's web page. Sometimes, they can still be bought on disks and installed like that, although physical PC games are slowly decreasing in popularity. As PC platforms are so fragmented, there are no unified regulations that games should adhere to in order to be published. Very often, these requirements are either loose or not actively checked out by platforms.

If you are a PC gamer yourself, you might have noticed that even big studios release games on PC that still have lots of technical issues. Games such as *EVE Online*, *Rainbow Six*, and *Diablo III* all had serious bugs in them when released, and some of them couldn't be played for hours or even days! You can read more about the most well-known botched launches on PC here: `https://www.pcgamer.com/the-worst-pc-game-launches/`.

On PC platforms, compliance testing is often skipped, or it's left to developers to decide themselves what is acceptable quality for their target audience. It's not unheard of for players themselves to commit patches and bug fixes on published games, even ones from big gaming studios.

We now have an idea about compliance testing on various game platforms. Next, we will take a deep dive into localization QA.

Localization QA

Localization QA is a type of testing, where we verify whether game content is properly displaying the target language and using game-appropriate vocabulary.

Games are truly global phenomena, and they are played everywhere. This became even more prominent with the penetration of **smartphones** to all corners of the world and with the rise of F2P games. As a result, the entry barrier to playing games became low; almost any modern phone can run at least some games, and people can play without purchasing games in advance or ever spending any money. With the democratization of gaming, there is an increased need to make game content more appealing to local audiences. For instance, traditionally many people who were gamers were also deeply interested in tech and, used English as the lingua franca; however, many mobile gamers nowadays have little to no interest in technology. There is literally a game for everyone out there – from children to the elderly, from competitive, hardcore gamers to casual ones. Additionally, some huge gaming markets, such as China and Korea, don't have as many English speakers as in Scandinavia or India, for example. And even in European markets, where English is relatively common as a second language, some research showed that players still prefer to consume content in their local language, especially when it comes to purchasing something in the games.

While **software localization** has been around since we started making software, it has become really important during the last decade in the gaming industry.

Figure 3.2 – The localization process

When a gaming studio decides that they are going to do localization, they must first prepare for it. Localization is usually done in the later stages of game development, after the UI is finalized and all in-game texts are finished. If we start the localization process too early, we might have to repeat the cycle again after adding more texts to the original game.

As localization is done by an outsourced team, the game studio needs to prepare for successful localization. Game teams should follow these procedures:

- **Game texts** should be exported into separate files that the localization team can work with.
- The product owner should decide which **fonts** will be used for specific languages, especially if they are complex script languages.
- Game producers should prepare internal **bug flow** and how a team will handle localization bugs. We will learn more about bug flow in *Chapter 7, It Works on My Machine: Bug Flow*
- Designers should prepare all available **game documentation**, including videos and screenshots of a game, to be able to give the best possible overview of the game to the localization team.
- The development team should have technical clarity on how to **implement** new languages into an existing game.

Following these points will allow for a more smooth localization QA process and minimize localization errors. After localized texts are implemented in the game, game builds with integrated localizations will be sent to the localization QA team for testing.

Next, let's take a quick look at the different levels of localization.

Different levels of localization

We should recognize that in games, there are different levels of localization. They will depend on a studio's business strategy, game target audiences, studio financials, and many other factors.

Basic localization

Only marketing assets and game descriptions are translated. This means that when browsing through the platform store, a player will see a localized screenshot and game description that will give them a better idea of what a game is about, but the game itself won't be localized. This is a relatively cheap way to test international audiences and for studios to decide whether full localization would be profitable for them.

Full game localization

In this case, we translate not only the marketing assets but also the overall texts in the game. That means that all the menus, dialogues, instructions, and any other texts in the game will be localized. In this case, a player will usually have the option to select the desired language from the *settings menu*.

Internationalization

When we aim for significantly different markets than our initial one and we want to make sure that a game will do well, studios will invest in full internationalization. Not only do we localize text but we also adopt the look, feel, UI, UX, and even story to better match local tastes. This means that the same game can look significantly different and even play very differently, depending on which country you got it. This type of localization is very expensive, time-consuming, and requires lots of effort, so it's usually done only for major global markets. Rather than adopting existing games, internationalization is frequently done as a separate version of the game, intended only for specific markets.

Things we look out for during localization QA

Localization is usually done by specialized companies. There are localization companies that also specialize primarily in games, and their translators are gamers. These companies often offer localization QA or localization testing services. In localization testing, we do much more than just check whether localized content in a game is localized correctly. We also look for the following:

- Translation consistency
- Translation quality/wrong translations
- Whether the translation fits the overall game
- Missing translations
- Wrongly displayed text

- Cultural awareness
- Functional bugs

We will cover these in more detail in the following subsections.

Translation consistency

Sometimes, the translation of **in-game text** might be done by several people in order to increase the speed of translation. Translators very often don't have the full context of the game, and if it's text heavy, they might use synonyms or different words later in the game. The job of localization QA is to find such *inconsistencies* in the game and report them. Even if they might not seem like a big problem, they could potentially confuse a player and even give wrong information.

Translation quality

Depending on the language, there are usually at least several ways to say the same thing. Good translation quality will be easy to understand and follow and not necessarily involve a word-for-word translation. It won't have many spelling and grammar mistakes. We can notice sometimes with games coming from developers where English is not widely spoken, such as China and Japan, that the English translation can be somewhat odd or even completely nonsensical. The very popular mobile game *Love Nikki* is a good example of it. While the main story is relatively well translated, when it comes to item descriptions, they are very often unintentionally funny, confusing, or just bizarre. For example, low-level common dress has the following description: *"Collect all ordinary sets and you'll unlock the achievement of Nobody. You can do it!"* It's a localization QA job to flag this type of issue.

Another relatively common issue is **wrong translation**. This is not necessarily because translators don't know the language well enough. Without the full context of the game, sometimes it can be challenging to translate correctly. For example, in one of the games I worked on in the past, we had a case where you had the option to retire a character – that is, not use them anymore. The German translation of the game came out saying something along the lines of "character goes to pension." The translation wasn't exactly wrong, but it made no sense within the game context.

Does the translation fit the overall game?

A good translation will try to match the feel and spirit of a game. For example, if we are translating text spoken by an in-game character that is a Regency-style nobleman, we would aim to have a more formal and stiff expression than if we were translating the dialogue between two skaters in a park. This can sometimes be very hard if we have characters from a specific era or style that don't exist in our target country. It might be challenging to find the right vocabulary to realistically paint the Wild West to an average Chinese player, for example. At the very least, localization QA needs to check that translations are *era-appropriate* and that they describe the *spirit of the game* in the best possible manner.

Missing translations/text

This is one of the most common bugs we find in localization QA. It is not necessarily because text wasn't translated; it's often due to a **technical mistake** made during the integration of localized text files. In cases when text is missing, we might see placeholder text, text in the original language, or fully missing text. These are all considered bugs and should be reported.

Wrongly displayed text

Text can be displayed incorrectly in multiple ways. It commonly happens that text doesn't fit in a UI box and is *spilling* over, or is cut off. In one language, a word for something can be very short, while in another, the same word may be exceptionally long. If you want to say that you got lost in German, you will need to use much more space than in English to accommodate "*abhandengekommen.*" If UI boxes are not designed to be scalable or translators are not given a **character limit**, we will find these types of bugs often.

Additionally, we can also find issues where text covers part of the screen, and in the case of complex languages, it might be displayed in the wrong direction or display only certain characters incorrectly. Besides text, localization QA also verifies whether date, time, and currency are displayed properly, as these formats vary significantly between countries. All these bugs would make reading and understanding a game very difficult and can sometimes even mislead a player.

Cultural awareness

While we all have many things in common across the globe, every country has its own cultural specifics that are hard to understand if you are not local, or if you haven't spent time in that country. Even some things that are considered universal, such as emojis, might have a different meaning in a different country. There are also certain things that we presume are just part of gaming iconography, such as seeing lots of fairly realistic violence in first-person shooters or skeletons in RPGs. Anyone who has ever played *Diablo* or *Skyrim* can confirm that you will encounter plenty of those! However, your game might get banned in Germany if it contains too much violence and gore. While skeletons and skulls are not banned in China, they are considered culturally insensitive.

Hand gestures are another thing to be very careful about. One of the most universal signs, the sign for *peace*, if shown with the back of the hand visible, is insulting in the UK, Ireland, South Africa, and Australia. Part of localization QA is to be aware of these cultural differences and flag them to developers.

Lastly, we will mention humor. Games often contain light humor, jokes, and wordplay. These can be quite difficult to translate, as they often don't do so directly, but a localization agent needs to adapt them to local tastes.

Functional bugs

By now, we have an idea that localization QA involves quite a bit of testing. In practice, localization QA involves going through all aspects of a game where text appears, and that means **end-to-end testing** of the game. While localization QA is organized differently and has different goals compared to *functional testing*, due to the thoroughness of localization QA, it will also very often find functional bugs that might have passed through unnoticed.

Now, when we know more about how we do localization QA, it's important to mention who is undertaking it. **Localization testers** are a specialized branch of QA, who are generally native or near-native speakers of the language. Very often, localization testers have a background as translators who pivoted in the technical direction. It can sometimes happen that a localization QA specialist moves to functional QA, especially after gaining more testing experience. As localization QA is not always needed in game development, it's generally one of the most commonly outsourced services. Only large studios have their own internal localization QA teams.

While localization testing might not be seen as important as game testing as such, that is not the case. If a gaming studio already invests money and time in localizing a game and commits to marketing spend on a target market, poor translation can affect players negatively and even make them leave the game.

Finally, what languages do we most commonly translate? This is also affected by the platform – it can be much more cumbersome and time-consuming to localize and do localization QA for console-based games than for mobile ones.

Generally, games are localized in what is commonly called **EFIGS**, which is an acronym for **English, French, Italian, German, and Spanish**. We should recognize that this means European Spanish, while LATAM Spanish is generally considered a different language. Besides those, other common translation languages are Brazilian Portuguese, simplified Chinese, traditional Chinese, Korean, Japanese, and more recently, Arabic and Turkish.

Now that we are familiar with how localization QA works and how to execute localization QA, we will take a look at regression testing next.

Regression testing

When we work with large games or games that have already been live for a long time and have lots of different content in them, it becomes quite difficult to map all areas of a game. We develop live games with development plans that range from 6 months to a year in the future, but some of the most successful F2P games now run for over a decade. *Candy Crush* was released for the first time in 2012 and is still topping gaming charts.

With these types of games, it becomes necessary to occasionally do regression testing and check how new features, new content, and even more complex bug fixes affect already existing parts of the game. We can conclude that the purpose of regression testing is to ensure that a game still functions as it was intended after any update, code change, platform update, or bug fix has been made to the game, or if a new feature has been added. Regression testing is sometimes also considered part of functional testing, as at its core, it validates whether a game works as it should.

Let's have a look at the main differences between functional and regression testing.

Differences between regression and functional testing

As mentioned previously, regression testing can be considered a subset of functional testing, since their overall purpose appears similar, but these two sets of tests do have some differences. Let's take a look at some of them.

Testing goal

In functional testing, our goal is to find out whether a game or feature functions as intended. However, in regression testing, our goal is to find out whether a newly added feature or fix has broken already existing code.

Testing approach

In functional testing, we identify how the new code should work and verify that it does what it is intended to do. In regression testing, we identify what areas of a game might be affected by new code and test whether that is the case or not.

Test cases

In functional testing, as we are dealing with a function for the first time, we usually have to create new test cases based on user scenarios or game documentation. In regression testing, we use already existing test cases that we might only slightly modify.

Timing

We execute functional tests when new functionality or a feature is developed for the first time. On the other hand, we execute regression tests when we are adding new features to an already existing system or deploying bug fixes.

Now that we have a brief idea of what regression testing involves, let's check out some of the approaches that we adopt to perform regression testing.

Different approaches to regression testing

The idea of regression testing might come across as overwhelming. Retesting a whole game would take a lot of time, money, and work. How do we decide what to test? There are several different ways to approach regression testing.

Collaborative approach

The best way to approach regression testing is to consult with the coder and game designer in your team. As a tester, the better you understand the risk, the better idea you will have of where to focus your regression testing efforts. You can jointly make a solid assessment of the impact new changes can potentially have and the inherited risks. To even further optimize your testing efforts, regression testing can be done along with functional testing, and if a feature is new, as well as using **basic acceptance testing** (**BAT**), the testing team will probably need to develop some new test cases. We will learn more about test cases in *Chapter 6, Friend or Foe – Test Cases*.

While functional testers focus on testing new functionality that was introduced by implementing new code, regression testers focus on the immediate impact of the changes in that part of the game. This type of testing should find potentially the most problematic issues relatively early and help optimize a development effort, avoiding a last-minute crunch.

Thorough regression

With a game that has existed for some time, the testing team usually has at least some regression tests prepared that can be run when needed. Difficulties in using those tests arise when the code changes are either so significant or out of the ordinary that generic tests will not be enough to ensure that the risk brought by the changes is properly addressed. This is especially important in cases when a game is already widely popular with players and we are implementing a major new feature. For example, if a game has been live for, let's say, 6 months, has millions of players, and we decide to add on a multiplayer feature, there will probably be marketing campaigns about it and player expectations will be high. However, the actual code implementation would be complex and impact several areas of the game.

In cases like the aforementioned, it's always recommended you do a more thorough regression. While we also start with a collaborative approach, in thorough regression, we should also investigate areas of a game that are not directly impacted by the change but that might be indirectly. In this type of regression testing, a QA specialist can often use already existing test cases that might need to be modified to adapt to new changes. In *Chapter 10, Eat, Sleep, Test, Repeat: Test Methodology*, we will cover in detail different **testing methodologies** that will help us prepare in the best possible way for regression testing.

Quick regression

We do quick regression in cases where a game has already been thoroughly tested and all major bugs have been identified and fixed. Quick regression is done with the intent to give assurance to product managers and the rest of the team that new changes are working well and don't negatively affect the rest of the game. While quick regression is never supposed to be used as a substitute for full regression, it often happens that it's the only type of regression done, due to time constraints and the fast-paced cadence of game releases.

In this section, we provided an in-depth overview of regression testing and how to execute it. In the following section, we will briefly cover other types of testing that are relevant in the gaming industry.

Other types of testing

There are other numerous types of testing that are used in the gaming industry. We will briefly cover the most significant ones that are frequently used.

Basic acceptance testing/acceptance testing/smoke testing

Basic acceptance testing (BAT), **acceptance testing**, and **smoke testing** are terms often used interchangeably. They are all considered to be part of functional testing, but with the specific purpose of validating only the basic functionality of the game or feature under test. These tests are time-limited, so we always have a benchmark on how long it takes to run one BAT/smoke test.

Stress testing/load testing

Stress testing is often performed by backend developers themselves or in collaboration with QA. In stress testing, we simulate potential stressors to game performance – multiple players joining a game at the same time, a rapid increase in game downloads, players focusing on only one part of the game, and similar. **Load testing** generally requires at least some coding work, and it can be automated.

Playtesting

Playtesting is most commonly done by a selected group of players. If it's done by a QA specialist, they should try as best as possible to put themselves in a player's shoes and try to play the game as the player, and not as a QA professional. Playtests can be done in many different ways – as a one-on-one, within a focus group of 5 to 10 testers, or as an extended playtest, where the player plays the game for several days.

> Note – one-on-one playtesting
>
> Playtesting is a user-centric testing methodology that is used to validate how end users will perceive and interact with the software we are developing. It's usually done in a game while it is not completely ready, as we try to get these crucial insights as early as possible. Otherwise, it would cost us lots of time and money to redesign a product that is almost finished. In one-on-one testing, we have a test moderator and playtester. The test moderator guides the playtester throughout the game, providing instructions on what to do next and asking questions. One-on-one playtesting is usually recorded and the moderator also takes notes. The moderator is either a UX designer or someone who is very familiar with the design of the game.

The goal of playtesting is to get an idea of how players perceive a game, how well they understand the tutorial, and how players interact with the game. Playtests can be arranged by game studios themselves, or they can use specialized agencies that provide these types of tests. When we do playtests, it's important that the game is mature enough that players can have a relatively smooth and bug-free experience, that players who participate are the right target audience (screening surveys help to determine that), and that players are not biased toward the company or game.

Ad hoc testing

Ad hoc testing is a unique but very common type of testing, where we don't use documentation, test cases, or a predetermined process. This type of testing is generally done by experienced testers who have already been working on a game for some time. They have such sufficient knowledge of the product that they already have an idea of what might be broken or not working well. Generally, this type of testing should be done only after more formal testing is done, but due to fast-paced game development in live ops and integrated QA, ad hoc testing is sometimes executed as the only testing as well.

Beta testing

Beta testing is unique in the sense that it is not done by the QA team but, rather, by the players themselves. It's very common in the gaming industry and used on all platforms, especially on PC and consoles. For games for mobiles, it's more common to do a **soft launch**. We will talk more about soft launches in *Chapter 9, It Works, but It Hasn't Been Tested: Testing Approach*.

Beta testing can be open or closed. **Open beta** means that a game is available on the target platform for a wide range of target audiences. Most of the time, to test the game in open beta, a player doesn't have to fulfill any special requirements besides sharing their email address.

Closed beta is when a game is open only to a selected group of players. They are chosen based on different parameters – geographical location, their gaming preferences, familiarity with the IP, or something else. For some highly anticipated game releases, there is quite a demand to get access to closed beta testing.

Why do we do beta testing? This is the last, big test before a game is released globally and studios start to spend big amounts on their marketing. It is beneficial to have beta testers included in the **game community**, such as forums or *Discord channels*, where studios can follow discussions, players can report bugs, and share their first impressions of the game. Beta testing allows game developers to do final fine-tuning of the game's difficulty, fix any outstanding issues, and get an idea of how the game will be received when released publicly.

Summary

In this chapter, we got a deep insight into what type of testing we most commonly undertake in game testing. First, we covered functional testing, the most common testing in games. After that, we got more familiar with the localization process and how localization QA works. We also learned the best ways to perform regression testing and how it is different from functional testing. Lastly, we briefly covered several other types of testing that are used within the gaming industry.

In the next chapter, we will turn our focus to gaming platforms, their importance in game QA, and how to execute testing based on each platform's specifics. We will cover in depth all the main gaming platforms, including mobile, consoles, and PC.

4

Deeper Look – Testing on Various Gaming Platforms – Mobile, PC, and Console

In this chapter, our focus will be on gaming platforms, which are exceptionally important in game QA. The choice of platform determines the entire flow of testing and can completely shift the focus. We begin this chapter with an explanation of platform relevance. Next, we focus on modern mobile platforms and how one mobile platform is differentiated from another. We take a deeper look into why console platforms are so different from others and finally, we wrap up this chapter with a look into how to handle testing for PC and other platforms.

In this chapter, we will learn the main reasons why platform testing is important and master the skills to organize testing for platforms. We will learn how to overcome the most common platform-testing challenges and uncover the strategies for efficient execution of platform testing. These are the topics we will address:

- Platform relevance
- Testing for Google Play
- Testing for the Apple App Store
- Testing on other mobile platforms
- Testing on consoles
- Testing on PC and other platforms

Platform relevance

Before we go into the details of why the choice of platform matters so much in game QA, it's important to define what we mean by *platform* in gaming terms.

What is a platform?

A platform is a digital space/ecosystem where our games are published and can be obtained by players either purchasing it, or for free. In order for developers to publish games on any platform, they have to meet a set of predetermined requirements. In some cases, the platform will test the game that its developers are attempting to submit. The process of submitting a game to a platform is called **submission** and is an important part of game development that also heavily involves QA. We will talk about it in more detail in *Chapter 11, Are You on the Right Version? Live Ops and QA*.

Players usually obtain the game from the platform by downloading it fully or partially to their own device. It's the player's responsibility to ensure that their device is on the specific version of the platform needed to run the game. It is rare and, in some cases, impossible for a given game to run on all existing versions of the platform. We can break down the process of the player obtaining the game into the following steps:

1. Finding the game on the platform – usually in some type of online store

2. Purchasing the game – either for a fee, through a subscription, or by obtaining it for free with the option of **in-app purchases** (**IAPs**)

3. Accessing the game – usually by fully or partially downloading it onto their own device

In broad terms, we can split the platforms primarily into the groups of devices used for playing games: mobile, console, and PC. There are significant differences between these three groups. Not only that games have to meet very different requirements to be published on each of those platforms, but even the games themselves need to be developed with different code structures to be able to run on those different platforms. The same game will not run on mobile, console, and PC by default. If you want to develop a game that will run on each platform, you need to create different versions of it. Furthermore, if you want your game to be successful and work well for a long time, your game architecture also needs to be optimized differently for each major platform. Of course, with additional work, the same game can be released on different platforms via a process we call *porting*.

What is porting?

Porting is the process whereby we export the game to other platforms than the one for which it was originally developed. Porting includes making all the required technical changes as well as changes in usability, the user interface, and compliance for the new platforms. Depending on the game, porting can be a very quick and straightforward process – for example, it's very easy to port a game from one mobile platform to another. But, in other scenarios, porting can be a lengthy and challenging process. For example, when we ported Angry Birds from mobile to consoles, we not only had to change the code and add content, but we also reworked lots of visuals, as screen resolutions are very different on mobile and TV screens.

We can already see that there are major differences between the approaches required for each platform. To make it even more complicated, each of these major platforms can be further split in others, with their own unique characteristics.

Mobile can be split into two major platforms: **Android (Google Play)** and **iOS (App Store)**. Android is not only Google Play; it also hosts other stores, the major ones being *Amazon*, which is a standalone Android-based platform, Samsung, Huawei, and others. They usually offer the Google Play Store as well as their own stores on the Android platform. The iOS platform runs only on Apple-made devices and as such has only one store and unified platform rules.

On the other hand, **consoles** are split into the Sony *PlayStation*, Microsoft *Xbox*, and *Nintendo*. There are other consoles in existence as well, but they are either obsolete and can't be purchased anymore or they don't hold a significant enough part of the market to be notable. Each of these consoles usually has one major current model.

Lastly, there are **PCs** and **Macs**. PCs have been used for gaming ever since they became a common household item, while Macs have traditionally not been used for gaming that much. This has changed recently and both computer platforms are used for playing games nowadays.

Now we know more about the platforms themselves, but *why* are they so important? Platforms set the rules about what can be published in their digital stores. Sometimes those rules are simple and easy to follow, but more often those rules are strict and require quite a bit of skill to implement and test for. Most of the platforms also perform their own QA. If you submit your game to a platform, it will be tested to check whether it meets the requirements. If it does, no problem. But if it doesn't, your game will be rejected, and you will need to fix the issues the platform discovered in the game. As you can imagine, this can potentially be time consuming, demanding, and very expensive, especially if your studio is running big marketing campaigns announcing a specific launch date. If your game fails to meet the platform requirements in time, your game will not make it to the platform's store and your marketing spend will have been wasted.

Now that we know why platforms are so important, let's continue with a deeper look into Google Play.

Testing on Google Play

Android is today the most widely used platform in the world. Over 3 billion people used Android phones in 2022 (source: `https://earthweb.com/how-many-people-use-android/`). While iOS is the most common platform in the USA, almost everywhere else in the world, Android is dominant, giving it a global market share of 86.1%.

While *Google* bought Android in 2005, we need to be careful not to use the term Android and Google Play interchangeably, as Google Play is just one of the marketplaces on Android, albeit by far the most popular one.

Google Play is one of the most approachable platforms; it is relatively easy to publish games and the requirements are not particularly strict. To be able to publish games and other apps on Google Play, you just need to register as a developer, which is a simple and relatively cheap process. The requirements for Google Play submission are easy to follow and are not excessively strict. You can always find the most recent requirements on the Android developer pages at `https://developer.android.com/quality`.

Up to now, this has sounded very easy and simple, but now we come to the biggest challenge that we meet with testing for Android. As we learned, Android is the most popular platform in the world, and even if it's owned by Google, it allows for other stores and multiple phone manufacturers. While having so much diversity is great for users as they can choose from very basic and cheap models all the way to the latest technological marvels, that same diversity causes headaches for testers. It is estimated that there are more than 10,000 different Android devices currently in existence. Having such a wide range of devices and manufacturers means that when a new version of the Android operating system is rolled out, it doesn't always hit all the devices at the same time. Some devices never get updated to certain Android versions at all.

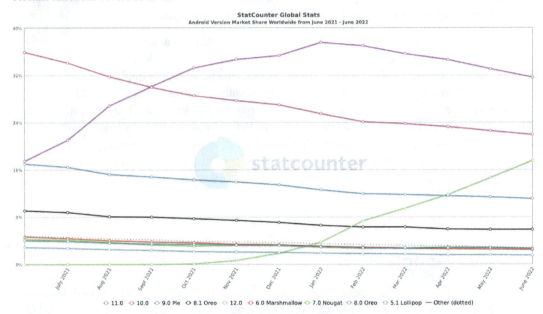

Figure 4.1 – Android version market share graph (Source: https://gs.statcounter.com/android-version-market-share)

You can find a more detailed breakdown of this at `https://infogram.com/android-os-market-share-1h7j4dvwrw18v4n`.

As we can see from the preceding chart, there are multiple versions of the Android operating system in use simultaneously. That means that if we want to ensure that our game will work across those versions, we need to test our game on them.

You can imagine that with such a high number of devices and operating systems in use, choosing which ones to test on can quickly turn into every tester's worst nightmare. We will talk more about how to select the optimal test set in the next chapter, *Chapter 5, It Must Be Hardware: Testing Hardware in Modern Game QA*. That still leaves us with the open question of how to test on so many versions of the Android operating system. Your strategy for handling this should focus on creating the least possible testing permutations that will give you optimal results. The first thing is to exclude versions that you know are not supported or that represent only a very minor fragment of your player base. Then, it's time to pick the "main one" – the OS version that is a must for your game. That will be your *principal version*. It will not necessarily be the latest one available – it's the version where most of your players are. How do you figure that out? If your game is not out yet and you don't have this type of analytics available, you can do some deductions yourself. Is your game casual or mid-core? Is it in 3D, with lots of content, animations, and action scenes? Or is it in 2D, with simpler gameplay and not too heavy a load on players' devices? Mid-core, resource-heavy games will target mostly newer devices where they will run the best, while if you are working with a lighter, more casual game, chances are that most of your players will be also on mid-range devices. That means that your principal operating system is probably the one that is most distributed and works on the widest range of mid-level devices. This is where you should focus most of your testing efforts. With that said, if you are aiming to get the biggest spenders and most visibility from the platform, it's very important to make sure that your game works on flagship devices, which generally means the latest version of the operating system.

One thing that can help us with testing for Google Play is the possibility to "*blacklist*" certain devices. If we discover during QA that the game doesn't run on a specific device, we can just blacklist it. That means we exclude the game from being visible on that device altogether. In that way, we won't get bad reviews in the store saying, "the game doesn't work" and we buy ourselves time to fix the problem in the next release.

Even if Google Play platform testing is relatively straightforward, we can already see that there are many different permutations that we need to take into consideration and that testing might become challenging, not because of the complexity of the platform but rather because of its popularity. For that reason, it's really important to prepare your test sets for Google Play testing on time and have appropriate testing resources to achieve sufficient coverage.

Besides that, it's good to have testing strategies ready that will optimize tester time. For example, how do we handle bugs found on a particular version of an operating system? Do we test for that bug on all other versions? If we do that, this prolongs testing and makes it very difficult to finish, especially if we work with lots of bugs. The best strategy to deal with this is the following:

1. Determine whether the bug is low, medium or high impact (we will learn more about bugs severity in *Chapter 8, I Thought I Fixed That: How to Write Efficient Bug Reports*). If it's low impact, we don't need to do anything else about it.

2. If we deem the bug to be of medium or high impact, we should verify whether the same bug appears on the lowest and highest supported versions of the OS.

3. If the answer is yes, the chances are that the bug is present in all versions of the OS.

Now that we have learned more about Google Play, it's time to switch to its main competitor, the **App Store** on iOS, and learn how it is different.

Testing on the Apple App Store

The App Store is the main store for Apple mobile devices. These mobile devices run on *iOS* or *iPadOS*. The whole ecosystem is fully controlled by Apple; unlike Android where we have many different manufacturers and stores, all Apple devices are made by one manufacturer, and it has only one store. While that potentially means fewer challenges in selecting test sets, App Store testing has its own unique challenges. Apple phones are predominant in the USA, UK, and Japanese markets, but can be bought almost anywhere in the world. It is considered that Apple users are on average bigger spenders than Android users and practically all Apple smartphones are considered premium devices. Compared to Google Play, the App Store also has somewhat more demanding testing requirements. The team at Apple proactively tests games that are submitted to the platform, and game build can be rejected due to bugs or other issues.

Apple's game requirements change relatively frequently and it's important to always keep up to date with them. You can find the latest **App Store requirements** here: https://developer.apple. com/app-store/review/guidelines/.

When it comes to operating systems, Apple works slightly differently than Android in that Apple always pushes their users to update to the latest version of iOS. Even if some users purposely keep their devices on older versions of iOS in order to reduce bloatware, most Apple users upgrade to the latest version of iOS as soon as it's available. With that in mind, it's still important to also test on older versions of iOS, especially if our game has already been live for some time.

Another thing to pay attention to is that unlike Google Play, with the App Store, you cannot blacklist devices. The game will show up on all devices, regardless of whether it works on them or not. What it is possible to do, though, is to exclude certain versions of the operating system. So, if you tested your game on an older version of iOS and you noticed it doesn't work, you can choose not to publish the game on that particular version, regardless of which phone it is installed on. This is handy when dealing with cases where the game doesn't work well on older versions of iOS. Often it is more economical just to cut support for that version of iOS than spend weeks trying to fix the game.

As mentioned earlier, games and apps submitted to App Store will be tested. What is usually tested by the team at Apple?

- Core gameplay on flagship devices
- Purchases

- Any Apple integrations
- Does the game meet the App Store guidelines?

Make sure that your internal testing team includes all these tests in their testing plan. That way, you will avoid the disappointment of your game being rejected by Apple.

Testing on other mobile platforms

As previously mentioned, these are not the only mobile platforms. The other most significant mobile platform is Amazon. while its OS is based on Android, it does have its own devices and its own app store.

Amazon is predominant in the USA and even if it doesn't have such a big chunk of market share as Google Play and Apple's App Store, it has significant revenue and almost half a million available apps to download. Amazon users are also known as very good spenders, and generally spend more than even Apple users. Developing for the Amazon platform is relatively easy as it's based on Android, but, of course, Amazon has its own set of requirements that need to be met in order to publish games on its platform.

There are other significant mobile platform stores owned by phone manufacturers. The most significant ones are the following:

- Samsung Store
- Huawei AppGallery
- TenCent MyApp (which is based on the QQ instant messaging service)
- Sony Apps

Lastly, we will mention *Netflix*, the latest platform to join the mobile gaming market. Netflix's mobile platform is, at the moment, restricting who can publish games. Developers who want to publish on Netflix have to make arrangements directly with the firm. This makes it a much more difficult platform to reach than Google Play or the Apple App Store. For now, all games on Netflix are free and developers make revenues through direct agreements with Netflix. Netflix also has its own strict list of requirements that games need to meet, but those are not publicly listed. Besides Netflix's internal requirements list, every game published on Netflix also must meet App Store/Google Play requirements.

Now that we are familiar with mobile platforms, let's next move on to consoles.

Testing on consoles

While there is a lot of similarity across gaming consoles, they all have their own unique sets of requirements. In the following diagram, you can see the main consoles on the market and the major differences between them.

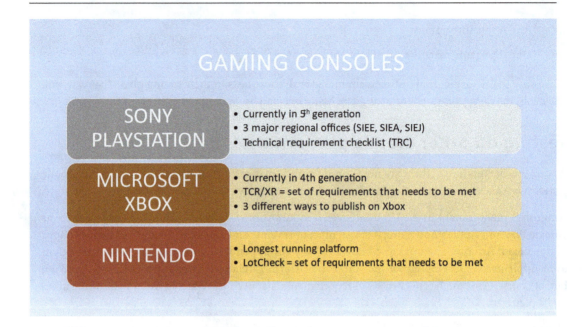

Figure 4.2 – Gaming console breakdown

All console testing consists of gameplay testing, which follows a similar methodology as any game testing, but it has specific achievements and compliance testing. At a high level, console testing includes the following:

- Gameplay testing

- Social gameplay (if implemented)

- Achievements (if implemented)

- Legal compliance based on specific checklists provided by consoles

Gameplay testing

Gameplay testing and stability are important parts of platform testing for any platform. You can be sure that each platform will thoroughly test your game and make sure that there are no issues with loading, performance, or glitches within the gameplay. To make sure that your game passes the submission process, it is recommended that the QA team does in-depth testing and ensures there are no major bugs. This also includes all forms of multiplayer or social gameplay.

Achievements

Many console games have numerous achievements, some of which are exceptionally hard or time consuming to reach. Game developers do this deliberately – it makes the game more interesting for the player and adds to the fun and long-term playability. While achievements work great as a motivator for the player, they can create lots of headaches for testers. Consider the following example. When I worked on the Angry Birds trilogy for consoles, one of the achievements we had in the game was to finish all levels with maximum efficiency, 3 stars. The game had over 400 levels and some of them were very challenging! But in order to ensure that an achievement can be reached, testers need to reach the achievement manually at least once. As achievements testing can be very demanding and time consuming, it is often outsourced to specialized testing companies.

Legal compliance

Legal compliance is different for every platform, and it is challenging to achieve. Each major console has its own set of regulations. They are not available publicly – to get access to them, you need to be a part of the development program with the target platform. As part of these programs, you are under a **non-disclosure agreement** (**NDA**) and hence it's not possible to disclose the full scope of those checklists. What can be said is that the checklists are very thorough and include items such as ensuring that games work well, that legal concerns are met, that all documentation is created and correct, all in-game texts are displayed correctly, and many other things. Some of the requirements can be challenging even to fully comprehend, which makes testing extra demanding.

It is important to note that Sony and Nintendo have multiple offices across different regions. If you want your game to go live globally or in multiple regions, you need to submit it to each main territory's office separately. There might be slight differences within the compliance requirements for each territory even on the same platform, so you should consider submission to each office as a separate process with separate QA required.

Specifics of console testing

When we plan for console testing, we need to bear in mind the pressures of time. Console games are usually very large productions with *fixed release dates*, and QA must be done in a timely manner. The development process works very differently than mobile F2P games, where we can fix live bugs, push content, or balance the game very quickly. On consoles, every change takes time and there is lots of pressure on QA to find all issues promptly.

Another major difference between testing for console versus mobile is that in mobile games, we don't have to worry too much about *balancing* the game. Very often, studios make very generic game-balancing decisions (i.e. character strength, weapons capacity, ease of passing levels, etc.) and wait to see game data to optimize the balance in the best possible way – making it both entertaining for players and profitable for the studio. On consoles, with a different development process where quick changes are very difficult to do, we prepare for the launch of the game as a finite product, they have beginning and the end. Game balancing needs to be thoroughly tested prior to launch, as it will be challenging to adjust quickly once the game is live.

Lastly, we shouldn't forget about *sounds and music*. This is another important difference between testing mobile and console games. Every game, on any platform, will have at least some sounds and music. It's impossible to even imagine a game that has no sound. But as mobile games are often played "on the go" – in public transport, while waiting in queues, even in schools and workplaces – the sound is often muted. Furthermore, mobile games are designed to be easy to pick up and easy to leave, and even if atmospheric music is great, it's not necessarily such an important part of the mobile gaming experience.

With consoles, the situation is very different. Console games are usually played in longer sessions rather than short spurts and provide much deeper levels of player immersion. Therefore, as they are part of the core gaming experience, sound effects and music have a much more important role in console games. For that reason, sound testing with console games is a very important task that needs to be done in a timely manner.

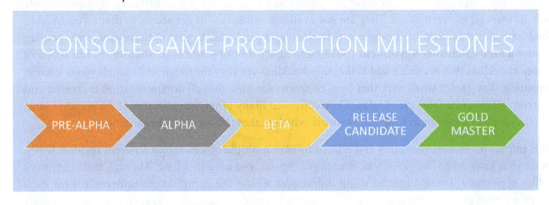

Figure 4.3 – Console game production milestones

In the above diagram, we can see the traditional console game production milestones. These days, if the game is not going out on physical disk, instead of "release candidate" and "gold master", we use only one milestone, sometimes called **gold candidate**. These production milestones are different from those used in mobile game development. In console game development, the **Alpha** milestone signifies that the game has all features and content complete and QA usually starts there, being done intensively until the **Beta** milestone is reached. QA is not finished at Beta though. At the Beta milestone, all major bugs should be finished, and no major changes should be made to the game, but there will still be QA activities focusing on improving the polish of the game and taking care of any outstanding regression, acceptance, and localization testing.

Console compliance testing is generally considered the most demanding type of game testing, and it's most often done by specialized teams. Large studios that regularly produce console games have their own internal testing teams, while smaller studios most often outsource console compliance testing to external partners.

As with the other elements of compliance testing we mentioned in this chapter, compliance checklists are often updated and changed, so it is important that your team regularly checks for any changes.

In this section, we went into the details of testing on consoles and how it differs from mobile and other popular gaming platforms. Next, we will look into the basics of testing on PC and other smaller platforms and how this is different from the platforms we covered already.

Testing on PC and other platforms

The PC has been around for a long time and since the early 90's has been widely used for gaming. The PC is a unique platform as it doesn't have a predominant store or preferred way to get games. As a player, you can get your games from various online stores, directly from the developer's web pages, or buy them as a physical product. Today, the most popular way to get games for PC is through the **Steam Store**. Steam has the largest selection of games, from AAA productions to indie offerings. Steam, as a marketplace, does some testing on games submitted to its platform, but those tests are not as strict or comprehensive as the ones for consoles.

Besides Steam, there are other online stores where players can purchase games, including *GOG.com*, *Epic Games*, and *Itch.io*. These generally have very few requirements that need to be met. Of course, that doesn't mean that PC games shouldn't be tested – it only means that their quality won't be scrutinized by professional testers working for stores on the platform.

Of course, the PC is not the only remaining platform. Games are also played on Macs and on computers running other operating systems, such as Linux.

The biggest challenge in testing PC games is ensuring that they run on a wide range of PCs. Even though they have similar characteristics, there are thousands of different specific hardware configurations out there, including some that are custom-made by players themselves. It's virtually impossible to ensure that game will work on all of them. As a rule of thumb, bigger and more hardcore games usually require more powerful machines to run, while smaller and more casual games can run well even on average computers. We will talk more about how to test hardware in the following *Chapter 5, It Must Be Hardware: Testing Hardware in Modern Game QA*.

Besides computers and consoles, modern games can also be played on *smart TVs*, *smart watches*, and other technical gadgets. They all have their own compliance requirements that games need to meet and be tested for, just like with any other platform. As a rule of thumb, regardless of the platform on which you are going to publish your game, you want your game to run smoothly, look great, and meet all the requirements of the given platform. In this way, not only will you make the target platform happy, but you will also help provide a wonderful experience for the players. Make sure that you take platform compliance into consideration early, ensuring you have sufficient time to fix any outstanding bugs and respond to any comments the platform might have.

Lastly, we will touch on **browser games**. Although they are theoretically PC or Mac games, as you do need an actual computer to play them, these games are slightly different, as they are played in the browser and not launched on their own. As such, there are specific QA tasks required for the browser platform. Browser games are different than other PC games in several ways:

- You need an internet connection to play them

- They don't take up space on your PC

- You don't need a specific hardware configuration to run them

- Very often, they are free to play

Browser games are not that popular anymore, but are still relevant. One of the simplest browser games, *Wordle*, took the world by storm just last year when it seemed like absolutely everyone was playing it. We need to consider when testing browser games that there are many different browsers in use, as well as many different versions of those browsers! To ensure that games work properly, QA needs to take this into account.

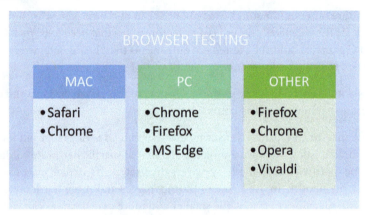

Figure 4.4 – Browser testing

In the preceding figure, we can see the range of browsers by popularity on each computer platform. When you are planning testing for browser games, make sure that your game is tested on the most popular browsers among your target market, as well as on the main versions of browsers currently in general use.

Summary

In this chapter, we learned more about the specifics of testing for each platform and strategies to handle platform compliance tests. You have learned how the platforms differ from each other and the main challenges of developing and testing for each platform. We also learned more about player behavior on each platform and how this affects QA.

In the next chapter, we will continue with our study of platforms and go even deeper into platform differences by investigating how to test on different hardware and how to prepare optimal hardware test sets.

5

It Must Be Hardware: Testing Hardware in Modern Game QA

While this chapter is relatively short, it's also really important to take into consideration when testing games. It's exceptionally difficult, if not impossible, to test games without using specific hardware to do so. In this chapter, we will explain how to build your hardware **test sets**, with an emphasis on **mobile game testing**. You will learn how to plan and optimize your test sets in order to meet your schedule and avoid issues in live games. At the end, we will wrap up the chapter by sharing tips on how to select and use your hardware for other gaming platforms.

In the previous chapter, we spoke in great detail about the differences in testing between different platforms. In this chapter, we will dive deeper into the core difference – hardware. What is hardware testing in the context of game QA? We can look it at from two angles:

- Testing whether the game works on a wide range of existing gaming hardware
- Testing whether gaming-focused hardware performs well when we play games on it, especially new, popular games

In this chapter, we will primarily focus on the first option – testing whether the game works on a wide range of existing gaming hardware. As this book is focused on game testing, this angle is much more relevant for us as it's part of any modern game testing effort.

The second option is important as well, especially if the *hardware manufacturer* is aiming to sell to the gamer market, but this type of testing is generally not done in gaming studios, but rather in special labs on the manufacturer's premises and often using testing rigs.

Is hardware important in modern game QA?

Hardware is one of the most important factors we need to take into account when testing games. The platform itself is in many ways defined by the hardware used. For some platforms, such as *consoles*, hardware testing is not particularly demanding. On the other hand, hardware testing for *mobile* is complex and requires good planning. In this chapter, we will focus mostly on mobile hardware testing and go into depth on how it affects game QA.

When talking about *mobile*, we need to make a clear distinction between iOS (Apple) and Android. While Apple has an increasing number of mobile devices and tablets on the market and in active use, they are all manufactured by the same company. It does take some effort to make sure that all supported devices are covered, but it's generally manageable even with a relatively small testing team. The big challenge testers face with testing for iOS is when Apple releases new models of phones. This usually happens in September each year, and it's hard to get those devices ahead of time. If you have followed Apple throughout the years, you have probably noticed that new phone launches are big events, with dedicated fans waiting for hours in line to get the newest device. Those people are called "early adopters" and they are known for being very good customers, who are most likely to convert to spenders. That's the market you probably don't want to miss with your game. But if you didn't get a chance to test the game on a new device before it became available, and this particular model is significantly different from the last generation of Apple phones, your game might not work as it should.

It's possible for well-known studios to get access to new devices relatively quickly after launch, but for many smaller gaming companies, making sure that game works on the latest Apple device might be challenging.

On the other hand, *Android* has its own set of challenges. Android is an open source platform and many manufacturers use Android as the operating system for their devices. The result is that the hardware in each device is supplied by numerous different companies.

Source: https://gs.statcounter.com/vendor-market-share/mobile/worldwide

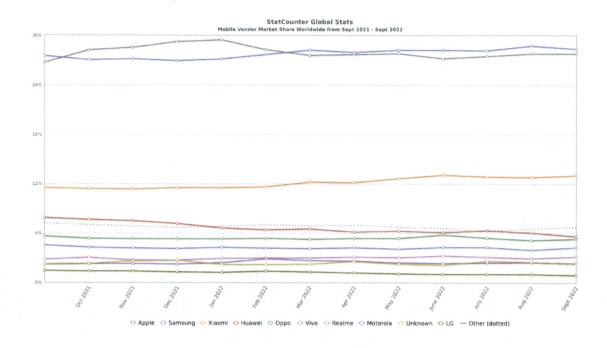

Figure 5.1 – Global mobile manufacturers breakdown

In *Figure 5.1*, we can see that Apple (iOS) and Samsung (Android) have been in positions of global primacy over the last couple of years. In *Figure 5.2*, we can see a breakdown of the current market share between major mobile manufacturers.

Samsung	Apple	Xiaomi	Huawei	Oppo	Vivo
28.43%	27.73%	13.04%	5.66%	5.32%	4.29%

Mobile Vendor Market Share Worldwide - September 2022

Figure 5.2 – Global mobile manufacturers breakdown in %

As we can see in *Figure 5.2*, the Android manufacturer with the biggest portion of the market is Samsung. Even if Samsung's market coverage varies from country to country, they have such a big chunk of the market overall, that we can safely say they are the leader in the Android market. How is this information useful to game testers? If you had a limited pool of devices to purchase and test on, picking up a *Samsung* flagship mobile phone is a good choice.

In this segment, we learned how important hardware is for game testing and the main challenges that come with it. We learned more about mobile manufacturer market segmentation, and more broadly about how different platform hardware is utilized in game testing. Next, we will learn how to prepare test sets for game testing, with a focus on mobile games.

Test sets – how to build one

Every game, besides console games, needs to be tested on at least several devices. That means the QA team needs to have a set of testing devices that can be used as required. The collection of devices used for testing our game build is called the **test set**. But how do we go about building an optimal test set? We will be focusing primarily on mobile devices here.

We always start from the **principal device**. This is the device that we use the most and should be representative of the majority of our target audiences. Very often in small studios, developers just use their own personal devices. While that's better than nothing, it's not necessarily the best approach to testing on devices. If the device is made only for the local market, for example, or is different from what our target audience uses, we might prioritize bugs differently and have an unrealistic idea of the priorities in the project. We will learn more about how to prioritize bugs in *Chapter 8, I Thought I Fixed That: How to Write Efficient Bug Reports*. For these reasons, it's important to select a principal device that is the most relevant for our target market.

While many testers are passionate about technology and might have good ideas about the ideal smartphone to use for testing, this isn't necessarily always the case nor is it a QA specialist job requirement. Before we choose the principal device, we need to ask ourselves the following questions:

- What *country or territory* is our main market? Which phone brand/model is popular there?

- What is our *target audience*? Are we making educational games for kids? Casual games targeted mostly at middle-aged women? Or a new twist on first-person shooters that would appeal to younger male audiences? Every segment of the audience has different gaming and device preferences.

- Are any new flagship devices coming out very soon, or have just been released? Often, those devices can quickly take over from previous models in terms of popularity, and may also have implemented new technological advancements that affect how your game runs on them.

When we have answers to those questions, we can narrow our choice of device down to a manageable list. After the principal testing device, we should prepare our **"must work" set**. These are the devices on which our game must be confirmed to work well. The following are some reasons why games are required to work on specific devices:

- We are trying to secure being *featured* on Google Play or the App Store and it's one of their requirements

- A big portion of our *players* in some of our major markets uses this device

- Players who use these devices are known to be better spenders than average; that's usually case with *early adopters* who purchase new technology, meaning new phones as well

- We have a *partnership* with a manufacturer or other stakeholder, and this is one of their requirements

As you can see, there could be numerous reasons why we might want to include certain devices in our test sets. Even with these parameters, though, as there are so many active devices out there, we can still end up with lists containing thousands of devices. How can we narrow it down to something more **manageable**? What would our studio consider as manageable?

The overall size of your test set also depends on the size of your QA team. If the team consists of only one or two testers, having 100 devices in a test set will not be helpful. There is only so much time that one person can spend testing on each device. Unfortunately, there is no "ideal" number of devices that one tester can cover, as the frequency and intensity of testing change throughout the project. If you need to verify a quick bug, you might be able to do it on a dozen devices. While I was a localization tester at Lionbridge (now Telus), I managed to test one specific task on 11 devices, and it took me only about an hour. But when your testing task is more than a quick check, it might take an hour per device, or even more. And sometimes it can take a significant amount of time to upload the testing build to each and every device, and this time requirement should not be taken lightly.

In cases when your test round lasts for a couple of days on one device, it might take way too long to test on more than one or two devices. I usually suggest having three devices per tester (one high-end, one medium, and one low-end), as that setup is also ideal for quick bug verifications and early identification of how widespread a bug is. Therefore, taking the math of three devices per tester, if your testing team has, let's say, five testers, the size of your "must have" test set should be about 15 devices.

But how we can make sure that we have the right devices? Even if the number of available Android phones is overwhelming (and Apple is also steadily increasing its number of supported devices), most of them have very similar *configurations*. They might be from different brands and look different on the outside, but they can be surprisingly similar "under the hood."

DEVICE	PROCESSORS	GPU	DISPLAY	SCREEN RATIO	MEMORY	ANDROID OS
Samsung Galaxy S22 Ultra	Octa-core (1x2.8 GHz CortexX2 & 3x2.50 GHz Cortex-A710 & 4x1.8 GHz Cortex A510) - Europe	Xclipse 920 Europe	Dynamic AMOLED 2X, 120Hz, HDR10+, 1750 nits (peak), 6.8 inches, 114.5 cm2 (~90.0% screer-to-body ratio), 1440 x 3080 pixels	19.5 : 9	512GB 12GB RAM	Android 12
Google Pixel 6 Pro	Octa-core (2x2.80 GHz CortexX1 & 2x2.25 GHz Cortex-A76 & 4x1.80 GHz Cortex-A55)	MaliG78 MP20	LTPO AMOLED, 120Hz, HDR10+, 6.7 inches, 110.6 cm² (~88.9% screen-to-body ratio) 1440 x 3120 pixels	19.5 : 9	128GB 12GB RAM	Android 12
Oppo Find X5 Pro	Octa-core (1x3.00 GHz CortexX2 & 3x2.50 GHz Cortex-A710 4x1.80 GHz Cortex-A510) - Global	Adreno 730	LTPO2 AMOLED, 1B colors, 120Hz, HDR10+, BT.2020, 500 nits (typ), 800 nits (HBM), 6.7 inches, 108.4 cm2 (~89.6% screen-to-body ratio), 1440 x 3216 pixels	20 : 9	256GB 12GB RAM	Android 12

Figure 5.3 – Android phone comparison

In the preceding table, we can see one of the possible ways to group devices. It's generally considered safe to pick one of the devices from a group with the same characteristics – if your game works on one of those devices, it should work without major issues on others as well. The preceding table also has specifications for three high-end devices. We can notice that while they have lots of similarities, they also have important differences. Additionally, we can see that at least some of them have alternative configurations intended for different markets: the Samsung Galaxy S22 Ultra for the rest of the world outside Europe, and the Oppo Find X5 Pro for China. If our main markets were, for example, in the US, we would need a different model of Samsung Galaxy S22 Ultra, and likewise if our main market for the Oppo Find X5 Pro was China.

We already spoke about the importance of testing on different versions of operating system in *Chapter 4, Deeper Look - Testing on Various Gaming Platforms – Mobile, PC, and Console*. Your game might work great on devices running a specific operating system version, but not run at all on the same device with older or newer versions of that operating system. So it's important to take this into account when creating your test set. Make sure that you have several devices running different supported operating systems. Here it is important to mention that you need to control who can update the operating system version on your test sets. Unfortunately, once when you upgrade the operating system on a phone, it's exceptionally difficult to downgrade it, and you want to make sure that this is not done before prior approvals and considerations.

It's worth noticing that, we add devices considered **"good to have"** or for which we are recommended to check. We generally approach this group *heuristically*. Based on our previous experience, we might know which devices could potentially create problems and want to take them into consideration. We also look at the general availability of devices on the market where our players are. The product team might have plans to take our game into *new markets* or *localize* it for a specific market to increase downloads and revenue. We would want to know in advance how the game will perform on the devices popular in those markets, and we should definitely consider including them in our sets.

In this section, we learned in detail how to prepare our test sets for mobile and the things we must take into account to do this efficiently. In the next section, we will learn more about hardware testing outside mobile: how this is different from mobile and the things we need to consider when working with those hardware platforms.

Hardware testing beyond mobile

Let's investigate in more depth how to organize hardware testing beyond mobile games.

Console hardware testing

Console games are usually made for one model of the current generation of consoles, although many do offer backward compatibility. Consoles of the same generation don't have too much differentiation. They might have more or less memory or look slightly different on the outside, being painted in different colors or patterns, but the console hardware itself is pretty much the same.

When we test for consoles, we can't test on commercial versions of the console hardware that you buy in the store. In order to test consoles, the studio needs to be registered as a developer with the target console platform (Sony Playstation, Nintendo, or Xbox) and order *development and testing consoles* directly from the manufacturer. While the process of ordering and getting the target console might be lengthy, testing the hardware itself is not. You only need to test the game on one test console, so tests don't need to be repeated on a series of devices. It is necessary to order the dev and test console, as you won't be able to use a burned disk or USB stick to install a working version of the game. **Commercially available consumer units can only run commercially released games.** They are set up in that particular way by the manufacturers themselves to combat game piracy. Besides the ability to run the game from different storage media, the test set can also be adjusted to *different regions*. This way, your team won't need to get separate testing sets for each region in which your game is going to be launched. We briefly spoke about testing for consoles in different markets in the previous chapter. Lastly, console test sets have the capacity to store data dumps and do certain automation checks in order to assist in the testing efforts. This is an important feature that helps developers fix bugs timely and efficiently.

Lastly, test and dev consoles can look quite different to consumer units. As they are intended only for internal and professional use, there is no need for them to have appealing aesthetics.

PC hardware testing

We already briefly mentioned in the previous chapter how challenging it can be to test on different *PC hardware configurations*. Not only do we have numerous PC manufacturers, but PCs are often modded or even assembled by users themselves.

Most PC users also use additional peripherals: keyboards, mice, and cameras, among others. It would be impossible to test all possible hardware permutations.

Usually, this challenge is handled by establishing *minimum hardware requirements* that need to be met in order to run a specific game. These are clearly marked in the descriptions of games when buying them online, or on the actual box if you are purchasing a game in physical format. This, by default, excludes the need to test the game on every possible permutation. But it still leaves lots of possible different hardware on which the game can be installed. When we are preparing to test PC games, we should ask the following questions:

- Which supported graphic cards are most commonly used by our target market? Sites such as `https://store.steampowered.com/hwsurvey/Steam-Hardware-Software-Survey-Welcome-to-Steam` are a good source of information.

- What is the minimum CPU on which the game will run?

- What is the minimum GPU required?

- What are the minimum memory requirements?

Testing the game on the minimum supported hardware is a good indicator as to how the game will perform on more powerful configurations. If we realize during testing that there is lots of lag in-game, or other issues that arise with this configuration, we can choose either to fix the most concerning bugs or increase the minimum system requirements. This way, we can save time in development and avoid a deluge of post-release customer tickets on the player support system.

While it is recommended to test your game on a wide variety of supported configurations, these days, lots of studios, even big ones, are skipping this step. The cost of time and effort to run such an extensive operation toward the end of the game development cycle is often considered not worth investing in, especially if it would lead to the game launch being delayed. Big gaming studios usually have very well-planned launch schedules, with marketing activities that start months before the actual launch date. Announcing last-minute delays would potentially enrage fans and lead to marketing budgets being wasted. For that reason, PC games often go out with quite a few bugs that are only fixed after launch. Even if this might sound counter-efficient, PC gaming fans are mostly used to it.

Summary

In this chapter, we learned how hardware testing relates to modern game testing, the things we need to take into consideration when preparing mobile hardware test sets, and how to differentiate hardware testing needs for different platforms. Among other things, we also learned how to approach preparing test sets for Android phones. The skills learned in this chapter will enable you to optimize test sets for the size of your team, make the necessary hardware procurements, and by making smart hardware choices, avoid serious bugs in production. In the next chapter, we will start our journey into test cases: the first step towards testing execution, the key activity of QA.

Part 2:
Test Strategy and Execution

Part 2 of this book is all about test execution, the main activity of QA. We will learn how to create great test cases, set up different types of bug flows, and write effective bug reports. We will wrap up this part with deeper insights into how agile methodology affects game QA and learn more about the best testing approaches.

This part has the following chapters:

6

Friend or Foe – Test Cases

For a long time, test cases were considered a staple in game testing. With the adoption of agile methodologies and the gaming industry's increased focus on **Games as a Service** (**GaaS**), test cases had to evolve as well. In this chapter, we will talk in detail about the importance of test cases, how to approach them, how to recognize good ones, and most importantly, how to create them. In modern game testing, we don't necessarily always use test cases. We will also look into the most common test-case alternatives in more detail.

In this chapter, you will learn how to write great test cases, when to use them and when alternatives are a better choice, and lastly, how to create and use test-case alternatives.

We'll cover the following topics:

- What are test cases, and do we need them?
- How to write great test cases
- Test case alternatives

What are test cases, and do we need them?

A **test case** consists of instructions to testers that need to be executed in order to find out if a game is working as intended. Very often, when creating test cases, testers uncover issues with game design and logic. In simple terms, test cases are *instructions* about how we execute testing. While they have been a crucial part of traditional testing, in more modern approaches, test cases are sometimes not even used at all.

Do we need test cases? As with many other game testing-related questions, the answer is, *"it depends"*. There are instances when test cases are exceptionally useful, while in other situations testing might be more efficient without them. Let's investigate this a bit deeper.

TEST CASES ARE USEFUL	TEST CASES ARE NOT USEFUL
Onboarding new team members	When testing team is senior
Working with outsourced testers	When test cases require heavy maintenance
Working with a new game	When they are used as only measure of testers efficiency
When we need to split work among multiple testers	Can prevent testers from using their initiative
Estimating test coverage	When they stop producing bugs/testing fatigue

Figure 6.1 – Test case usefulness

Test cases are useful when we are just starting work on a new game that hasn't been tested before. In those early stages, the process of **designing test cases** based on game documentation, use cases and requirements can reveal flaws in game logic, missing components, and similar things. As the process of designing test cases is consecutive, utilizes testing strategies, and follows logic, it can be relatively easy to spot missing steps in design.

Another time when test cases are highly useful is when we get a new tester on the team. Having well-written test cases ready for execution drastically decreases the onboarding time for new testers. By following test cases, they can start contributing to the testing team's efforts almost immediately. This works in a similar manner when we work with *outsourced* QA partners. It's easy to send them batches of test cases and monitor their execution. If test cases are well prepared, testers rarely need additional instructions or training to start working on our game.

We also need to keep in mind that our team members might move on to different departments or even different companies. When people leave, they take lots of know-how with them. Having solid test cases makes handovers much easier. We can conclude that any testing involving teamwork can benefit from having test cases. I remember a situation from my time at Rovio, where we had a very tight deadline for one of Angry Birds games and testers were offered overtime to make sure that we were on time for launch. We had quite a large group of testers, but without well-defined test cases, some time was wasted. We had cases where a few people tested the same areas of the game, while others were not tested at all. At the end of the day, everything worked great, and the game launch was a great success, but looking back, we could probably have done it with a bit less stress and in a bit less time.

We have spoken in detail about when test cases are useful, but what about times when they are not useful? There are numerous situations when test cases are not really that useful. When you are working with a very *experienced* group of testers working on the same game for a long time, sometimes test cases can be more of an obstacle than a useful tool. Those testers are very familiar with how the game works, and they might find more bugs *heuristically* than using test cases.

Another case is when test cases are so detailed that it takes more time to maintain them than execute them. If you realize that you are spending more than 20% of your time maintaining test cases, it's time to check in and re-evaluate their usefulness.

Lastly, test cases might not be appropriate when used as a key indicator of testers' *efficiency*. Having test-case execution speed as a major (or the only) measure of testers' efficiency will definitely give us an incomplete picture of the team's work. It might encourage testers to speed through the test cases to meet the targets and get better management reviews. This can lead to a lack of focus, superficial execution, and as a result, missed bugs. When we document test cases and they are approved, it's human nature to think that we have done our job and we primarily rely on the test cases, minimizing thoughts about other ways to test games. That can lead to "mindless repeating" of work and missing important bugs. Even the best-conceived test cases eventually suffer from testing fatigue and stop producing bugs. Therefore, testers should stay vigilant and even when using test cases, always keep their eyes and mind open. We will talk more about the future of testing in *Chapter 13, There Are No BUGS Without U – QA and the Game Team*.

Now that we know when test cases can be useful, let's take a more thorough look into them.

Test cases can be very different in style, length, detail, and how they are managed. While they are often kept as Excel sheets, there are also sophisticated tools for creating, managing, and executing test cases. These are called **test management tools**. These tools allow us to link test cases directly to bug reports. This way, not only can we get much better reports about the efficiency of our test cases, but it's also much easier for testers to do bug verification in later stages. We will talk about bug verification in more detail in *Chapter 7, It Works on My Machine: Bug Flow*.

While there are many different ways to create test cases, they should all have the following:

- **Unique identifier**

  By using unique identifiers, we can recognize much more easily which test case was the one that revealed the bug. Depending on how we set up our identifier system, we can also easily recognize which part of the game the test case covers or what type of testing it employs. If we don't have defined identifiers and we have multiple test cases, it's much easier to get confused, especially if you are working in a team of multiple testers. Dividing work, collaborating, and rechecking are all much easier with identifiers attached to the test cases. Generally, we use numeric identifiers (think 1.1, 1.2, and variations of these) but there are no strict rules on that. As long as you and your team can easily identify them, it is good enough.

- **Any required preconditions**

  When we work with games, some test cases naturally come later than others. The simplest example of that is when testing specific levels. Usually, you need to pass earlier levels before you can move forward to the following levels, unless you use a cheat menu. But some preconditions might be less obvious than that. For example, lots of test cases covering aspects of multiplayer functions usually have specific preconditions. While some preconditions might not be necessary as they are obvious (i.e., start the game, make sure it runs), some might be very important but much less obvious (i.e., start the game, leave it idle for 15 minutes). Here, it is important to use your common sense and decide when it's acceptable to skip the preconditions, and when they are a must.

- **Clearly written steps on how to execute the test case**

  Here, we come to the main part of test cases – test case steps. There is no rule on how many steps a test case should have. It's often only one, especially with more generic test cases aimed at more senior testers. Test case: "Check the start screen" is completely valid (and is also an important test case to pass as it can have severe legal consequences if the game isn't displaying the right logo and visuals). Of course, not all test cases can have only one step, and often need a few. While it is good to split more complex test cases into smaller executional units, being too granular is not recommended. When I worked at Nokia, I often encountered test cases that had over 20 steps. Not only was it quite difficult to keep focused on the test case, they were also a nightmare to maintain. The team did not have enough resources to properly maintain them and we ended up with a large number of test cases that were obsolete and could only be used as high-level guidelines.

  Games slightly change with every update, and in free-to-play games, we continuously add new content. That means that test cases should be adjusted to reflect the changes made to the game. If you create your test cases with too much detail, very soon you will find yourself spending most of your time updating them. This can end up with us having a lot of test cases that took significant effort to create, but they become useless relatively quickly.

  Another thing that we need to mention here is the language we use when we create test cases. Use simple, straightforward language and clear, industry-standard terminology. Keep your sentences short and clear. While at Rovio, we used an outsourced QA service provider that created test cases featuring sentences that were three rows long. Nobody was sure what those test cases meant or how exactly to execute them. Reporting bugs from a test case that is hard to understand or execute can easily result in bugs being downgraded to lower severity than reported.

- **Desired outcome/what is considered pass**

  This is another field that can either be very obvious for the tester, or exceptionally confusing. In my career, I used to have very passionate fights about whether a test case passed or failed, as we didn't have the desired outcome mapped in the test case. The developer kept claiming that the game worked as intended, while the QA team, in the team to represent the players, kept claiming that this test case is a fail. When we clearly define the expected outcome, doubt is removed, and we can rest assured that bugs found through this test case will be taken seriously.

- **Possibility to mark the status of the test case** (pass, fail, can't execute, etc.)

  Testers should be able to mark the status and result of the execution of a test case. This is useful for several reasons. Firstly, we can follow the testing progress and have an estimation of how much work is still left. Secondly, we can get a good idea about the maturity of the build under test. If we see that most of our test cases receive a fail status, we know that the game is not mature enough to be released. Lastly, having the capacity to change the status of the test case helps us optimize the usage of the test cases themselves. If we find that many of the test cases help us find bugs, it suggests they are very efficient and that by running these tests, we will get good results. On the other hand, if many of them have statuses such as can't execute or n/a, it means that our test cases might be outdated, and that they need to be replaced with more relevant ones.

Let's look at a couple of real-world test cases:

Test Case Id	Test cases	Description	Expected Result	Result	Version Number	Comments
V0.6_1_01	Loading	1. Install the build 2. Launch the build	▓▓▓ Screen should be visible.	Pass		
V0.6_2_01	Game Launch	1. Install the build 2. Launch the build	Game should be launched with all correct scenes	Fail		http://youtrack.bo
V0.6_3_01	Art	1. Load the game 2. Observe all the cities, Resources and factories	Game should display all cities, Resources and factories	Pass		
V0.6_4_01	Tutorial	1. Load the game 2. Observe the tutorial text.	Tutorial text should be displayed correctly in the speech bubble	Pass		
V0.6_4_02	Tutorial	1. Load the game 2. Observe the tutorial text.	Check the tutorial text is spelled correctly	Pass		
V0.6_4_03	Tutorial	1. Load the game 2. Tap on the tutorial text to proceed 3. Arrow points at Apple request at city Seven rivers	The Camera should zoom in at City seven rivers. And Green arrow should point correctly at Apple request.	Pass		
V0.6_4_04	Tutorial	1. Load the game 2. Tap on the tutorial text to proceed 3. Tap on the arrow that points at Apple request at city Seven rivers	Yellow arrow should point at the facility Apple Orchard and blue spiral animation is visible at city seven rivers	Pass		
V0.6_4_05	Tutorial	1. Load the game 2. Tap on the tutorial text and request at city to proceed 3. Tap on the arrow that points at Apple Orchard facility	Truck moves from Apple Orchard to Seven Rivers delivering the Apples.	Pass		
V0.6_4_06	Tutorial	1. Load the game 2. Tap on the tutorial text and request at city to proceed 3. Tap on the arrow that points at Apple Orchard facility 4. Truck delivers apples	Request completed icon is displayed at the city. Arrow points at the request complete icon	Pass		
V0.6_4_07			Rewards animation is observed Tutorial text is displayed and tap to proceed to further			

Figure 6.2 – Test case example 1

The preceding test cases were written for a real game and stored in Excel. We can see that besides test case IDs, there are also game area markers that help determine which part of the game we are testing. Descriptions include the test steps and the expected results are clearly marked. The **Result** column indicates clearly whether the test case passed or failed and the **Comments** column can be used for linking to bug reports. These test cases are well written and easy to understand and follow.

	A	B	C	D	E
	Not Checked	Pass	Fail	Blocked	N/A
	14	0	0	0	0

% of Test Pass Complete	% for Review before Sign Off	Total Checks
0.00%	100.00%	14

Test Case	Expected	Status	Comments
		Tester Name	
		Device	
Facebook Connect			
	Verify that new user can connect to Facebook	Not checked ▾	
	Verify that progression loads correctly for already connected user	Not checked ▾	
	Verify User is able to disconnect the connected FB account using Logout in game settings.	Not checked ▾	
Invite			
	Verify that user can invite a friend	Not checked ▾	
Notifications should appear in Facebook app and browser	Verify that invited friend receives a notification	Not checked ▾	
	Verify that tapping received notification opens the App store for invited friend	Not checked ▾	
	Verify that if a invited friend is an existing player, tapping on notification opens the game	Not checked ▾	
Requests			
	Verify that Tapping on Ask button directs to list of friends in FB	Not checked ▾	
	Verify that the friend receives a invite request notification	Not checked ▾	
	Verify that tapping on received notification opens the game for requested friend	Not checked ▾	
Sharing			
	Verify that user can share an event on Facebook	Not checked ▾	
	Verify that Event share appears correctly on users wall	Not checked ▾	
	Verify that share appears correclty on users wall	Not checked ▾	
	Verify that user share has correct art and text	Not checked ▾	

Figure 6.3 – Test case example 2

The preceding test cases also use Excel as the repository, but the setup is more elaborate here. At the top, it has a summary of execution progress, which gives us a great overall view of how testing is going. We can see how many test cases are still left to run, how many have passed or failed, were blocked, or received **N/A**. In some cases, we need to execute test cases consecutively, passing the prior test cases before advancing to the following ones. One good example of this is where we have a test case to successfully join the guild in a game, and the following test case involves using the chat in the guild. If we can't join the guild, it would be impossible to use the chat, so that test case would be *blocked* if the prior one failed.

While we call this example a test case, it would be more precise to call it a **test scenario**. We will talk in more detail about test scenarios in the *Test case alternatives* section of this chapter.

We have now learned what test cases are, how useful they are, and how they can be presented. In the next section, we will learn in more detail how to write professional bug-finding test cases.

How to write great test cases

Before we fully jump into the instructions for writing great test cases, let's have a look first at those test cases that would be considered poor or not that useful. It takes skills and experience to create great test cases. The tester has to have logical thinking, really understand the game being tested, and also can write in an understandable manner. With experience, testers learn which types of test cases are more likely to find bugs and what type of language works the best. Let's have a look at an example of a poor test case.

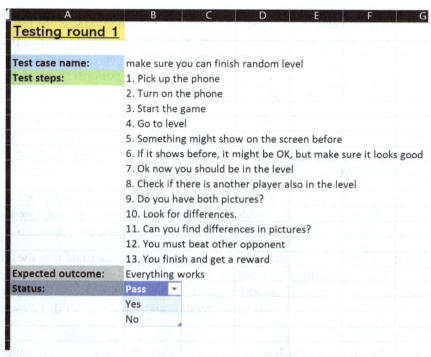

Figure 6.4 – An example of a poorly written test case

In the preceding figure, we can see a test case that is less than optimal. Let's analyze what is wrong with it. Firstly, this test case has no identifier. If we want to link to it, quote it, or re-use it, it would be quite difficult. Secondly, there are no preconditions mentioned. When we look at the test steps, we can see that preconditions are included. That's not necessarily bad, but it makes this test case quite long – it has 13 steps! Taking a closer look at the test steps, we can see that they are not really unified. Some are very generic, some are detailed, and others are more of an expected result than a test step that needs to be executed. There is no expected outcome per test step and the overall test case's expected outcome is way too vague. Lastly, we can see that the test case status is somewhat confusing. While "Pass" is understandable, "Yes" and "No" are too generic. Now we know what a poorly written test case looks like, let's take a much closer look at how to create great ones.

If we decide to use test cases in our testing processes, it's really important to create test cases that have these four attributes:

- Easy to read, understand, and follow

- Has a good chance of producing bugs

- It can be reused

- It's accurate and focused

We design test cases in the **test design phase**. Test design is the earliest stage in the test creation process. In this phase, we decide what *features* we are going to test, what our *test oracle* is (meaning, what are we testing against, e.g. use cases) and which *approach* we are going to adopt in the creation of test cases. For example, in this phase we might decide we are going to write thorough test cases with well-defined steps, or use a more high-level approach.

It is important to go through the test design phase, as it helps us unify our approach and prepare test-case writing standards that make it easier for testers to prepare tests themselves. Failing to do so, we might end up with test cases that are of different lengths, styles, focus, and granularity, all of which would impact testing negatively.

Besides test cases design, in this phase we will also decide how we *report bugs* and if they are going to be *linked* to the test cases. We will also decide on our test case *repositories*, the ways we will share them among testers, and what test reports will be created based on the test-case execution.

Depending on the size of your studio and QA team, the test design phase could take the form of a single meeting where you agree with all stakeholders how to approach writing test cases and prepare simple, one-page instructions. In bigger, more complex organizations, this process can be lengthier, and you might have to go through several layers of iteration and approvals. For that reason, make sure that you start the planning process early.

When we have decided on our approach for producing test cases, the work can start. Test cases are most commonly written by *testers* themselves. If the QA team is on the larger side, there are often one or two team members who might take the lead on the test-case creation task. Sometimes, test cases can be also written by game designers or producers, but these days this is not that common. They will provide the test oracle, the use cases, the **Game Design Document** (**GDD**), and other documentation to the testers to use as a base for test-case creation, but rarely have the responsibility of creating the test cases themselves.

As we mentioned previously, test cases are usually stored in some type of *repository*. While this is often Excel, Google Sheets, or something similar, there are also specific tools used for storing and executing test cases. If your team heavily relies on test cases, it's worth investigating the test case tools available and putting them to use. TestRail is one of the most popular test-case management tools, but there are multiple others such as Testiny, QACoverage, TestCase Lab, Tuskr, and Xray.

When we start creating test cases, we should create them in specific **test sets**. Test sets can be divided by *test focus*, where each test set covers one part of the game (critical path, multiplayer, tutorial, etc.). If we divide them into *testing phases*, we need to take into consideration in which phase of development the game is (user acceptance tests, alpha tests, regression) or *testing strategy* (negative testing, pairwise testing, etc.). Test cases can also be differentiated based on their purpose: while we use *basic acceptance testing* to verify that a game is working, *functional testing* helps us find functions of the game that are not working. We already examined the different types of testing in *Chapter 3, A Deeper Look - Types of Testing in Games*.

There is no specific order to the creation of test cases; it's always good to start from what we would consider the *critical path* – the most likely path a player would take when playing the game. After that, we can focus on writing test cases for other areas of the game.

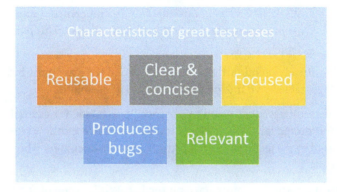

Figure 6.5 – Characteristics of great test cases

While test cases are relatively short and somewhat *technical instructions*, it's exceptionally important to use proper language when we create them. Always use sentences that are as simple as possible. Avoid too many abbreviations and uses of industry jargon – the gaming industry does not have a unified approach to this, and what is clear and understandable to you might be very confusing to someone else. It is not only much easier to follow and execute test cases that are concise and clear; they are also much easier and faster to update. Whenever possible, use short, actionable verbs such as "go there, push this, stop that." This type of language makes execution much smoother and faster.

Another very important thing to keep in mind while creating test cases is their *usefulness*. Testing time is always limited, and we want to focus our testing execution on the most efficient, bug-finding test cases. To find *relevant bugs* that are difficult to dispute, we need solid test cases that truthfully reflect the players' intended behavior. For example: while working on the Angry Birds Trilogy for consoles, one of the outsourced testers created a test case which, in brief, was about holding your finger on the controller's X button for six hours straight. It really didn't matter what happened as the result of that test case, because no player will ever hold their finger on one button for such a long time!

When we create test cases, although we know that they will eventually run out of steam and stop producing bugs, we do want them to be usable for as long as possible. We want to make sure that our test cases are easily *repeatable* and can be *reused* in the future.

Now that we have learned more about how to write and prepare test cases, let's have a deeper look into what test cases should consist of.

We already mentioned previously the must-haves for a good test case, but often they have even more information in them. We will go through them here:

- **Test case name**: Very often, test cases might have a name, especially if they are more detailed ones that take some time to execute or they need to be visibly distinguishable from similar test cases. If you use test case names, they should be clear, descriptive, and short. For example, *"First-time tutorial walkthrough without interruptions"* is a much better name than *"We will be going through the first-time experience of the tutorial, with a focus on the pure walkthrough and without any interruptions"*.

- **Test case ID**: We already mentioned this earlier as a good test-case must-haves. As long as it's unique and recognizable by your team members, it's a good solution.

- **Test data**: Some test cases require you to use specific test data, for example, email or social media logins. You should have test accounts and data available for these types of tests. It helps to have these listed in the test case or even better, a link to a document where this information is stored in one place.

- **Test preconditions**: Another must-have on the list. While some of the preconditions are very obvious, we should also not assume knowledge. It's much less harmful to skip known preconditions than execute a test case poorly while lacking the preconditions.

- **Test steps**: The core of the test case. While it's perfectly fine to have only one test step, it's not recommendable to have too many in one test case. If your test case has more than five steps, see if you can split it in two test cases. Make sure that each step is short, clear, and actionable.

- **Expected result**: Make sure the desired outcome is very clear to everyone.

- **Test case status and result**: It's important to be able to change the status of test cases. This helps us assess the maturity of the game under test (pass versus fail) as well as testing coverage. If we notice that many test cases have the *N/A* or *can't run* statuses, it indicates that it is time to quickly update the test cases as they are not relevant anymore.

- **Links**: Many test-case repositories allow testers to link to related test cases, but also to link to actual bugs found by the test cases. This functionality is great to assess the efficiency of the test cases as we can clearly see which ones are producing bugs. Besides that, having related test cases linked to each other shortens the search time and makes test execution faster.

We now know how to create great test cases and have seen real-world examples of how test cases can look in gaming studios. We also learned that test cases are not always the optimal choice. In the next section, we will take a closer look at the alternatives to test cases and how to use them.

Test case alternatives

We now know that test cases are not always necessary for the successful execution of testing. On the other hand, testers rarely test by making it up as they go along, without any guidelines. Here, we will cover the most popular test case alternatives used in the games industry.

Test scenarios

Test scenarios are short, usually one-line instructions on what to test. Rather than giving detailed instructions on how to execute the test case, it gives the freedom to the tester to utilize their experience and skills and follow trails that might lead to bugs. As test scenarios are usually brief and generic, they age well, don't suffer from testing fatigue, and can be reused for a long time.

	Test cases	Test scenario
What is it?	Detailed information on what to test, the steps to be taken, and the expected result	A one-liner stating what to test
It's about…	Documenting details	Thinking about and discussing details
Importance	Outsourced testers, coverage measure	Saves lots of time when team members can understand the details from the one-liner scenario
Advantage	Easy regression, faster and easier to write bugs (if you just add tc id)	Time saver, idea generation, easy to maintain, no testing fatigue
Beneficial	A foolproof test case document is a lifeline for new testers	Reduces complexity, makes people think rather than just following commands
Disadvantage	Time and money consuming	Needs more team effort, can be misunderstood

Figure 6.6 – Comparison between test cases and test scenarios

In *Figure 6.6*, we can see a comparison between test scenarios and test cases. As with any other tool, there are situations where one is more beneficial than the other, but test scenarios are very common these days. Their simplicity and ease of maintenance makes them a very popular choice, especially when working with *live ops* and *free-to-play games* that are frequently updated.

Use cases

Agile methodologies are very commonly used in the gaming industry, and thus so are use cases. These are used as a source for writing test cases and in many teams, use cases themselves are used as a substitute for test cases. In embedded teams, QA is part of the team and very familiar with all work being done on the game. Without the need to use traditional test cases and by reusing use cases, testers can work much faster and focus on testing the most critical parts of the game.

Test charter

Test charters are also frequently used in *agile teams*. They are primarily used for **exploratory testing**. Rather than giving detailed instructions to testers, they allow them to explore new areas of the game and record their findings. The **pairwise testing** technique is often used in executing test charters. In pairwise testing, we have two testers of different seniority levels executing tests together, one acting as a lead and the other as a follower. They test together, discussing the items under test, bouncing ideas off each other, and trying different approaches. The idea behind the usefulness of pairwise testing is that "two heads are better than one," and by working together, testers will generate more ideas.

Test charters, while lightly documented compared to test cases, still need to have certain information to be useful to testers. Each test charter should contain the following information:

- What should be explored
- What should be covered
- How long the testing session will last
- Who will do the testing
- Any specific setup that is required for test execution

During *test charter execution*, testers take notes, report bugs, and note down any issues they found while testing. This type of report can also be used as a foundation for writing traditional test cases.

Summary

We are now fully familiar with test cases and their alternatives. We learned how to write great test cases, examined some examples of what they look like, and learned more about when it's not ideal to use them. Furthermore, we also covered their alternatives, their advantages, and when they are appropriate for use. The desired outcome of a test case is a *bug* and in the next chapter, we will start our journey into bugs in great detail. We will build on what we have learned about test cases and see how bug reporting works, how it flows between the game team, and how QA fits into this process.

7

It Works on
My Machine: Bug Flow

Bug flow is a part of every game development. Even when it's not designed by anybody in particular, it still exists – it's impossible to write and fix bugs without it. Bug flow can be used interchangeably with the term **bug life cycle** – it's the set of stages that a bug goes through before it's finally addressed. I'm purposely not saying *fixed*, as not all bugs will be fixed (and they shouldn't), but all bugs need to be addressed. That means that each and every bug reported should go through a second set of eyes, and the team should decide how it is going to be handled.

In this chapter, we will learn about the importance of good bug flow and what can happen when bug flow is not optimized. Then, we will learn how to set up a great bug flow for any type of game team, with detailed examples that can be used as a base for creating bug flow in your own teams. We will also learn about good practices for creating and maintaining bug flow.

We will cover following topics in this chapter:

- The importance of bug flow in game teams

- How to set up a good bug flow

- Bug flow statuses and transitions

The importance of bug flow in game teams

If you are working in the gaming industry in any capacity, you have definitely heard about **bugs**. They are some of the most dreaded consequences of game development and, at the same time, the reason why **quality assurance** (**QA**) is so important in game production. Without QA, it would be difficult to find relevant bugs on time. But finding bugs is just the beginning of the story. How we handle them and what we do with them are equally important. Bug flow is the main way testers, developers, and producers communicate. While we often think of game teams as small groups of people working together in the office, today, this picture is very different. Games, especially ones on consoles and successful free-to-play ones are built and maintained by large teams scattered across different geographical locations. Studios also frequently use *outsourced QA services* as support or a main testing force. If our bug flows are not properly set, game production can experience severe problems and can even lead to delayed launches or faulty updates.

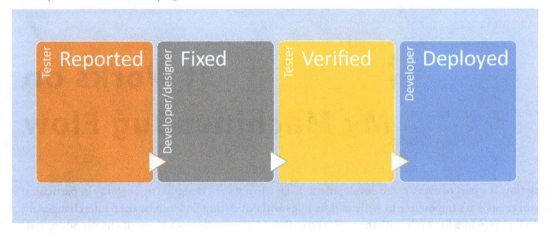

Figure 7.1. – A simple bug life cycle

In the preceding diagram, we can see a simple bug life cycle. Each bug has to be addressed in some way when it is found. Primarily, we want most bugs to be fixed. But that's not always possible or even advisable, as not all bugs are made equal. We will talk in more depth about bug reporting in *Chapter 8, I Thought I Fixed That: How to Write Efficient Bug Reports*. Even if the bug ends up not being fixed, it should be addressed. What does this mean for the game team? Each bug should be seen by someone in the team, either a developer or a producer, who will make the call about what to do with the bug next. This is where things can get complicated in bug flow. If we presume that the bug was fixed, it also needs to be verified and committed into the game. Let's investigate this in more detail:

1. The bug is found and reported in a **bug database**. The tester who found the bug assigns the bug to the next person in the bug flow. This is most often the developer, but it could also be the QA manager who checks whether the bug meets the required standards. If the bug is related to art, design, or sound, it might be assigned to that particular discipline lead.

2. The bug's destiny is decided – the bug is either rejected (there should be a valid reason for this) or assigned to the person who is going to fix the issue. Sometimes, it's the same person who reviewed the bug.

3. The bug is fixed by the developer and assigned back to the tester for *verification*. The tester will execute the same *test steps* that they did when they found the bug, making sure that they are in the correct testing environment and confirming whether the bug is fixed.

4. The bug fix is *committed* to the game under test – if we are not live with our game yet, the bug fix will be committed to the code, whereas if we are working with the game already in **live ops**, the bug fix will probably be committed as part of the next update, unless it's a major fix. We call those fixes **hot fixes**, and we will talk more about them in *Chapter 11, Are You on the Right Version? Live Ops and QA*.

When we look through the basic bug flow, we can easily see that there are many alternative ways in which the bug flow could possibly go. Depending on the team size, production methodology, and internal processes, we could also have different actors participating in almost all stages of the bug flow. Setting up the proper bug flow is not an easy task, and often we must go through a couple of iterations before we nail the process down to fit the whole team. There are many steps in the process where we could go wrong, and they might not really work as we imagined. So, what are the consequences of a poorly designed bug flow?

One of the common mistakes is *not designing the bug flow*, but rather letting bugs move through the life cycle in an organic way. In these situations, bugs take on a life of their own Everyone does what they think is right, and quickly, we lose track of bugs. Some crucial bugs can easily fall through the cracks and the team might focus on the wrong things and lose precious time. In general, the whole team might become disgruntled and start accusing each other of doing a poor job. Additionally, the bureaucratic load will significantly increase as it will be very hard to get a clear picture of the situation regarding bugs and, consequently, the game build maturity.

When I started working at Nokia as a QA manager for Nokia tools, I inherited a similar situation in the project. We had a bug repository with more than 1,000 bugs, and nobody knew if they were valid, fixed, or anywhere in between. It took a lot of time and effort to go through all of them and clear the slate.

Another mistake is creating *rules that are too tight*. Processes change, people change, and even the methodology we use can change. When we work with live products, we can also encounter lots of bugs that need to be addressed differently than bugs in pre-launch game production. If our process doesn't allow for that, we might end up with bugs that are not "flowing" through the system, or they are assigned to the completely wrong person who can't assign them further. I found this type of situation when I took over production at Next Games. Our bug flow was so tight that when a bug was assigned to a developer or artist, they could only assign it to the tester. While in theory, that might look like the ideal scenario, in slightly larger teams and more complex games, one bug might be reassigned to a different developer for a fix, or it might even go through several hands before we could confirm that it's really fixed. This is especially the case for audio or design bugs, for example, that might require two different disciplines to fix one bug. We resolved this situation by relaxing the bug flow but also training the team on the new process and explaining the responsibilities that came with it. In that way, we secured process adoption by the team and gave space for early questions and feedback.

In the following segments, we will look deeper into how we can set up efficient bug flows for different scenarios and what things we need to consider.

How to set up a good bug flow

While we already know that there is no one-size-fits-all solution, certain procedures will help you create the *optimal bug flow* for your team.

I'm a big fan of keeping what's not broken. That means that your first step should be to analyze the current bug flow. Even if it wasn't purposely designed, there is always some unwritten way the team generally handles bugs. Analyze what the team does, see what is working well and what the team considers to be problematic. The best way to do so is to interview each team member and ask them three questions:

- How does bug flow work? (You want to make sure that they all have the same understanding, or whether it's widely different between team members. It will also give you the full picture of the bug flow, including the parts that are not documented.)

- What part works well for you and helps your work?

- What part doesn't work for you, and would you like to see improved? Also, ask whether they have an idea for improvement themselves. That doesn't mean you will automatically adopt it, but it will help you understand the need of the person and give you an idea of their expectations.

When you collate the individual information, *analyze it,* and take it as a base for your bug flow creation. After that, it's usually a good idea to have a meeting with the whole team. If your game team is really large, have a meeting at least with the *discipline leads* and have an open discussion about bug flow. Present them with your solutions, get their feedback and suggestions as a group, and use them to refine the process further. It is important not only to get everyone on board but also to make different disciplines hear each other out and understand others' needs better. In that way, you will be able to create a bug flow that is understood on a deeper level by the whole team and accepted as their own. This is a very important step because if the team doesn't feel that process reflects their needs and they don't understand why things are done a certain way, you will struggle with bug flow adoption and might have to redesign it.

When this work is done, the next step is properly *documenting* the flow. I always recommend having a one-page document with a flow chart that is easy to access and clear to understand. When this flow chart is fully flushed out and clear to all, then you can add additional information explaining the *transitions* and transition statuses in more detail. Make sure that conditions for each transition are clearly explained, and try to stick to a limited number of transitions. If your transitions are way too complicated with ambiguous explanations, the team will probably not take them into use, or at least not in the way that you might have imagined.

One of the most important things to do when creating a bug flow is to appoint a person responsible or the *owner* of the bug flow. That is usually either the *game producer* or *QA manager*. This person is responsible for flow adoption, enuring that everyone is following it correctly and that all team members are familiar with it. Another part that comes with ownership is actual flow execution. This takes us to the last step in flow creation – *execution*.

When flow is charted, understood, and supported by the team, it's time to take it into use. In every studio, we use some kind of bug database. **Jira** is probably the most common one in the gaming industry these days, but there are numerous others in use.

The bug flow owner should adjust the bug database in a way that reflects the agreed flow. That can be quite a demanding job and it requires good knowledge of the bug database in use. Usually, QA leads and producers are very well trained in the usage of not one but several different kinds of bug databases. Very large teams might even have bug databases maintained by internal or external technical teams. In that case, the flow owner will present the documentation to the party who is in charge of the bugs database maintenance and oversee implementation.

While this might seem like quite a straightforward process, in practice, it can take days or even weeks, especially if we have an existing bug flow (and bugs) that would need to be transitioned to a new bug flow. Depending on the bug database in use and differences in old and new bug flows, there might be a need to make some additional manual adjustments after the flow has been implemented. As we can see, this process can be quite delicate and demanding, and it's best to do it during quiet QA times – either early in production or when we don't have any pending testing rounds coming soon. In this way, we will not interrupt any crucial work, and we will have time to smooth out any issues with adaptation to the new bug flow.

Now that we know more about how to create a good bug flow process, let's look deeper into bug flow statuses and transitions.

Bug flow statuses and transitions

When we are setting up *bug statuses and transitions* for the first time, it's easy to get carried away and try to include status and transition for any possible scenario. While this might seem like a good idea in theory, in practice it rarely works. We already learned earlier in this chapter that bugs flow through many hands. Your team members have lots of duties, and if you create very complex and lengthy transitions, most people will start to feel uncomfortable using them, especially if there is no easy way to see the exact meaning and purpose of every transition. For that reason, it's always recommended to make them as simple as possible but sufficient to support your team's *development methodology*.

We need to consider that every game development team is utilizing some type of methodology, such as *Scrum*, *Kanban*, *Waterfall*, and so on, but there are many variations on how work is actually executed within the methodology framework. QA work needs to fit into the existing methodology and processes, and how we handle bugs is a big part of that process. That's why QA can't create the bug flow in isolation without consulting with other team members and the producer.

Next, let's look at an example of a detailed bug flow:

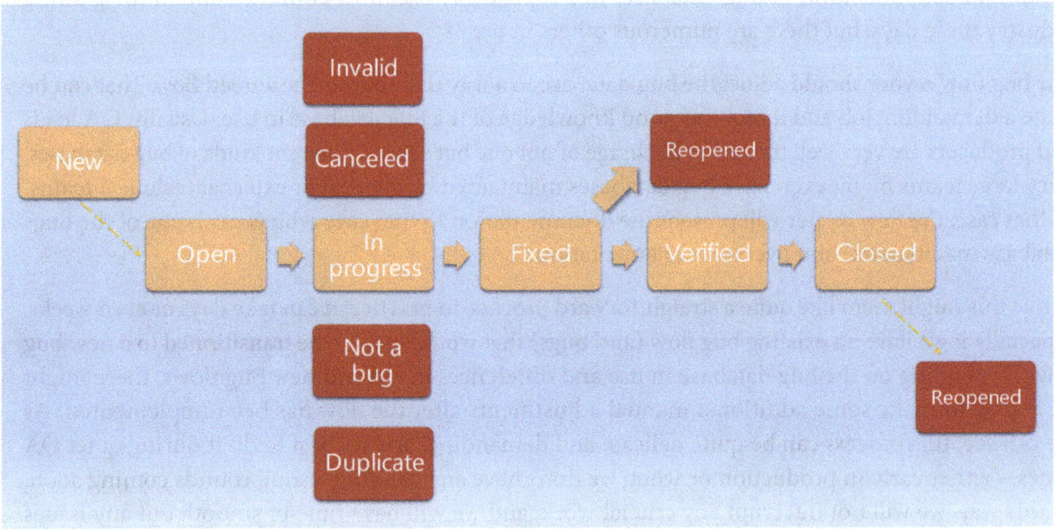

Figure 7.2 – A bug flow with multiple transitions

This bug flow includes all the major possible states through which the bug can transition. Let's go through them to understand the process better:

- **New**: While it can be used interchangeably with open, it's sometimes used as a separate step in a bug flow (as indicated by the dashed arrow in the preceding diagram). For example, when we work with outsourced QA or large QA teams, the first step is usually reporting a bug, and the bug reporting system we use will assign it automatically to a status of new. That means that QA has found a bug but nobody else had a chance to see it or work on it.

- **Open**: This status means that the bug has been accepted into the flow. It has been reported as valid by the tester who found it, or it has been approved by someone who is reviewing all found bugs. That is sometimes done by the QA supervisor or QA lead, but in some cases, it can also fall on the back of the producer, as they will have the best insight into the team's schedule and priorities.

  Next, we come into a phase where the bug can go into multiple states. We will go through each of them here.

- **In progress**: This means that someone is actively working on fixing this bug. We should keep an eye on how long a bug is in in progress for. If we have an efficient development methodology in the team, such as Kanban, developers can only take a specific number of bugs to work on, and they will generally be looked into relatively fast. On the other hand, if we work with Waterfall or some less agile methodology, it can happen that developers have assigned multiple bugs for fixing and put them in the in progress state, but in reality, they might be working on something else.

Of course, not all bugs get accepted by developers for fixing. So, let's go through other alternative transitions.

- **Not a bug**: This status indicates that the bug reported is not actually a bug and as such, doesn't require fixing. While many jokes have been made about it, "it's not a bug, it's a feature," in some instances we do really have cases when this is fully acceptable. For example, the bug appeared due to external influences, such as Wi-Fi availability or the tester testing on the wrong build. While I'm generally a strong proponent of the idea, if testers don't get it, it's a feature, and neither will the players in some cases; the bug really is a feature. The situation comes to mind when we got several bug reports about random eggs in the game. It was an Easter holiday game update, and the gameplay was inspired by the Western Easter tradition of hiding eggs in the garden and have an egg hunt. Our testing partner was from Asia, and they were not familiar with the tradition – of course, that game looked really weird to them!

- **Canceled**: This status indicates that work on this bug has been started, but for some reason, has been canceled. It might have been a business decision or the priorities shifted. Canceled is used interchangeably with **Postponed** or **On Hold**.

- **Invalid**: While similar to not a bug, it has its differences. Invalid means that this could potentially be a bug, but it's either not relevant (for example, we are dropping this feature) or the tester possibly did something wrong: for example, used the wrong preconditions, an unsupported testing device, or didn't provide sufficient information. For that reason, we also sometimes use the following status.

- **More info**: This status indicates that the bug is not rejected as such, but there is just not enough information for the developer to go forward with. We will talk more about how to write a great bug report in *Chapter 8, I Thought I Fixed That: How to Write Efficient Bug Reports*, and learn how to avoid getting bugs in this status.

- **Can't reproduce**: This is my favorite of all, frequently misused status. Sometimes it's also called **it works on my machine**. This means that the developer couldn't reproduce the bug the tester submitted. I generally like to avoid this status, just because it's used too often without further explanation. Sometimes bugs will be difficult to reproduce, or they will reproduce only occasionally. In those cases, we use repro rates when reporting bugs – we will talk more about them in the next chapter. While there is nothing wrong with having a *Can't reproduce* status, ensure that your development team understands that it should be used only in genuine cases. Lastly, we will talk about the following status.

- **Duplicate**: This status indicates that the same bug has already been reported. When we test and find a bug, we should always check whether the bug has already been found. In cases where we see that the bug has been found, but it might be reported for a different platform or device, it is usually sufficient to update that bug report with your finding. Alternatively, you can make a separate bug report, but you do want to link it to the original bug. Testers should have a good knowledge of how to use a bug database and search by keywords through reported bugs before reporting.

What should the tester do with all of these statuses? Firstly, they should read the **comments** from the developer and try to understand why the bug is in such a status. If they disagree with the developer's opinion, they should put a comment against the bug and add more information supporting their claim. Then, reopen the bug and send it back to the developer.

Let's go through the remaining transitions, in case everything goes as intended. After working on the bug for some time, the developer will move it to one of the following statuses:

- **Fixed**: This indicates that the developer or whoever the bug was assigned to perform the fix did work on this bug and claims it's fixed. Often, this is also accompanied by a developer comment, and usually, it's indicated in which build the fix is committed. This information helps the tester determine where and how they can verify the fix.

- **Verified**: The tester's job is not over when the bug is found, but only when the bug is fixed and they have verified that the fix works as intended.

- **Reopened**: Sometimes though, the fix doesn't really work. In those cases, the bug is reopened and assigned back to the developer. In this stage is important to add *additional information* to the bug and explain how and where the bug is verified and add new *screenshots* or *crash logs*.

After the verified status, the bug is usually put into a status of **Closed**. That means that all the work on the bug has been done and it doesn't need to be addressed anymore.

We should remember that sometimes bugs will reappear in the future. We have learned by now that game architecture can be quite complex and with continuous updates, parts of the code might end up being reused or some old code might get triggered with new changes. In those cases, we will change closed bugs to *Reopened* with the addition of the latest information on the bug. This happens surprisingly often, and sometimes even months after the bug was fixed and closed. We should just keep in mind that even if it's the same bug, new and updated information will help everyone understand that the bug is still valid and it will help with the new fix.

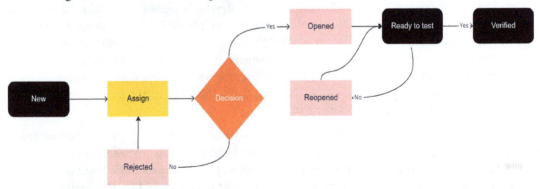

Figure 7.3 – A bug flow example

Now that we have learned more about bug statuses, let's have a closer look at the different types of transitions.

In the preceding diagram, we see a relatively simple way of bug transition. Here, we utilize the *New* status when a bug is found and *Assign* as a status for indicating someone is responsible for looking into this bug. It can be assigned, for example, to a senior QA team member for review or to a producer who will decide who the most appropriate person in the team is to handle this issue. After **Assign**, the bug can be in one of two statuses: *Open* or *Rejected*.

Opened means that the bug is entering the fix cycle, while **Rejected** indicates that nobody will work on this bug for the time being. Here, we notice that this transition is very simple, and we don't go into multiple options of why the bug is not accepted.

In simple transitions like this, it's always advisable to put a *comment* against the bug indicating why the bug is rejected. If the tester doesn't agree with the reason why the bug was rejected, they can assign the bug back to the person who rejected it or to someone else, depending on the reason for the rejection. For example, we might assign the bug to a developer who is not an expert in this area, and they think that this bug would be better addressed by another developer in the team. In that case, they will transition the bug into rejected status with a comment about who to assign the bug to instead. This might seem like a very cumbersome way of working, with lots of messaging going back and forth. Bugs are, in a way, exactly that – one of the main areas of communication within a game development team. Rather than just automatically transitioning bugs through the process, everyone included in the bug flow should pay attention to bug reports, read them carefully, and think about what to do next. It's always time better spent than hurrying along, reporting incomplete bugs, and trying to force our point of view on another team member without reasoning and proof supporting our claims.

Moving forward with our example, we can see that when a bug is open it means that it's being worked on. From that status, it transitions to *Ready to test*, which indicates to QA that bugs are ready to go through verification. That means that after testing, the bug can either be in a status of *Verified* or *Reopened*, informing developers that the fix wasn't working as intended. In this simple bug flow example, we don't necessarily use **Closed**, as we can conclude that all bugs that are in the **Verified** status have gone through the bug life cycle, successfully passed it and no additional work is needed.

This type of bug flow is well suited to internal teams or external teams that have been collaborating for some time and have a good understanding of studio workflow. It works particularly well for relatively small to medium teams who are utilizing an agile methodology. Due to the limits of the bug statuses, it would work great for periods when we don't expect massive amounts of bugs – for example; it would work well in live ops.

Now, let's look at another example, which has more complexity in transitions.

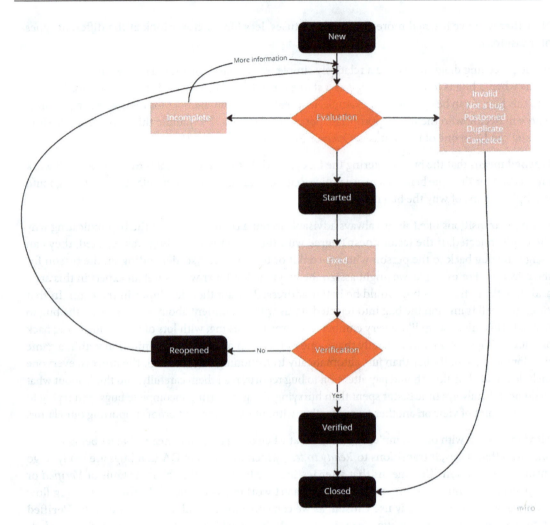

Figure 7.4 – A bug flow, example 2

In the preceding bug flow, we can see that we start with *New*, but after that, we transition into *Evaluation*. This status indicates that the team using this bug flow is not automatically accepting all reporting bugs, but instead, they have to go through the *process* of some type of evaluation. This can be done either as a simple evaluation by the QA manager or producer or with a working group of people who will decide whether the bug is accepted or not. As a result of the evaluation, the bug will be put in a range of statuses, which we covered earlier in this chapter.

The different status we use here is *Started*. It means the same as **Opened** in the previous bug flow example – it indicates that someone has actively started working on this issue. After that, the bug goes to the *Fixed* status, which corresponds to the **Ready to test** status in the bug flow presented in *Figure 7.3*. After that, the bug goes through verification, where it can either be confirmed as fixed or it has to go back to the beginning of the cycle. We see here that bug has slightly more transitions but far more statuses than in the example in *Figure 7.3*.

Having more bug statuses helps us filter the bugs and get useful data, not only about the quality of the game but also about the quality of the testing. For example, if we see that we have lots of bugs in the **Duplicate** or **Incomplete** status, we can conclude that testers might not have really paid enough attention while reporting bugs. It might indicate that we have to additionally train our QA staff to create and report better bugs.

This type of bug transition will be well suited for larger, dispersed teams, where we have a high rotation of QA staff. Evaluation is used as a *check point* that will catch all irrelevant bugs, and we have multiple options for each bug, which will help with reporting and traceability. This type of bug life cycle would also be well suited for periods when we do expect higher bug turnover, but in that stage, we need to pay attention that the evaluation process doesn't become a bottleneck for the bug flow. While this is a very informative and detailed bug flow, it can be too restrictive for agile teams where there is more emphasis on team trust and independent work.

Next, we will check out an example of a bug flow where we will also add actions and actors to the chart.

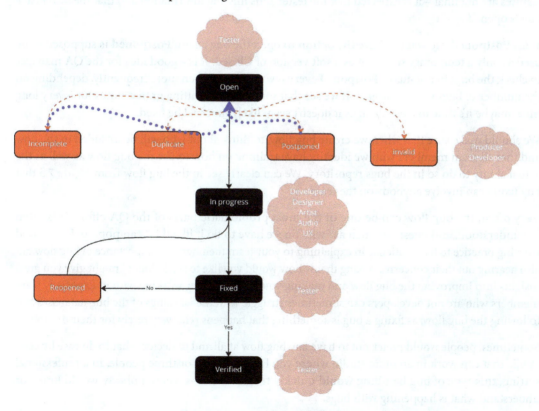

Figure 7.5 – A bug flow, example 3

As you can see in the preceding diagram, this is a relatively straightforward bug flow, similar to the one we already looked into in *Figure 7.2*. What is important here is to pay attention to who *transitions* the bug. We can see that in many statuses, several people could potentially address the issue. That's because bugs in games are not only software errors but could also reflect issues with art, sound, or the logic of the game design. In this example, after the tester reports the bug, it can end up in other statuses than In progress. As before, **In progress** indicates that someone is working on it.

In other cases, the developer will change the status to **Incomplete** or **Duplicate** and assign the bug back to the tester who reported it. The developer might also assign the bug to be in the **Invalid** state, but most often, it is the producer who decides that the bug is in the *Postponed* state. The bug can get postponed for multiple reasons, but most of the time is due to changes in focus and priority. As it's generally the producer who is the keeper of the schedule and milestones, it falls on them to postpone fixing the bug. In smaller teams that don't have producers, the developer or even the game designer might make the final call about it.

In this bug flow, we should also pay attention to the possible two-way transitions from the **Incomplete** and **Postponed** states. We can see them marked with a blue dotted line. This indicates that those two statuses are not final – it is expected that the tester adds missing information and that the *incomplete* bug is opened again.

With **Postponed**, we want to have the option to open the bug again. **Postponed** is supposed to be used as only a temporary state, not as a soft version of **Closed**. It is a good idea for the QA manager to check the bugs in a status of **Postponed** every few months or even more frequently, depending on the number of bugs in your project. If we see that some bugs are sitting in that status for a very long time, maybe it's time to close them as it doesn't seem likely they will be fixed.

We should make sure that when we create bug flow, to think about who will be included in the flow and that all team members who we identify have training on how to use the bug flow as well as the actual ability to do so in the bugs repository. We can clearly see in the bug flow from *Figure 7.5* that bug fixing can involve anybody on the team.

Very often, the bug flow can be one of the most problematic parts of the QA effort. It is often misunderstood, and questions such as "why do we have to do it like this" can pop up. It is a good working practice to have patience in explaining to your team members the importance of bug flow but also hearing out their concerns. Asking them "how would you like to see it done?" might give you great insights into improving the bug flow and making your team happier working with it. Especially team members who are not developers can sometimes struggle with the workings of the bug databases and following the bug flow, as fixing a bug is something that happens relatively rarely for their discipline.

Sometimes, people would prefer not to have any bug flow at all and to decide what to do case by case. While that can work in an indie studio where you have only two or three people, in a professional setting, this type of bug handling would quickly turn into chaos where nobody would know or understand what is happening with bugs.

Next, let's look at our final example of a bug flow.

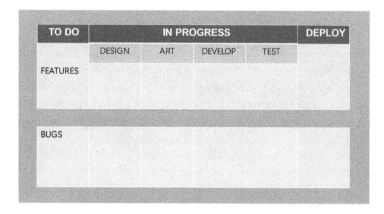

Figure 7.6 – An example of a bug flow in Kanban

The last example here will be bug flow for Kanban teams. This is a simplified bug flow I utilized in one of my previous jobs, and it shows that we are working with an agile methodology.

We can see that in the bug flow, bugs have much fewer statuses and go through very simple transitions. All new bugs will go into the *To Do* category after they have been accepted in the bug flow. As we used this in live ops and worked only with internal senior QA, there was no need for bug evaluation prior to being put on the board. In the actual board that contained bugs, we could see the **bug priority**, and that indicated which bugs should be addressed first. In Kanban, team members *pull* their own tasks from the column without having bugs assigned or having the **Ready to test** status. Statuses here are passive, as it's up to the team members to decide what to address next. In this Kanban board, bugs go through all the columns and are tracked just like any other task. But to make them more visible and have better tracking of bug progress, bugs have a separate, dedicated *swimlane*, as indicated by a separate segment of the board in *Figure 7.6*. While this type of bug flow might seem counterproductive and overly simplistic, when we are working with the Kanban methodology, everyone in the team has the agency to decide what tasks they will focus on next, and the bug flow, as such, follows this philosophy.

In some teams that are using Kanban, teams might have a dual way of tracking the bugs. One separate for bugs in the bug databases and on the common Kanban board. While this approach gives more flexibility to the QA team, this generally makes the QA process too heavy and requires administrative overhead that is counterintuitive to the Kanban methodology. It's a much better solution to work within the team's Kanban framework and try different approaches to bug flow until you find the one that works for the whole team.

As the name says, this type of bug flow is intended to work in agile teams using the Kanban methodology. It's particularly well fitted for games live ops as it gives high visibility and allows for fast and efficient movement of the bug through its life cycle.

Summary

We have now learned how to approach the creation of a bug flow; we got a deep insight into several different examples of bug flows and in what situations we should use them. We learned about all the possible transitions, their meaning, and how they relate to each other in the flow. We also learned why this part of QA is exceptionally important and how difficult it might be to implement properly. In the next chapter, it's time to learn about the core of the QA job – how to report great bugs.

I Thought I Fixed That: How to Write Efficient Bug Reports

This chapter takes a deep dive into the bread and butter of **quality assurance (QA)** – reporting bugs. While **bug reporting** is not the only activity QA team does, that's the one that is the most visible outside the discipline, and very often, QA's work is judged based on the quality and sometimes the number of bugs produced. This gives additional importance to this particular aspect of QA work. In this chapter, we will learn about the following key topics:

- Why bug reports matter
- How to write excellent bug reports
- Bug priority versus severity explained
- Bug reporting best practices

We will go into detail about how to write optimal bug reports and provide an in-depth explanation of how to differentiate bug **priority** and **severity** and what affects them. We will wrap up this chapter with practical tips and best practices for bug reporting. At the end of the chapter, you will learn why bug reports are so important, how to write excellent ones, and how to set up appropriate severity levels and you will gain valuable tips that will help you further in writing compelling bug reports that are rarely refused.

Why bug reports matter

Bug reports are the main mean of communication between different stakeholders: coders, QA, game designers, producers, art, and any other discipline involved with game creation. In the past, it was common to have the whole team sitting in the same room or not too far from each other, sharing the same office space. As *outsourcing* practices became more dominant and parts of game development were handled by outsourced partners, the importance of well-written bug reports grew. During the last few years, as a consequence of the pandemic, we saw more employees working predominantly from home. That further contributed to the importance of having high-quality bug reports.

Today, we have game teams that are geographically dispersed and might come from different working cultures and working in different time zones. If our bug reports are unclear, there is missing information, or they are written poorly, the coder can't just walk to QA in the next room and ask additional questions. If there is a significant time difference between distributed teams, it might take another day before QA in a different location will even see the question. With already relatively short testing cycles, especially in *live ops*, it's really important to have bugs addressed quickly and efficiently and the first step to that is having great bug reports.

Another significant reason why bug reports are so important is *legacy issues*. Teams change and people move to other projects or other companies. A basic bug report might have worked well between team members that worked very closely for a long period of time. But when that team changes, that same bug report might be poorly understood by others. Old bugs often resurface, especially in live ops, when we work with the same code base for long periods of time. It can be very valuable to the team if we can pull out an old bug report about the same issue we are facing again and see how it was handled. If the bug report was not named properly or it was written poorly, it won't be of use to the team.

While developers and QA work very closely, due to the nature of their work, sometimes there might be *friction* between them. Developers focus on building games, while QA is focused on finding different ways to break games. That's why it's really important to have mutual respect between these two disciplines and collaborate in constructive ways. But if QA keeps producing poor-quality reports, that will negatively influence developers opinion about QA. They will start to doubt their *reliability* and will become more prone to ignoring bugs or arguing about them with QA. Consistently producing high-quality bug reports helps build respect and ensure that QA and bug reports are taken seriously.

Now that we know why it's so important to write good bug reports, let's take a deeper look into how to write them.

How to write excellent bug reports

The bug report format will very much depend on the bug *tracking tool* you use. Most of them already have a pre-made template. But in every good bug reporting tool, those templates can be adjusted to better suit the needs of your team. In the following screenshot, you can see a couple of examples from different bug-tracking tools:

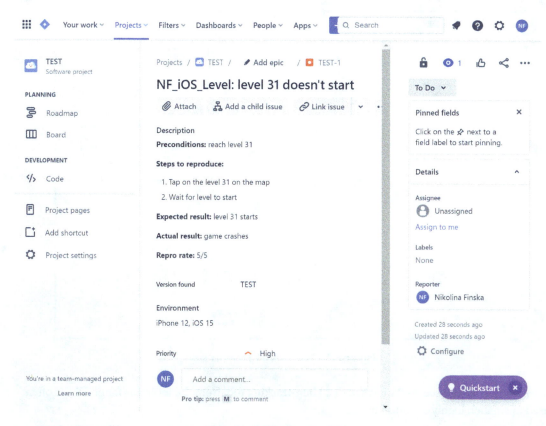

Figure 8.1 – JIRA bug sample

Figure 8.1 showcases **JIRA**, one of the most commonly used bug-tracking tools in the gaming industry. Its popularity is partially due to the fact that it also acts as a project management tool, and it can be integrated well with other tools, for example, player support databases. JIRA is regularly updated with new features, and it's highly editable, so it might look very different from one team to another.

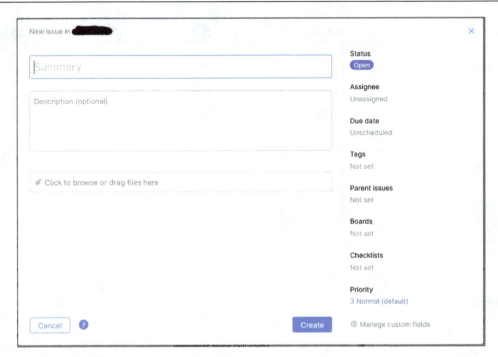

Figure 8.2 – YouTrack bug template

In *Figure 8.2*, we can see the **YouTrack (YT)** bug-tracking tool from the JetBrains family. YT is often used in smaller, highly technical teams.

Figure 8.3 – Monday.COM bug sample

Figure 8.3 showcases **Monday.com**, a popular project management tool that now also has incorporated a bug-tracking tool. This tool is simple to use, and it's been designed to perfectly fit agile teams.

Figure 8.4 – GitHub bug repository

In *Figure 8.4*, we can see a bug report template from the **GitHub** bug repository. GitHub is a tool that is frequently used in the gaming industry. It's convenient to also use their bug repository, which has been updated to be user friendly.

Keep in mind that bug databases are tools that are regularly updated, and the **user interface** (UI), design, and layout will change with time. It should also be mentioned that these are not all the bug databases out there – there are dozens if not hundreds of different bug databases actively used. When we look at them, we can see from these examples that even if they have differences in the UI, they all contain very similar basic fields that form the core of your bug report. We will go through them next.

Headline or title

While it might seem obvious, it's very important to have a *standardized* headline for bug reporting. It's much easier to identify bugs with a good headline, and this also helps to optimize bug database searches. Long-lasting projects can easily have tens of thousands of bugs in their repository and you want to make sure that you get relevant hits when looking for something specific.

There is no common, agreed format for the headline across the industry, but as a baseline, it should consist of key information about the bug. That consists of the platform, the part of the game where the bug was found, and a short summary. If you work with outsourced teams, you might want to have a way to indicate that bug came from an outsourced partner. For example, the format could look something like this: (partner initials)_(platform)_(game segment): (short description). In the database, it would look something like this: TestingPartner_Android_UI: Shop items names displayed as logical strings.

Depending on how your testing is organized, the headline can also include the *build version*, *test environment* (Live or Dev), or anything else that would be useful to your team. The most important thing is that the naming convention is standardized and that everyone in your team reporting bugs knows how to properly name them.

Description

This is part of the bug where you need to describe the issue that you found in the best possible way. We should always start the description with *preconditions* if there are any. There is no need to write "start the game, but we might want to indicate some more specific preconditions such as "while the device is charging," or "while using Wi-Fi," for example.

After that, we will need to write the *steps to reproduce the issue*. Here, we need to describe in detail how we executed the test that produced this bug. If we followed a specific test case, we can either copy and paste or link to the *test case* in question. If we deviated from the test case or we found this bug by not using previously specified steps, we would need to write them down as they happened. Again, it's a good practice to use common sense: you don't need the step "open the game" unless the bug is found in the process of opening the game. But you don't want to create steps that are too generic either. Very often, the bug's root cause it's not obvious, and something that might look irrelevant at first might provide a key clue in finding out why the bug is appearing. When writing steps to reproduce, please stick with one or a maximum of two short sentences per step. Use language that is easy to understand and avoid abbreviations that are not industry standard.

Lastly, we need to add the *expected result* (or expected outcome, they are used interchangeably) and the *actual result*. This is important to mention, as sometimes it's not obvious what behavior, sound, or visual is an expected result. For example, we might have updated the UI in a new version of the game, and while testing, we see that the old UI is still displayed in a part of the game. The UI that we see in the game is still usable and there is nothing obviously wrong with it. But we know that this is an old UI that had to be replaced with a different looking one. This brings us to the next item on the list.

Screenshot/video or similar

The previous example perfectly illustrates how important screenshots can be. Very often it's difficult to describe visual or behavioral problems in the game. Attaching a screenshot or a video makes the job much easier for the person fixing the bug. That doesn't mean that you should skip writing steps. A screenshot or video on its own, without explanation, can be as confusing as text without a picture. The best-written bugs will have both. In cases where we report issues with a game crashing, for example, it's also useful to attach any crash logs, as they provide very valuable information to coders who are working on the fix.

Version tested

This is one of the often overlooked parts that is crucial to include in bug reports. It's easy to just forget about it when we are in the middle of the testing round, just before the launch, and everyone is on the same build because the code is frozen. But throughout development, there are usually a couple of versions of the game available, and not all of them are meant to be tested. Sometimes we have multiple builds per day and only some are supposed to be tested. It is vital for the tester to note in which version they found the bug, as coders might be working with completely different versions already where the bug doesn't appear. This brings us to the loop of frustrated communication with "It works on my machine" and "invalid" bug statuses going back and forth. Sometimes, if it's impossible to get a build version, you can use the build date and time to identify it.

Furthermore, when the game goes live, we deal with the live version, test version, and development version. It becomes crucial to know on which build the bug was found. This can also affect bug **severity**. For example, finding a crash bug with a high **reproduction rate** (**repro rate**) in a live game will have a much higher severity than finding a crash bug in the first round of testing on a newly implemented feature in a test environment. We will talk more about live ops in *Chapter 11, Are You on the Right Version? Live Ops and QA.*

Reproduction rate

The repro rate indicates how many times the bug appears when we repeat the test. It's generally displayed as a fraction, for example, 1/10, meaning "1 in 10 times the bug will appear." While the repro rate is not a particularly useful indicator when we report bugs such as graphical glitches or other visual bugs, it becomes very important when we report game crashes, freezes, or lag. The repro rate also affects the bug's severity: a game crash that is 9/10 will have a much higher severity than a crash that is 1/10. When using the repro rate, please don't use 1/1 because that doesn't really say much besides "I did this test and it failed." The only time this is acceptable is if your repro rate field is obligatory to fill in the bug report and the bug you are reporting is about a visual glitch or a minor issue.

A good practice is to have at least five attempts, but every case is different. Reproducing bugs can take from very short to quite long periods of time, so use your common sense and experience when deciding how many attempts you will make.

Platform and OS version

If you are testing on multiple platforms, it's crucial to indicate on which platform you found the bug. We spoke in *Chapter 4, Deeper Look - Testing on Various Gaming Platforms – Mobile, PC, and Console,* about how important the platform and **operating system (OS)** is for testing games. We should always indicate the following details:

- What platform we tested on (iOS, Android, PC, Mac, Xbox, etc.)
- If it's mobile testing, what device we found the bug on (Samsung Galaxy S22, iPhone 13, etc.)
- The version of the OS (Android 13 or Tiramisu, iOS 16.4, Windows 11, etc.)

Sometimes, bugs will appear only on one platform, even if we develop and test simultaneously for several platforms. The same situation can happen with the versions of OSs and devices: bugs will not necessarily appear on all of them. In case we want to quickly check whether the bug is appearing across multiple OSs and devices, a quick shortcut to that is to try to reproduce the bug on the lowest supported OS/device and the highest available version of the OS/device. If a bug appears on both ends of the range, it's highly probable that it appears on all of them. Knowing how widespread a bug is across the platforms and OSs will also have an impact on its severity and priority.

Comment

This field is best used to provide additional information that would not fit in other fields. The **Comment** field is usually a *free-style text field*, and we can express our opinions, suggestions about the bug, or anything else we find relevant. This field is often used for additional communication between team members, so when a bug gets assigned to you at any stage, it's always advisable to check the **Comment** section as well.

Assign to

In this field, we can assign the bug to someone in the team who will make sure that bug enters the bug flow. Generally, each team has its own rules on how this is handled. It is assigned to the QA manager or producer who will make sure that bug is reviewed before being assigned for a fix or it can be assigned directly to the person who is supposed to fix the issue. These rules vary, and they are highly dependent on the team's organization. We spoke in great detail about the bug flow in *Chapter 7, It Works on My Machine: Bug Flow*.

We learned now how to write efficient bug reports that are informative and clear and provide the required information for coders to start their work on fixing them. In almost all parts of the description, I kept mentioning priority and severity. These are also fields that every bug report will contain, and now that we understand a bit more about how each piece of information affects them, let's have a deeper look into how to work with them.

Severity versus priority

Severity and priority are sometimes used interchangeably, and that causes even more confusion in understanding what they really are. In fact, severity and priority are very different, and they should be looked at separately when writing bug reports. Priority indicates how urgent it is to fix or address something. Severity indicates how big an impact this bug has on the end user. When QA reports bugs, they act as a representative of the player, and they should have a good grasp of the severity of the bug. But a decision about priority is rarely in the hands of QA. While QA can certainly recommend how quickly something should be fixed, it's up to the producer to decide the final priority of the bug. The producer will have the full picture of the roadmap, stakeholders' interests, and team capacity and will make decisions based on those factors.

In the following table, we can see what the main distinctions between priority and severity are:

	SEVERITY	PRIORITY
PERSPECTIVE	Technical	Business
WHO DECIDES	Tester	Producer, product manager
DECISIVE FACTORS	Effect of the bug on the player	Impact on the business, roadmap, stakeholders' interests, and availability
STATUS	Rarely changes	Can change frequently

Figure 8.5 – Differences between severity and priority

In *Figure 8.5*, we can see the main *differences* between the **Severity** and **Priority** fields. We can summarize it in the following way: severity indicates what the effect of the bug is, while priority describes when the bug will be fixed.

Generally, high priority is also high severity. But high severity might not necessarily mean high priority. For example, if we find a bug with a high severity very early in game development, that doesn't mean that this bug will automatically have a high priority to be fixed.

As we are focusing primarily on QA activity, we will talk in a bit more detail about severity, as this is something that is up to QA to decide and effectively communicate to the rest of the team.

Severity

How do we determine severity? Sometimes, it's obvious – let's say that game under test crashes while loading with a repro rate of 10/10 on all platforms. That means that nobody can play it, and it's definitively the highest severity. But not all bugs are so clear to determine. When working on a new game or early on in the production cycle, it might be more challenging to decide the severity of the bug. When deciding, it's useful to ask yourself these questions:

- What's the *impact on the average player*? Each game has a target player, and we should try to imagine how this bug would affect their gameplay.

- Does this bug have any *legal or financial consequences* on the game? For example, not crediting someone on the credits or using a brand name without permission can potentially lead to complicated legal situations.

- Does it affect *game revenue*? This is especially important for **free-to-play** (**F2P**) games.

- Will this bug potentially cause the game to be rejected by the platform? Most platforms have strict rules that need to be met in order to publish your game. You can read more about this in *Chapter 4, Deeper Look - Testing on Various Gaming Platforms – Mobile, PC, and Console*.

- Will it affect the company's reputation? Some bugs can be so severe that they might cause damage to the company's reputation and even decrease the company's valuation. One famous example of that is Assassin's Creed Unity. It was so buggy that it dropped Ubisoft's share value by more than 12%. You can read more about it here: `https://www.pcgamesn.com/ assassins-creed-unity/ubisoft-stock-price-falls-significantly- following-troubled-assassin-s-creed-unity-launch`.

- Will it affect *game ranking* or public perception? Higher downloads or revenue rankings and positive reviews help increase organic sales of the game and decrease marketing costs.

- Is this a potential *root cause* for other bugs? Sometimes, one bug might be the root cause of several other ones. Fixing that issue will be much more efficient than focusing on fixing consequential bugs.

All these questions will help you determine the severity of the bug you found. Keep in mind that bugs with high severity might only take a couple of minutes to fix. Adding someone to the credits or changing the spelling of the company name is generally considered a quick fix even though the bug is classed as high severity. On the other hand, we also have bugs that might have a low severity but can take a really long time to fix and involve several people. Those types of bugs are not worth fixing, as the effort required might make no sense for the benefit that we gain.

We have spoken a lot about "high" and "low" severity. Let's have a look next at how to set up *severity levels*. They are usually set up on a scale between low and high. Sometimes, we will also have a scale that goes to *critical*. This is not the only scale that is used. It depends on the bug database your team uses and how your game production processes are set up. Severity can also be determined on a numerical scale, where the highest number indicates the most severe cases or vice versa. Whatever type of severity scale you use in the team, it is advisable to use something simple that's easy to understand by everyone.

There is no need to have more than three to four *severity statuses*, as anything more than that will make the process unnecessarily complicated. If your team doesn't fully understand severity statuses, you might end up with all severity statuses as the highest ones. In that situation, the severity categorization will become useless, as we know that not all bugs that are marked as high severity are that severe.

If you are using any other scale beside the straightforward "low to high" naming convention, have a document with a brief explanation of each status easily available to anyone on the team. Remember that even if the severity is determined by QA, bug reports are read by multiple team members, and some things that are obvious to us might be very confusing to someone working in a different discipline.

Now that we have looked into severity in more depth, let's touch on priority.

Priority

While QA will not necessarily determine the priority of the bug, it is important to understand it. Priority is usually determined using a similar scale as severity and it's important for QA to understand what it means in practice. For example, if we find a bug that will prevent *submission* or it will cause submission to fail because this bug is about failing to meet platform submission requirements, it's up to QA to flag this issue as of utmost importance to fix it as soon as possible.

Even if QA doesn't make a final call on priority, it should communicate the urgency clearly and with good reasoning. This is best done by writing a compelling bug report and adding comments that will present your case in more detail. At the same time, QA should not hold priority hostage. When testing, we often find issues that bother us, and we believe that they should be fixed first. But it might happen that the producer or product manager disagrees with us. If we didn't manage to prove our point, we should not take it personally. Instead, it's good to learn the reasons why the bug wasn't prioritized according to our opinion and use that knowledge to better understand the overall game production. The following are some situations that can affect bug priority that QA might not necessarily be aware of:

- It takes *several people* from different disciplines to fix the bug.

- It requires input from a *different department* with no bandwidth to help for a certain period of time. This frequently happens in game studios that also develop their own engine or custom backend. Bug fixes might require work from a separate team working on the engine, but they have their own milestones and priorities that are not necessarily aligned with the game team.

- *Data from analytics* shows us that there is another issue in the game that is affecting players much more severely.

- *Company management* requires another item on the list to take priority due to business reasons.

- The studio is planning to *drop support* for a specific platform where the bug is found, but it hasn't been announced yet.

- *Team members* are leaving the studio, but it hasn't been announced to the rest of the team yet. The producer knows that there will be no capacity to fix this bug but can't share the reasoning with QA yet due to privacy reasons.

These are just some of the situations that can affect how priority is set. *The producer's role* is, among others, to act as a connection between the game team and other stakeholders, and they will have insight into a much wider company picture and overall company priorities. Having a *transparent organization* helps with teams working better together and aligning on company goals. Sometimes, due to legal reasons or the way the company was initially set up, it's not possible to have open information sharing with all levels of the organization. Testers should ask for reasoning if they find prioritization confusing or they disagree with it, but they shouldn't take it personally if they don't get a definitive answer. It might be that it's just impossible to share that information.

Now that we know more about how to handle severity and priority, let's have a look into bug reporting *best practices*.

Bug reporting best practices

We have learned now about what should be included in a good bug report and how it should be structured. While every gaming studio might have different *production practices*, there are certain bug-reporting practices that can be implemented in any game team. Let's look into them more closely.

Reliability

The bug report should be *factual* and present the real issue as it happened, without embellishment or additions. While it's incredibly useful to add additional information and *supporting documentation* and files, such as screenshots, QA should restrain from presenting opinions as facts. Bug reports have a commentary field where QA can express their opinion on the bug, but as such: an opinion. Presenting it as a fact might cause a lack of trust in QA, throw the coder on the wrong track, and, in return, can affect bug-fixing rates and timelines. When we report bugs, we want to make sure that developers and other stakeholders reading bugs can find them reliable – that they truthfully describe what has happened to the best of the tester's ability.

Related to this, QA should always report bugs in bug reports, not their ideas about how to improve the game or a feature. QA insight and feedback into game design and playability are exceptionally important but a bug report is not the right place to write those observations. Depending on your internal *production process*, your bug report might go directly to the coder. They don't fix design, they fix technical issues. Your suggestion is probably going to be rejected as "Not a bug" or "Won't fix." If your bug reports turn out to be mostly suggestions, this will affect the reputation of the team and most of your bugs might end up ignored. The right way to handle suggestions is to have separate processes or forms to do it. For example, in Next Games, our bugs database setup allowed us to report bugs or suggestions. While bugs went directly to the lead developer, suggestions were assigned to the producer to be discussed with the feature team.

Lastly, when we talk about reliability, we should mention bugs that are not really bugs. After many rounds of testing and utilizing the same test cases, QA might come to the point where there are simply no more bugs found. It can be tempting to report something that's "suspicious" or an edge case bug that will happen in exceptionally rare circumstances. These bugs are most often a waste of time. If you find something that doesn't feel or look right in the game and if you have time, it's recommendable to investigate it further. But presenting it as a bug without justification is not going to help the team or the game. When your tests don't find any more bugs, you should change the approach or just stop testing.

At the end of the day, what matters the most is the *quality* of reported bugs, not quantity. Several well-written and well-justified bug reports about critical issues are much more valuable to the team and to the success of the game than dozens of quickly written low-severity bugs.

Objectivity

While it might be hard to precisely determine the severity of the bug, especially early on in the project or when the tester is new to the team, we should always strive to be as objective as possible. With time and experience, testers become much better at determining severity and priority. While making mistakes early on is acceptable and understood, it is expected that the tester progresses with time and becomes more precise at determining severity. Unfortunately, sometimes it happens that QA loses its objectivity and reports bugs that are valid, but not necessarily as severe as QA sees it.

While I worked as a game producer, I had a case where QA flagged the release of one of the highly anticipated games that I was in charge of. The QA manager claimed that the quality of the game was too low to be accepted. There were lots of bugs that were categorized as high severity, but upon a closer look, I didn't really consider them to have been objectively assigned. This caused *tension* between QA and the development team and I took the decision to release the game as planned, respectfully declining QA's recommendation. The game became a great success, and it was the most popular game ever released by our department. While QA wasn't wrong about reporting some quality issues, and many of them were fixed with time, those were not really affecting players in a significant way, and there was no need to postpone the launch because of it.

When we talk about objectivity, it's impossible not to mention the eternal *bug versus feature debate*. It's probably the most dreaded comment that QA can receive: it's a feature, not a bug. There are many opinions about this issue in professional software development circles. When we talk about games, we talk about a product that is made for a worldwide audience, software that is intended for thousands, if not millions, of players out there. Some of them might be experienced gamers who play multiple games for a long time. But with the increase of mobile F2P games, we now have players who don't fit into the traditional picture of the gamer: these are people who play only on mobile, they favor one or two games, and they don't have the same understanding of game mechanics or game rules as someone whom we would consider a *hard-core gamer*. These days, most players in the world fit into the category of occasional gamers. If we are creating games primarily for this audience, which we call *casual gamers*, we have to make sure that our players will understand game features. Testing teams consist of professionals who play the same game over and over again. Most of the time, they play other games as well. If a tester who spends months and months playing the same game can't figure out that something is a feature, not a bug, there is no chance that players will.

Clarity

We previously mentioned that bug reports are one of the main means of communication between different stakeholders within game teams. That means that bug reports should be written with clarity and structure that it's easy to understand. Always use simple, precise language, and if in doubt, too much information is always better than not enough. A bit of extra information that turns out to be useless it's much less damaging than having a bug report that is missing key components and has to be bounced back between QA and development several times.

Timeliness

It does matter *when* bugs are reported. While it can be easier for QA to spend blocked time testing and write reports at the end of the testing time, this is not ideal for the rest of the team. For example, if you test from 9 am to 3 pm and only after that time do you start writing down all the bugs you found in the database, the developer will see them just before they leave to go home at 5 pm. That means that no bug fixing will start before the next working day, or, even worse, the coder might have to stay to work overtime and fix bugs after working hours. Besides that, reporting a bug when it is fresh, we still have all the small details in our heads. Reporting a bug hours after we found it, we might lose some of the small detail, which can affect the bug report quality. It is exceptionally important to report bugs promptly when we are doing testing rounds just before the launch. In those moments, time is really precious and we should raise the issue as soon as possible. Reporting bugs two hours before the submission is much better than reporting them when the submission process has already started.

Bug examples

Now that we know how to create great bug reports, let's look into a practical example:

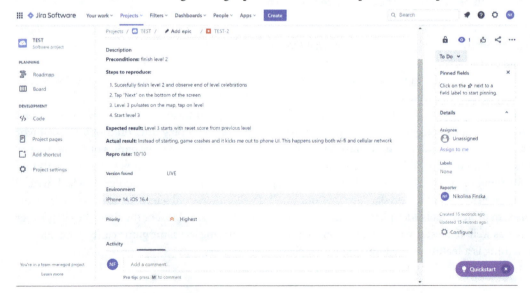

Figure 8.6 – A good bug example

In *Figure 8.6* we can see an example of a bug in JIRA that *follows good guidelines*. The headline is informative but not too long. We can clearly see who reported the issue, on which platform and OS it is happening, and a short but relevant summary.

When we check the description, it's *well structured* with a clear description and is using straightforward language. The issue described is easy to understand and reproduce. We can also see that the tester provided *extra information* – they confirmed that the bug is happening regardless of what type of connectivity we use. This information might be of use to coders. An alternative way to handle this information is to report two separate bugs: both bugs will look the same, but they will be reported once for a Wi-Fi connection and once for a cellular connection. In that case, it is advisable to link those bugs. JIRA allows us to link bugs that are related to each other, and this is a good example of how to utilize this functionality.

We can also see that the bug has a **Repro rate** value of 10/10. That affected the **Priority** value, which is set to **Highest**.

The current version of JIRA has a **Priority** field as a default with the option to add a **Severity** field. In this case, the tester made the judgment that this is the highest priority to fix. The reasons for that are that bug is severe (prevents the player from moving forward) and it appears relatively early in the game. The majority of players will reach level 3. Priority would probably be lower if this happened among the last few levels in the game. Only a small proportion of players reach that far in the game. That doesn't mean it shouldn't be fixed as soon as possible – those players are loyal fans of the game and important for monetization and organic growth, but in a limited time window, the priority decision might be taken by a bug that affects more players.

Next, let's look at the same bug, but this time in a poorly written report:

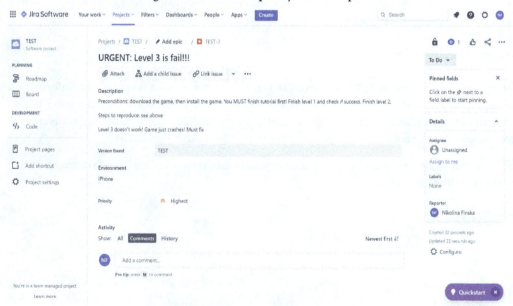

Figure 8.7 – A poorly written bug report example

Looking at it, we immediately see that the headline doesn't look *professionally written*. While it communicates perceived urgency, and we can conclude something is broken, it doesn't give us much other information.

Reading the bug description, there is a lot of *confusion* in the text. The **Precondition** field has too detailed preconditions and then there are steps to reproduce in the same field.

While we can conclude by ourselves that the *expected outcome* is that level 3 works, saying "Level 3 doesn't work" doesn't give us enough information. How doesn't it work? Does the game crash at the beginning or at the end of the level?

Adding "Must fix" is an unnecessary suggestion. We do have a **Priority** field where we can determine that this issue should be fixed with urgency. Another thing we are *missing* here is the **repro rate** value. When it comes to crash bugs, it's always beneficial to have a repro rate. If this crash happened only once, it might not be of the highest priority.

Lastly, let's mention the **Environment** value. While we have some information here, it's not enough. *iPhone* has numerous models that are still supported. iPhone users are always urged to upgrade their OS to the latest version but not all users do so. Not knowing on which device and which OS the bug appeared on makes it even less likely to be considered a high priority.

Bugs such as this are easy to *misunderstand* and commonly are bounced back to testers with a status of **more info** or **can't reproduce**. When time is tight and we find a bug that has a high impact on the player and the quality of the game, we might rush and write a report that takes shortcuts. Although we try to save time by doing so, we end up spending more time on bug fixing, as the bug might be initially ignored or has to go through several rounds of bouncing back between the tester and the coder. For that reason, it's better to take a few minutes more to write a good quality bug report that will be taken seriously at first glance.

Summary

In this chapter, we learned in detail how to write great bug reports, what is appropriate information to include, and how it should be laid out. We learned what the difference is between severity and priority and how we should determine them. Lastly, we became familiar with several different bug report layouts and compared a well-written against a poorly-written bug report.

In the next chapter, we will look into the testing approach and review testing in agile teams and learn more about testing strategies.

9

It Works, but It Hasn't Been Tested: Testing Approach

The testing approach we choose depends on many factors, from the methodology we use to develop games to the game type we are testing and much more. By now, we have already learned about the limitations we face in everyday game **quality assurance** (**QA**). There is never enough time, there are conflicting priorities, games are getting bigger and more complex, and teams are getting more and more distributed. Picking up the right testing approach will help us optimize our time and plan the most efficient way how to organize and execute testing. Because even with the best-written test cases and flawless execution, if we choose the wrong testing approach for the game we are currently testing, we might miss important bugs and spend our limited time on aspects of the game that might not matter that much.

In this chapter, we will cover the most common scenarios in modern game development, but we will not forget about lessons learned from the past. Our journey in **test strategy** starts with learnings we have from utilizing the waterfall model and analyzing which aspects of this model are still valid and useful today.

From there, we will move to agile methodology and talk more about embedded QA and provide useful, hands-on tools, and how to select the right **testing focus**. We will do our first deep dive into live ops and discuss approaches to testing when we deal with live games, and we will have a deeper look into how to organize testing in agile gaming teams. Finally, we will learn more about different types of testing strategies that can be utilized in any environment. In this chapter, we will review the following key topics:

- Lessons learned from the waterfall model

- Agile approach – embedded QA

- How to pick the right testing focus

- Testing strategies in live ops

- Types of testing strategies

Lessons learned from the waterfall model

The dominant methodology in game development these days, especially with **games as a service (GaaS)** (live ops), is *agile*. That doesn't mean *waterfall* is no longer used – it's still heavily used in more traditional game development. But, there are many elements of waterfall that are still actively used even if modern game teams are overwhelmingly adopting agile development.

One of the most commonly used waterfall features is the usage of *milestones*. Game development milestones are deeply embedded in the ways of working, and they are used as quick indicators of the readiness of the game. Not all studios use exactly the same milestones, but these are the ones that are most commonly still in use:

Figure 9.1 – Milestones in game development

Milestones are used predominantly in game development prior to live ops. Once the game is live and the team is working on updates and features, milestones are no longer used. There are several reasons for that. Firstly, development cycles are much faster, and teams are working with **minimum viable features (MVFs)**.

> **What is an MVF?**
>
> The nature of MVF is such that it is usually released as "good enough," and evaluated by the players. Good enough means that the feature is playable and doesn't have major bugs, but it might still be missing some components, polish, and gameplay depth. After it's confirmed through the game **key performance indicators (KPIs)** that the new feature has a positive impact on player experience, it's further developed and polished through one or several incremental updates.

Secondly, a live game is more determined by the reactions of the players than by set milestones. We will talk in more detail about how development works in live ops in *Chapter 11, Are You on the Right Version? Live Ops and QA*. While we have a pretty clear roadmap for pushing the game out on certain dates, the schedule for live ops is much more fluid and it's constantly changed. That's why live ops are always done utilizing the agile methodology.

When we talk about testing, though, we still follow the cadence of testing tasks that we utilize in the waterfall model:

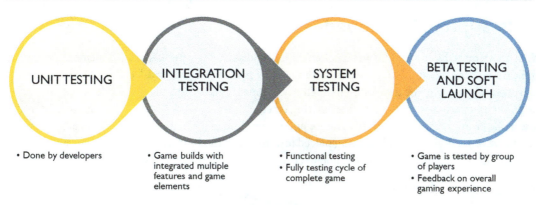

Figure 9.2 – Testing cadence

In *Figure 9.2* we can see that regardless of the methodology we use, we start testing with **unit testing**. After that, testers will take over and perform **integration testing**, making sure that all components of the game work well. In larger projects, work is sometimes split among several developers, and different parts of the game might be coded by different people, even different teams. It's important to validate that the integrated builds work well when all the parts are combined.

Integration testing is followed by **system testing**, where we test all aspects of the game and how they interact with each other. Among other types of testing, the bulk of testing done here will be functional testing.

After the game is deemed ready and greenlighted by the QA team, it can be validated by the players. The game is released to a selected group of players either as an open or closed **beta** and in the **free-to-play** (**F2P**) world, the game is in a so-called "soft launch."

In traditional QA, we call this stage **user acceptance testing** (**UAT**). In this phase, we should no longer get any serious bugs and rather focus on gaining insights into how players perceive the game and which parts they like or dislike. This is done through game analytics (KPIs) and through direct feedback from players via player support, game forums, and social media.

There are game teams that are working with a more agile approach to testing and relying almost exclusively on *exploratory testing* or an extended version of **basic acceptance** (**BA**) testing. In some very mature games that have been live for a while, QA is done by the whole team relying on **heuristic methods**. We will talk about them in more detail later in this chapter.

Now that we have learned about the testing methods of the waterfall methodology that are still present in game development, let's look into the agile approach in more detail.

Agile approach – embedded QA

What do we mean by embedded QA? It's often understood as having a permanent QA member assigned to the development team. But, it means more than just that. In truly embedded QA, QA becomes an instrumental part of game development in all development phases. QA takes the role of *representing the player* and participates not only in validating whether features work but also provides insight into how a player might interact with the feature and suggests changes that will benefit the game from a qualitative angle. Rather than just being placed towards the end of the development cycle, embedded QA participates in game development and decision-making from idea to execution.

Working in this way has several *benefits* for the team:

- Firstly, having QA involved so early helps decrease the number of bugs and the team can learn early on about the inherited risks of features they are looking to implement.

- Secondly, you can get an idea of how players will respond to changes in the game before you actually commit the feature to development. QA plays the game more than anybody on the team and works closely with player support in the live ops phase. They will have lots of qualitative information about how players perceive the game, and this knowledge can help product managers and game designers translate game KPIs into applicable features.

- Lastly, it helps teams to be more cohesive and work together towards the common goal: a great game that players love to play.

In traditional game development, it often happens that there is friction and misunderstanding between QA teams and developers. QA is often seen as "making problems" or "being negative," especially if they have found a significant number of bugs late in the development cycle. Working together throughout different development phases helps the team to see the real value of QA and experience their work as *collaborative* rather than against the developer.

To work in this way, the tester has to develop a different mindset as well as skillset than in traditional QA, where the finished product is just handed over to the QA team for testing. In this type of work, the tester needs to learn more about the role of each discipline in game production as they will work directly with the team. There will also be more *ad hoc* and *exploratory testing* versus thoroughly planned test case execution. Additionally, the tester will need to understand the product in detail – that means familiarity with the game under test and also with the competition and overall current gaming industry standards.

When we use the waterfall methodology, the game comes to QA mostly too late for any significant changes in core design and architecture. While QA finds valuable bugs, if we find issues with design or usability, those suggestions are usually dismissed as it's perceived to be too late to make those kinds of far-reaching changes so late in development. This approach often results in the game's initial reception being negative and facing lots of criticism from the players. Having embedded QA helps mitigate these situations and enables QA to provide valuable insights in a timely manner.

Lastly, when we utilize embedded QA, very often, we still have increased QA efforts in a similar way as we do in waterfall methodology toward the end of the development cycle. While embedded QA will participate in the development and execute tests along the way, in order to get really deep testing coverage, especially when we are working with significant changes in the game, we will utilize outsourced QA to run a set of functional tests. Outsourced or external QA is generally utilized more traditionally when we already have available game builds and major development work is wrapped up.

Now that we have learned what embedded QA is and how it works in agile teams, let's next look into how to pick the right testing focus.

How to pick the right testing focus?

By now, we have learned that games, regardless of their genre, are complex systems, and when we talk about games in live ops, these complexities are even further enhanced. With fast-paced development, it is crucial that the QA team is utilized efficiently. How to pick the right testing focus is one of the crucial questions that we need to answer in order to make high-quality games on time.

Testing focus is dependent on the following:

- The development stage
- The game business model
- The target market
- The game KPIs

Let's look into these in more detail.

The development stage

Depending on where we are with game development, QA will have a different focus and use different tools. We can see this in detail in *Figure 9.3*:

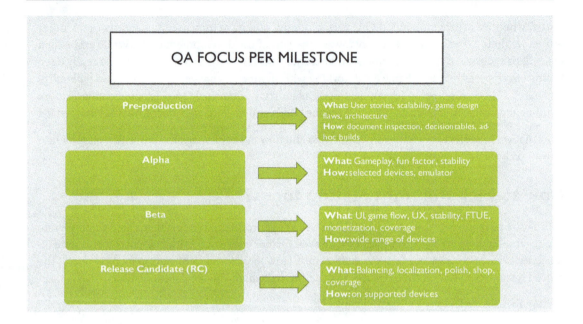

Figure 9.3 – Game milestones and their testing focus

Early in the production phase, certain aspects of the game are just not ready. Even if they are in the game, they might be initial, rough versions or placeholders. Testing parts of the game that are not ready is not only a waste of time, but can also cause tension in the team. Making sure that QA tests parts of the game as they are being developed and completed helps the development team to optimize their work and work through any major issues early enough in the process. That makes the whole development faster and cheaper.

When we move to the live ops stage and away from traditional milestones, we will need to rethink how we focus testing. Especially because now we will be facing two different tracks: live feedback from players through player support and game KPIs and the development track, where the live ops team develops new content and features. We will talk more about this later in this chapter.

The game business model

Historically, games used to be predominantly *premium*. You purchase the game for a fixed price and enjoy it for as long as you wish. These days, the games market is very different, and the predominant business model is *F2P*. Besides F2P, there are also other business models on the market. Let's have a deeper look at them and see how they affect the testing focus.

F2P is a business model where the game is obtained for free but the player has the option to make **in-app purchases (IAPs)** to enhance their gaming experience.

In order to make *IAPs* attractive to the player, games are trying to keep the player in the game for as long as possible *(player retention)*. The idea behind this is that the more committed player is to the game, the bigger the chances are of them purchasing something in the game. F2P games are built to be endless – there is no end game. They are also built on *scalable architecture* that allows for endless content updates and quick changes in game balancing. When we test F2P games, we need to focus on additional things such as purchasing flow and game updates. If we have the capacity to make changes in the game without submissions to the platform, we need to make sure that we have developed a process for testing those prior to them being pushed into live production.

Many games today are not only F2P but also have the addition of *ads*. Ads can be in different formats: video ads, playable mini-games, interstitials, or a banner. The most financially lucrative type of ad is a video ad and it's most often implemented as rewarded ads (player watches the ad for some kind of in-game reward). In order to make sure that the player doesn't gain too many goods from watching the ads, those are generally capped at a certain amount that is available to the player to watch.

When we test games that have ads, we need to also incorporate *ads testing*. That includes testing whether ads are properly implemented in the game, whether they display correctly, whether they break anything in the game, and whether they give appropriate rewards.

Besides IAPs and ads, games also sell *subscription* types of purchases. That means that players can buy "subscriptions," which can be daily or monthly, and for as long as the subscription lasts, they will gain a reward every time they log in to the game. Subscription generally works in a way that more valuable items appear later during the subscription. If our business model also includes subscriptions, we will need to test whether the subscription model works as intended. For example: is it possible to log in every day, what happens when you skip a day, do you get the appropriate reward?

Now that we have learned more about different game business models and how they affect testing, let's have a look at target markets.

Target markets

When we develop games, we usually have *geographical market* that we consider the most important. Statistics show that the most important gaming markets in the world are the USA and China (source: Newzoo: `https://newzoo.com/insights/rankings/top-10-countries-by-game-revenues`), but when we scratch the surface, we can see that there are many other global markets that like games and are willing to spend money on them. After all, gaming is a global phenomenon. If developers want to take full advantage of other markets, they usually perform *localization* of the game for that specific market. We discussed localization in *Chapter 3, A Deeper Look - Types of Testing in Games*. Unless we specialize in localization QA, we will not work directly with it, but we have to take into consideration the additional amount of time that will be given to localization and localization QA.

Besides geographical target markets, we can also talk about players' overall game style preference or *casual versus core players*. Those groups of players have different expectations from the games they play and will approach gameplay differently. Casual players play more recreationally – short gaming sessions of a couple of minutes, while on public transport or to have a quick respite. Mid-core players might engage in a longer session (30 minutes plus) and have a deeper gaming experience. In *Figure 9.5*, we can see the main differences between casual and hard-core players:

CASUAL GAMER	CORE GAMER
Short gaming sessions, up to 5 minutes	Longer sessions, 30 minutes or more
Plays for fun, to kill time	Passionate about game, dedicated to skilling up
Solo play or light multiplayer (like leaderboards)	In game community, multiplayer preference
Infrequent player, might be days between sessions	Sometimes plays multiple times per day
Looking for fun, relaxation, and completion	Looking for competition, excitement and, challenge
Doesn't buy specific or high-end HW just for gaming	Will purchase HW for optimized gaming, early adopter

Figure 9.4 – casual gamer versus core gamer behavior patterns

We can see from *Figure 9.4* that there are quite a few differences in how players engage with the game and what type of game experiences they are looking for. Knowing who our target audience is will help us immensely in deciding on our testing focus, from deciding which test sets we will test the game on to creating test cases or test charters that realistically mimic player behavior.

Game KPIs

Game KPIs are not often mentioned in the context of QA, but it's an exceptionally important part of it. When we are working with F2P and live ops, KPIs are some of the most important information about the game that we receive. KPIs are a reflection of player behavior in the game and they tell us how players engage with the game, what they do within it, what and when they buy, how they interact with each other, and many other things. While KPIs are expressed in numbers and percentages, they actually tell a story of how successful our game design is, what things players like, and what they dislike. Obviously, this is an important part of the information, but how can we use it to help us with testing focus?

If there is an area of the game where players spend the most time, it is important to test that part thoroughly. This information tells us that if something is wrong or subpar with that part of the game, it will have a negative effect on a big proportion of players.

Is there an area where most of the players **churn** (stop playing the game)? While those player pain points are often in the game by design, sometimes it's an indicator that there might be something wrong with that part of the game. Make sure that you test it thoroughly. On one of the games I worked on previously, we had a case where we had a high churn in a specific part of the game, but we couldn't figure out why. Upon deeper inspection, we realized that churn was specifically high for players based in the USA. After some heavy testing and trying different approaches to the problem, we realized that our game had a very specific problem with one of the USA-based cellular networks. As the USA was our main market, even if this was a costly exercise, it was deemed valuable to figure out what was wrong and fix it.

Another area that we can look into is, for example, which percentage of players finish a certain level. While we know that some levels are purposely more challenging, if KPIs are not what we would expect, maybe it's time to look into game balancing more thoroughly.

These are just some examples of how game KPIs can help you with the testing focus. As we are measuring many things in the games, make sure that you read game KPIs and discuss with the product manager how QA can be of most help to the product team.

Testing strategies in live ops

Before we dive deeper into live ops, let's first define what it means.

> **What is live ops?**
>
> Live ops refers to a period in a game life cycle after the game has been released to a wide audience on the target platform. While live ops can be viewed from many angles (development, backend, marketing, and so on) we usually consider live ops all actions and processes that affect game behavior while it's in a live state. In successful games, the live ops phase is the one that lasts the longest. Some games today have already been in the live ops phase for more than ten years, for example, Candy Crush, Clash of Clans, World of Warcraft, and many others.

As we can see, live ops are as important, if not even more so, than other phase of game development. At the same time, working in live ops means working in a much faster environment with different stakeholders. We will discuss live OPS in detail in *Chapter 11, Are You on the Right Version? Live Ops and QA*.

One of the main QA challenges in live OPS is *prioritizing* testing tasks. QA has to work with two simultaneous tracks – a new development that is continuously integrated into the game and with the constant stream of feedback coming from the live game:

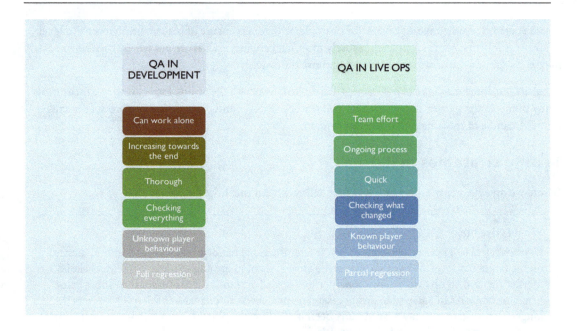

Figure 9.5 – The differences between QA in development and in live ops phases

We can see from *Figure 9.5* that there are significant differences between the characteristics of QA in game development versus live ops. When we are selecting an appropriate testing approach for live ops, we need to keep in mind these differences and be fully aware of the specifics of live ops development.

In live ops, we continuously add content and new features to existing games. Next, let's look into some strategies that will help us deal with *new code*.

It is important to understand what changes have been made in the game. Working in live ops is collaborative, and QA can take great advantage of that. It is perfectly fine to ask questions from the team. You could ask questions such as:

- Did you change anything significant in the code?
- Does the new feature in any way affect the old one?
- Will the new code make the game builds bigger?
- Do you expect any of the changes to affect game performance?
- Is there anything specific you would like me to test or pay more attention to?

Answers to those questions will give you great insight into the highest *perceived risk*, and QA will be able to focus their efforts where they will be most useful.

Team discussions don't replace the tester's own experience, skills, and critical thinking. When we gather information from the team, we should also ask ourselves: "As a player, how will I interact with this new feature compared to the old ones?", "How will this feature fit in the overall game ecosystem?", and "What are the inherent risks with this feature?"

Due to the *time limitations* we have for QA in live ops, the best testing strategy is always **risk focused**. When the game is live, we have thousands, if not millions of players, all over the world playing the game, enjoying its features, and spending money. If something seriously goes wrong with the game at this stage, it could mean the end of the game and incredible financial and reputational loss. In production, risks are significant but not necessarily that impactful to the game, possibly even for the studio's survival.

A risk-based testing strategy is based on four main phases:

- **Risk identification**: Utilizing available documentation and discussions with the team members, the tester will identify the main risks with the new feature and code we are implementing.

- **Risk analysis**: Here we investigate the impact: what would be the consequences if something goes wrong with this feature? What are the consequences for the player, for the game, and for the company? In this stage, the tester can also have discussions with the product owner, game designer, and player support to get the full picture of *risk, probability, and impact*. For example, suppose we implement a new way of saving game progress due to changes on the server. The developer tells us that they didn't have enough time to explore the new system properly and there is a high chance of bugs; we can already tell that probability of risk is high here. It doesn't take much investigation to figure out that not being able to save your progress in the game is going to cause lots of inconvenience for players and there is a chance that many players will leave the game due to that. The remaining players might start to doubt the reliability of the game and decrease their purchases due to a lack of trust. We can see that this is definitively a high-risk, high-probability case, and we should prioritize testing this feature in detail. It is important to remember that in agile teams, QA acts as a representative of the player, and the tester should not be afraid to voice their concerns.

- **Risk handling**: In this phase, we decide how we will address the risks that we have identified. What testing methodology will we use? How will we prioritize our testing tasks? We should always prioritize testing the areas with the highest risk probability and most severe impact. Your test allocation should always follow your risk assessment.

- **Risk monitoring**: This means that you should analyze the results of your approach. Were your concerns correct? Did you find any new, unexpected bugs? Did you learn something more about the game behavior or the usefulness of the tests? Do you need additional time or tools to ensure risk is appropriately addressed? Make sure that you note down your learnings and use them to improve the process for the next update.

Here, we learned the best test strategy to implement in live ops. Next, we will look in more detail at other types of testing strategies that can be used in any phase of game development.

Types of testing strategies

The **testing strategy** is choosing the right approach to testing and successfully assessing the quality of the game. A good testing strategy should be the following:

- **Product specific**: It takes into account all unique aspects of the product and uses the strategy that is most suitable for the game.

- **Risk-focused**: Risks with the most impact and highest probability should always be the ones that we will want to focus on.

- **Diversified**: We should implement different testing approaches to ensure that QA didn't leave any "blind spots."

- **Practical**: A test strategy needs to be easy to understand and implement. If our approach is too theoretical or difficult to implement, it will make testing efforts ineffective.

When we test the game for the first time, we are not familiar with its features and characteristics yet. We don't have firsthand knowledge about how it is supposed to work, whether there are any inherent risks with the code base, or how players are supposed to interact with it.

The first step in choosing the right strategy is learning about the game through available documentation, discussions with the development team, and participating in meetings. If QA is embedded in the team, they can utilize the iterative process of creating test sets by having short, focused testing sessions and trying different approaches in order to find the optimal way to test the game.

Let's look more closely at different testing strategy models that are commonly used in agile development teams.

The heuristic testing model is based on using a set of patterns that will help us select optimal tests. This testing model is not absolute, and it can change depending on the game's needs, but its core system can provide us with guidance on what to think about when creating tests.

In the heuristic testing model, the *testing techniques* we choose are affected by the game environment, quality criteria, and elements of the game. The output of testing techniques is "perceived quality." We use "perceived quality" rather than just "quality" as we are aware that we can never fully know the quality of the product, but based on our testing efforts, we can make a good assessment of it.

What do we mean by **game environment**? In this context, we don't only talk about technical environments such as hardware, operating system, test environment, and platform we use, but also includes testing resources, team relations, testing team size and limitation, available documentation, and any other resource or situation that can affect testing either positively or negatively. Acknowledging and accepting that we do have specific limitations and advantages and taking these into account will help us choose more realistic and effective testing techniques.

Quality criteria are rules, values, and sources that help the tester determine whether the game under test has problems. While we might think that quality criteria are clear and it's easy to recognize whether the game we test is buggy or of poor production quality, that's not necessarily the case. Quality criteria can be very different between teams and organizations, and they can often be contradicted by mixed expectations from different stakeholders. When we look into quality criteria, we should look at the game from the following angles:

- **Capability**: Does the game do what is supposed to do?

- **Security**: How secure is our game against hacking, cheating, or exploitation?

- **Usability**: What is the first-time user experience? Does the game **user experience** (**UX**) flow in a logical and easy-to-follow way?

- **Fun factor**: Is the game fun? Will it meet the player's expectations?

- **Scalability**: Can the game be updated regularly? Can we add new features and content?

- **Performance**: How does the game perform under stress? What is a frame rate? Is there a lag or delay?

- **Compatibility**: Does the game meet all of the platform standards? Does it work on all target devices and operating systems?

- **Installability**: How easily can updates be installed? What is the game size? Does the game remove "cleanly"? Where are the game files stored?

Lastly, we will briefly look into what we mean by **elements of the game**. We spoke in *Chapter 2, All Engines Go - The Basics of Game QA*, about what we test in games. We can also look at it from a different perspective and group game elements into the following categories:

- **Architecture**: Here we look into game architecture as the backbone of the code and with a wider lens, including any services that run independently from the game (third-party integrations), non-executable files, and anything else that is part of the core structure of the digital product.

- **Function**: This is everything that the game does that would fall into the category of functional testing.

- **Interfaces**: This includes the **user interface** (**UI**) and the UX.

- **Platform**: We spoke in detail about platforms in *Chapter 4, Deeper Look - Testing on Various Gaming Platforms – Mobile, PC, and Console*.

- **Operations**: While in function, we focus on testing everything that the game is supposed to do, in operations, we look into the game from the angle of how the game will be used. Here, it is crucial to put ourselves in the players' shoes, and besides optimal use, we focus on testing unfavorable and extreme usage as well.

- **Time**: This is any relationship between the game and time. Here we look into things such as installation time, loading time, speeding things up and slowing them down in the game, doing multiple things at the same time, and so on.

You can learn more about heuristic testing methods on Michael Bolton's blog: `https://developsense.com/`

Another strategic approach to testing we are going to look into here is the **five-fold testing system**. It was first described by Kaner, Bach, and Pettichord in their book *Lessons Learned in Software Testing*. The core of this strategy is the idea that every type of testing we do can be described through five different dimensions. Those dimensions are detailed here:

- **Testers or who does the testing?**: In agile teams, it's common for the whole team to be involved in some sort of testing activity. We might use internal QA or external QA. Are we doing beta testing, and are actual players testing the game?

- **Coverage**: What is being tested? Games are increasingly complex ecosystems with many different components. From how many different angles are we approaching it?

- **Potential problems**: Against which risks are we testing? What is the impact of a possible failure?

- **Activities**: How do we execute tests? What approach and methodology do we use?

- **Evaluation**: How do we evaluate whether tests passed or failed? While it may be obvious to the tester, a failure might not be understood equally by all stakeholders.

There are many different approaches we can take when thinking about our testing strategy. Rather than being a repetitive set of actions, testing is really about investigation, discovery, and continuous learning. Testers should make sure that they keep an open mind, are capable of critical thinking, and build testing models that are flexible enough to be easily changed when the project requires so.

Summary

In this chapter, we learned about aspects of the waterfall methodology that are still useful, how to focus testing in live ops, and several different methods to help us select an appropriate testing strategy. Now, you know how to approach testing in live ops and have the skills to approach the best strategy for handling testing in agile game development projects. You can speak with confidence about the waterfall and agile QA approaches. In the next chapter, we will dive into more detail about testing methodologies and learn practical methods that will help us execute the most efficient tests and secure game quality.

10

Eat, Sleep, Test, Repeat: Test Methodology

In this chapter, we will cover different methodologies that we can use to optimize our testing efforts. We will look into methodologies that are most commonly used in agile teams and help us deal efficiently with fast-paced development, with frequent updates and introductions of new code. While these methodologies are frequently used in agile game development, they are also very useful for more traditional teams.

Besides this deep dive into various methodologies, we will also look at the best practices when dealing with new code. While every game has a different architecture and each studio has slightly different processes, there are some good practices that can be used across the board.

In this chapter, we will learn about the following key topics:

- **Risk-based testing**
- **Exploratory testing**
- **Equivalence partitioning** and **boundary value analysis**
- **Decision tables**
- **Strategies for dealing with new code**

First, let's start with one of the most important methodologies we can use when dealing with continuous change and multiple stakeholders: risk-based testing.

Risk-based testing

Risk-based testing is one of the most valuable tools in any tester's arsenal, regardless of which development framework we use. But it's agile and live ops where it really shines, and it's always a staple of **quality assurance (QA)** efforts. We often do risk-based testing without even realizing that we are using a specific methodology. Whenever we approach the game from a player-focused angle and ask ourselves, "How will this affect the player?", we are doing some sort of risk testing.

Of course, risk-based testing also has its standard rule and best practices. While we already touched briefly on risk-based testing in *Chapter 9, It Works, but It Hasn't Been Tested*; here, we will dwell a bit longer on this methodology and how to use it in an optimal manner.

The efficiency of risk-based testing is highly dependent on the initial **risk analysis**. For that reason, it is important to do risk analysis in a way that is optimal for the project and which will give us the most reliable information.

How to do efficient risk analysis? This depends on several factors:

- In which game development phase are we?
- What is the goal of this testing round?
- What is a current business goal?

We can see that risk analysis depends a lot on the perspective from which we are looking at the product. When we do risk analysis in *pre-production*, one of the risks can be, for example, that game is too innovative, and we might not be able to finish it in a given timeframe. In *live ops*, our risk will be something along the lines of, "There is a risk that players will not understand the new feature." Both of these risks can appear in almost any game development phase, but the same risk might have different impacts and probabilities.

It is a good practice to *group risks* as well. We can do it either at the beginning of the **risk identification** process or at a later stage. Grouping risks early on helps us guide our thinking and ensures that we don't leave part of the game or some risks unaddressed. We can group risks in various ways. Some of the categories we should think about including are as follows:

- Code base
- Player
- Business
- Process
- Team
- Timeline

The next step is the risk analysis process, where we estimate the **risk, impact, and probability**. This is the most demanding part of the risk analysis, as it requires us to have deep insight into the game architecture, design, internal and external studio factors, familiarity with the player persona, and previous experience from similar game projects. It is rare that one person has a realistic view from all different aspects. That's why it's always recommended to involve other disciplines when doing risk analysis. Getting input from coders, artists, designers, and product managers helps us make the most objective risk assessment, providing a strong foundation for further testing activities. Let's look into more detail how to do all aspects of risk-based testing.

Risk identification

Let's have a look first at risk identification. We should never rely exclusively on our own knowledge when doing risk identification. Even if we have years of experience, there could always be some unknown factor that we haven't thought about. Having multiple perspectives helps us not only to identify all relevant risks but it also helps us make optimal estimates for risk probability and impact. Let's have a look at what the risk identification process looks like.

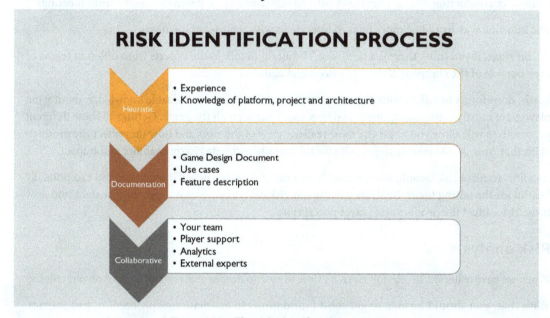

Figure 10.1 – The risk identification process

Initial risk identification starts with the tester. They use their experience, knowledge of the product, knowledge of the studio processes, and knowledge of the technical platform, architecture, and game engine to prepare an initial **risk list**.

> **What is a risk list?**
>
> A risk list is usually a spreadsheet document, which lists all identified relevant risks, but we haven't identified their probability and potential impact just yet. This document will be our starting point.

Next, we should read available *documentation* about the feature that we are about to test: the **Game design document (GDD)**, use cases, or any other readily available documentation. We expand our risk list with new things we have learned. We must keep in mind our time limitations here. If we are just starting the project and we are in the early phases of development, we can take more time to study documentation. But, if we are in live ops and we are talking about a new feature, we should focus on documentation about that feature only.

After we have added our own input, it's time to talk to the rest of the team. Depending on your studio structure and processes, you can do it in either a *formal* or *informal* way.

The formal way would be organizing a risk identification brainstorming session first, then an analysis workshop, conducting official interviews with all stakeholders, or having a specific team meetings.

The informal way would be more relaxed interviews with your team members.

At this stage, if you think there is a need, don't be afraid to talk to the experts from different teams or even outside of the company if there is a need and allowance for that.

Lastly, don't forget to talk to your *player support team*! They will have valuable knowledge about what players are mostly complaining about and how they interact with the game. Getting all these different perspectives will allow you to get the most realistic view of the risks and how they affect the product. With that, you should be able to get solid foundations to estimate risk probability and impact.

As a final result of risk identification, we will have a list of risks that is well thought out and exceptionally helpful for the testing focus. Next, we will use our risk list and analyze it to get more insight into how those risks affect the product and player perception.

Risk analysis

When we have collected all relevant risks, it's time to go into deeper analysis and expand on our risk list.

With that, you should be able to get solid foundations to estimate risk probability and impact. *Probability* tells us what the likelihood of the risk happening is. For example: after discussing with the technical team and based on your experience with the game backend, you feel fairly confident that the backend can take over 100,000 concurrent users and can be scaled up seamlessly. You also know that the development team did extensive load testing on the servers. The risk of the backend failing is relatively low. It is common to use a numeric scale to mark the probability and we would assign a value of 1 or possibly 2 to this risk, indicating that the probability is at the low end of the scale.

The *impact* is the effect that risk has on the product and even more importantly, on players. If we look at the impact of the previous example, it would be catastrophic. The game would become unplayable, and we would lose lots of players and lots of money. A similar situation happened in real life too. Electronic Arts released *The Simpsons: Tapped Out* mobile game without properly optimizing servers and underestimated players' interest in the franchise. Besides backend issues, the game was also riddled with bugs that severely affected players. It got so bad that game had to be removed from the App Store, and it took developers six months to fix all issues and publish the game again. The second time around, *The Simpsons: Tapped Out* became a great success.

This example tells us what can happen if we don't analyze our risks correctly. Developers severely underestimated the interest players would have in a the Simpsons-themed game as well as what impact bugs would have on players. This mistake cost the studio a staggering amount of money, with some estimates even going up to $200 million.

You can read more details about this story here: `https://www.cnet.com/tech/mobile/how-electronic-arts-resurrected-its-doa-simpsons-game/`

What is the best way to determine impact? In agile teams, QA's role is to represent the player. We should put ourselves in the player's shoes and see how each specific risk can affect them. If you are new to the game, make sure that you check feature requirements and talk to other team members.

Risk prioritization

After we have completed the analysis, we should *prioritize risks*. This will help us test the most vulnerable parts of the game, and it will help us choose the correct testing strategy. So, how do we prioritize risks?

At the top of our list, we will put risks that have a high impact and high probability of happening. Those risks are the most dangerous that can cause the most damage if not properly addressed, and we want to make sure that we test against them sufficiently to ensure that they won't happen. But how do we prioritize other risks?

If you identify numerous risks and you are unsure how to prioritize them all correctly, it is useful to use the **risk score**.

> **What is a risk score?**
>
> A risk score is a number that we get when we multiply probability with impact numbers. That number is then assigned to each risk, and we use it as a guideline on how to prioritize risks, starting with the ones that have the highest numerical value.

When we talk about risk prioritization, we should also mention **as low as reasonably practicable** (**ALARP**). Even if the term is not very often used in the gaming industry, the idea of ALARP is commonly included in risk-based testing.

> **What is ALARP?**
>
> ALARP recognizes that it's not always possible to eliminate all risks. There could be financial, operational, or project constraints that will not allow us to do that. ALARP is the principle that weighs the risk against the constraints and focuses on defining and addressing what is the lowest acceptable risk.

To get extra assurance, or if you still end up with many risks with the same risk number, it is good practice to discuss with the team and jointly decide how to prioritize them.

Developing a test strategy based on risks

By now, we have ready a risk list with the final analysis and risk score. It is time to look at our *test strategy* based on risk. Our priority is to ensure *good coverage* for the risks that have been identified with the highest risk score, meaning having high probability and impact. We can be sure that if we find a bug related to those risks, it will be taken very seriously.

We also want to ensure that we spend the most time and resources on risks with the highest score. In risk-based testing, it's better to spend most of the time on high-risk items and barely touch the ones at the bottom of the list than spend testing effort on everything equally. Very often, one bug from a high-risk item can have a much bigger impact than dozens of bugs found on the low-score risk items combined.

Our test strategy should include a combination of testing techniques to ensure comprehensive testing of areas that are considered high risk. Depending on the type of risk we identify as highest, we should consider using exploratory testing, equivalence partitioning, and boundary value analysis and it is highly advisable to do regression testing as well. We will speak about all of these methods later in this chapter.

Before we start test execution, it is a good practice to set up **test objectives** based on our risk analysis. Test objectives should always follow the *SMART framework*, meaning they should be the following:

- Specific

- Measurable

- Achievable

- Relevant

- Timely

Using test objectives helps us keep testing efforts focused, particularly if we are using a geographically dispersed or outsourced testing team.

What makes a good test objective? Let's presume that our highest rated risk is "Changes to the backend architecture might cause problems with game saves that can lead to a situation where players' progress can't be saved anymore." A test objective based on this risk would be something like this, "Ensure that multiple players can save their gameplay progression in any stage of gameplay." A test objective like this one fits within the SMART framework and would be a great guideline for testing team efforts.

Monitoring and managing risks

After we have executed our test plan, our work is still not completely over. We want to make sure that reported bugs will be fixed and that we do have some type of *contingency plan* if the worst-case scenario happens. Sometimes even with the best testing efforts, we can't ensure with absolute certainty that risk will not happen. There are times constraints and often various technical challenges that will not allow us to test every possible permutation that can potentially cause problems.

One good example to illustrate this would be releasing a new game update with a massive new feature that heavily affects the whole game architecture. For example, something like introducing events to the game or introducing multiplayer to a single-player game even if Working on something so massive probably took a while, there were many changes in the code on the frontend and backend, done by many different people. Even after thorough testing in the staging environment, we might still have some reservations about the game's stability. In cases like this, it is important for the team to develop a contingency plan.

In our example, we should implement an automatic alert system that will notify us immediately when something is wrong. Furthermore, our team should develop a clear process on how to revert changes easily and get back to the last stable game update, to minimize game downtime and prevent losing players. While this contingency plan sounds pretty simple, in reality, it takes quite a bit of time to implement properly. The best practice is to start thinking about "How can this fail" as early as possible in the project and include a contingency plan in your development schedule.

We have learned more about risk and how to execute risk-based testing. Next, we will learn about exploratory testing.

Exploratory testing

Exploratory testing is one of the most used methodologies in agile teams as well as in live ops. By its nature, exploratory testing relies on testers having the freedom to explore and discover. It's about exploring the unknown in the game we test, and as a result of exploratory testing, we gain insights and knowledge that will help us in further testing efforts.

We use exploratory testing in situations where we have very *limited documentation* or other knowledge about the game we are testing. It is also an excellent methodology to use when we are testing *new code* or testing the game for the first time.

While being an exceptionally valuable testing method, exploratory testing is a little bit more than that. It's also about learning about the game we are testing "and" testing execution and a great way to teach new testers in the team. In that way, exploratory testing is a unique method that is a valuable tool for any team:

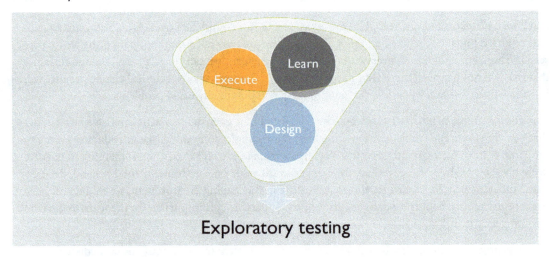

Figure 10.2 – The benefits of doing exploratory testing

Very often, exploratory testing is used interchangeably with *ad hoc testing*, and it is presumed that you just "dive in" and do not care too much about the planning or style of execution. While *unstructured exploratory testing* can be useful and it is sometimes necessary, we can also use this methodology in a more structured approach that helps us focus testing efforts and maximize our learnings. Let's have a look at how to do *structured exploratory testing*.

While exploratory testing is a flexible and fast method, in structured exploratory testing, we have the following steps that make our testing sessions more focused and efficient. This is particularly helpful when exploratory testing is done by multiple people and on a wide area of the game:

1. Firstly, we set up a *test charter*. A test charter is a short statement that tells us what our objectives are and what we are trying to achieve with this testing round. When the testing objective is reached, we can consider that this round of exploratory testing is over. A test charter can be something relatively high level such as "Make sure that the newly implemented event system works well, in single-player as well as multiplayer mode." We do want to be careful not to limit testing efforts too much, as then exploratory testing will lose its advantage of flexibility. Testers won't be able to "follow the trail" or explore deep enough.

2. *Planning* for exploratory testing should be minimal. It's more about providing the *testing framework*: deciding who is going to test, what tools will be used, and how long the testing round will last. Generally, we box testing time in blocks of one, two, or four hours. We want to allow testers to use different approaches and techniques as they find fit.

3. Lastly, it's *documentation*. During exploratory testing, testers should report bugs but also take **testing notes** about techniques they used, observations about the game they are testing, and anything else that might be useful for the team. We have spoken in more detail about how to properly report bugs in *Chapter 8, I Thought I Fixed That: How to Write Efficient Bug Reports*. At the end of the testing round, testers should provide a testing report where they note down what bugs they have found and the most important learnings, including any new risks they might have discovered. Very often, notes from exploratory testing can be used as a *source document* for the creation of test plans and test cases.

While exploratory testing is an incredibly important and powerful tool, it also has its *disadvantages*. Testers who are doing exploratory testing must have confidence and curiosity to really dive deep into the unknown. Junior team members or testers who prefer working with clearly defined work steps and detailed instructions might struggle with loosely defined rules and minimal guidance. In those situations, it's wise to pair junior team members with more senior ones to get the most out of testing sessions.

We learned how to do exploratory testing and its advantages and disadvantages. Next, we will learn more about equivalence partitioning and boundary value analysis.

Equivalence partitioning and boundary value analysis

Equivalence partitioning is a great method when dealing with *different data ranges*. It's not possible to test all possible permutations and values that we have in the game, but we do want to make sure that they work as intended. Using equivalence partitioning, we can significantly shorten the testing time and ensure optimal coverage.

The premise of equivalence partitioning is that we can split testing conditions into parts that can be considered the same. Testing one value from each partition is equal to testing each and every value from the same partition. Let's look at the following example of this:

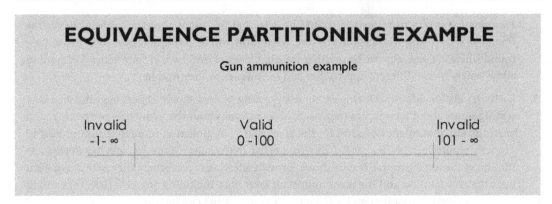

Figure 10.3 – Equivalence partitioning

In the example in *Figure 10.3*, we can see how equivalence partitioning would work in the case of gun ammunition. Let's imagine that this specific gun is designed for our new, sci-fi-themed game and that it can hold 100 bullets. We can see that we have three distinguished *partitions*. One is a *valid* one, with values from 0 to 100. It indicates that this is a valid range and the gun can contain any number of bullets in this range. Then, we have an *invalid range*, which is anything from 101 onward. We know that the gun is designed to hold only 100 bullets, so it shouldn't be able to hold more than that value. This is another partition.

Lastly, we have a partition in which numbers are between -1 and infinite negative numbers. It means that guns are not designed to have negative bullets. It is enough to test only one value from those partitions and consider that all remaining values in the partition are tested as well.

How would we test this? For example, our test case might include steps where we try to load more bullets into an already full gun. What happens? Or when we try to shoot even after we have spent all the bullets. What happens?

This is only one example of how *equivalence partitioning* can be helpful in game testing. We can also use it for testing soft currency in the game, points, or any kind of numerical strings. By using equivalence partitioning, we can confidently test those ranges in a much shorter period and with high reliability.

When we talk about equivalence partitioning, we need to talk about boundary value analysis as both methods go hand in hand. Let's have a deeper look into boundary value analysis next.

There are certain statistical indicators that tell us that bugs frequently happen in borderline areas. Boundary value analysis is a method that allows us to test boundaries between different partitions:

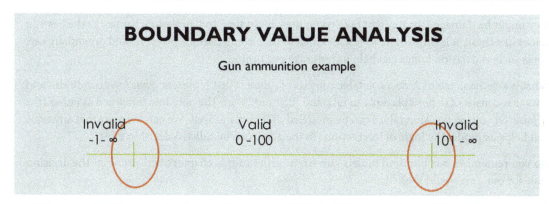

Figure 10.4 – Boundary value analysis

In *Figure 10.4*, we can see how boundary value analysis looks when added to the example in *Figure 10.3*. Here we see that we should focus on testing values that are on the *border of the partition*. Here are some test scenarios we could use for our gun example: what happens when we only have one bullet left, but we turn on gun burst mode? What happens when we have 91 bullets left and try to load a new charger of 10 bullets?

This method is also exceptionally useful when we have any *data entry fields*. Even if that's not too common in games, we do often have the option to enter our email for in-game registration or our age to ensure that the player is mature enough to be exposed to the content in the game. Those data entry fields can be successfully tested by using equivalence partitioning and boundary value analysis.

Benefits of these methods are that they significantly decrease the number of test scenarios QA needs to run without losing any testing reliability. But, the success of boundary value analysis very much depends on us doing equivalence partitioning correctly in the first place. If our equivalence partitioning is wrong, consequently, boundary value analysis will be wrong as well, and the test cases will not be valid.

When we deal with multiple permutations in software, sometimes these two methods are not enough to help us sufficiently decrease the testing load. In those cases, we can use another method, called a decision table.

Decision tables

A decision table is a *testing methodology* that helps us when we deal with *numerous permutations* in the game. This happens a lot in open-world games, where players have the option to interact with multiple objects and have the freedom to combine them or use them in multiple ways. For example, let's imagine you are working on an open-world **role-playing game** (**RPG**) game, a game similar to "Diablo 3" or "Skyrim." As a player, you have the option to move around in the world, fight enemies, and collect numerous weapons, different types of shields, and clothing items, among others. You also have the freedom to combine the items you find as you wish. While each of these games would have optimal sets for each situation in the game, as a player, you might not find all the optimal items, or they might be damaged, or it might take you quite a bit of time to figure out what works the best! In games like these, it is impossible to test all kinds of item combinations players could potentially use. Tools such as decision tables can help us optimize our testing.

What is a decision table? A decision table consists of *columns* that represent *game logic* conditions and rows that consist of *actions* players can take and their *outcomes*. The outcome is marked as either *true or false*. Of course, decision tables can be modeled differently as well. We can even say that any table that helps us model the logic of interactions in the game can be called a decision table.

Do you remember our hundred bullets gun from earlier in this chapter? Let's see what the decision table for our gun would look like:

	Wound	Daze	Kill	Enrage
Human	True (T)	False (F)	T	F
Alien 1	F	T	F	F
Alien 2	F	F	F	T
Alien 3	F	T	F	T

Figure 10.5 – A decision table for the gun effects example

In the table in *Figure 10.5*, we can see what different actions a gun can have depending on different entities that can be shot by the gun. As our game has a sci-fi theme, besides humans, we also encounter different types of aliens and guns will have different effects on each of them.

Using a decision table like this one, we can model the behavior in the game and help validate what would be considered a failed or passed test scenario.

Let's have a look at another example of the decision table.

CONDITION	ACTION	OUTCOME
Player enters active combat	Pulls out weapon	NPC attacks
Player runs out of ammo	Tries to shoot	Need more ammo! Message triggers
Player is in a safe zone	Pulls out weapon	Safe zone rules trigger and weapon is turned back to inventory
Player is in active dialogue	Pulls out weapon	NPC pulls their weapon and dialogue is stopped

Figure 10.6 – A decision table example modeling the outcome of gun actions

In *Figure 10.6*, we modeled our logic somewhat differently. Here we have columns showing us the precondition, the player action, and the outcome of that action. In this example, we are using a weapon in different scenarios and mapping what kind of outcomes we have from those actions.

Decision tables have many *benefits*. They help us understand how items can interact with each other, they make requirements much clearer, and they can also help us discover combinations in the game that we hadn't thought about earlier. Decision tables also help us discover illogical combinations, which would be very difficult to spot by only reading a textual description of the feature. They make a great base for writing test cases, they help us quickly verify whether something passes or fails in the game, and they are also a great tool for documenting game design.

Now that we have learned some of the most useful methodologies we can utilize, let's wrap up this lesson by learning about a few more strategies on how to deal with the new code.

Strategies for dealing with new code

In game development, especially when working with live ops, we deal with new code relatively often. Depending on the number of changes and, subsequently, new code that was implemented, we need to adjust our strategies to be able to successfully test those changes in a fast-paced environment. Here are some of the tips that will help you pick the right approach.

Start your testing with *mainstream tests* first. Those are the tests that cover basic functionality or optimal player path. These tests are usually simple and easy to understand, and if they fail, it would be taken as a serious problem. You want to find those bugs as early as possible in the development cycle.

At first, *test broadly rather than deeply*. This is particularly useful when we have no information about new code and we are unaware of any risks. Covering a wide area of the game will help us prioritize future testing and help us find the most risk-prone areas. This approach to testing works like a reverse funnel: we cover a wide area and slowly focus on the parts of the game that are most risky and prone to bugs. We should keep in mind that if we already have knowledge of the code and we performed risk analysis, this approach is not really useful anymore. We should instead focus on testing the most risk-prone areas of the game.

When your game passes mainstream tests, look for more powerful tests. Approach the testing from the angle of *"how can I break it?"* rather than *"I'll make sure that it works."* Utilize testing scenarios where you attempt to do illegal moves or follow less-than-optimal player paths. When approaching testing from this angle, make sure that the test scenarios you use are realistic and plausible. While it's great to explore edge case scenarios, we don't want to spend too much time on testing scenarios that might happen exceptionally rarely.

Make sure that you are using *exploratory testing*. We spoke about exploratory testing in length in this chapter. It's a perfect tool to use when we handle new code, and it can be used hand in hand with *risk-based testing* or as a precursor for any further testing efforts.

Lastly, don't forget to do *regression testing*. Even with the most carefully planned new features, there is always a possibility that new code, as well as a new design, might affect old features and the code base in unpredictable ways. By running a solid regression testing round, we ensure that there are no disasters lurking and that older parts of the game are still working well and make sense in the overall game ecosystem.

> **Regression testing**
>
> The purpose of regression testing is to ensure that newly implemented changes in the game don't break existing code and features or resurface old bugs. Regression testing is executed by running the same test cases we ran previously but on the newly updated software. Any bugs found in regression testing will be treated as new bugs.

Summary

In this chapter, we learned about the different methodologies that will help us in our testing efforts. We learned in detail about risk-based testing, equivalence partitioning, boundary value analysis, and exploratory testing, and we also reminded ourselves about regression testing. While all of these methodologies are useful tools regardless of how game development is organized, by now, we know that they are an important part of live ops. In the next chapter, we will go into the details of how QA works in live ops and how to organize it optimally.

Part 3:
Test Management and Beyond

In the final part of this book, we will first go in depth about working and testing in the live ops phase of game development. You will learn practical tips on how to organize and execute testing activities, keeping in mind the unique challenges of modern free-to-play games. Next, we will talk at length about working with the games team, as well as about a career in QA and where it can potentially lead. Finally, we will learn what the future might hold for games QA.

This part has the following chapters:

- *Chapter 11, Are You on the Right Version? Live Ops and QA*

- *Chapter 12, Beyond Testing – Introduction to Test Management*

- *Chapter 13, There Are No BUGS Without U – QA and the Game Team*

11

Are You on the Right Version? Live Ops and QA

In the last decade, **live ops** has grown to become a key phase of a game's life cycle. Live ops can (and should, if your game is successful!) last for years, and in the cases of several exceptionally popular games, we can see it continuing for over a decade. Live ops is a new game development phase that has become increasingly important with the rise of free-to-play games. However, although everyone is talking about it, there are almost no available guidelines on best practices. There is not even a unified explanation of what live ops means, as different disciplines in the gaming industry will look at it from different angles.

Throughout this chapter, we will get a bigger picture of what live ops is, how it fits in the game development process, why is it so important, and where QA fits in. We will analyze how QA for live ops is different, not only by the methodology that we use but also by how QA works with the rest of the team. Testers who work in live ops QA need to have somewhat different soft skills and preferred ways of working to be able to do their job efficiently in this phase and work seamlessly with the team.

In this chapter, we will take a deep dive into live ops best practices and learn the following topics:

- How it differentiates from *game development*
- How to deal with a continuous stream of *new content and features*
- What role QA has in *live ops submissions*
- Finally, how *live bugs* differentiate from "regular" bugs and what the optimal way to handle them is

The difference between dev and live ops

There is a lot of misunderstanding about live ops. It's a relatively new part of the development cycle, which became increasingly important with the rise of free-to-play games. Traditional games are made in the following life cycle, shown in *Figure 11.1*.

Figure 11.1 – Premium game high-level development cycle

Practically 90 percent of the work is done *before* the game is published. After the game is out and released to the target market, there might be some additional content available for purchase (called *DLC*) or some major bug fixes. Of course, there will also be the possibility for player to reach player support. However, we will consider development work is done when the game hits the market. The game team that worked on the game is either redistributed to other game development projects or let go. Premium game development is somewhat similar to creating feature movies. The team gets together, spends a couple of years working together on the same project, and then moves on to the next best thing.

Next, let's have a look at the F2P mobile game development cycle. We can see it in *Figure 11.2*:

Figure 11.2 – F2P mobile game development cycle

The nature of free-to-play games is very different. In *Figure 11.2*, we can see how the development cycle looks like for free-to-play games. We can see that more than 90% of the work is done *AFTER* the game is released. Game teams grow after release, and the live ops phase lasts for many years to come if a game is successful. As live ops can be explained and looked at from multiple different angles, let's identify it here first.

> **What is Live Ops?**
>
> Live Ops is a game development phase that happens after a game's initial release. Live Ops include all activities that are done on the live game that contribute to its ongoing operations and success. Activities can be technical, creative, promotional, supportive, or anything in between. They include things such as optimizing game architecture and updating technical components, creating new content and features, ongoing player support, user acquisition, and continuous testing.

In traditional game development, methodologies such as waterfall can still work quite well. That means that QA is considered a phase and game builds are "handed over" when development is considered done. If we approach game production and QA in the same way in live ops, our project will be in a lot of trouble.

During Live Ops, players get used to a regular *cadence of updates*. They expect a game to be fun and engaging, even after they play it for years. It's up to game designers to come up with new features that would fulfill players' expectations. Players' behavior in live ops is carefully measured through player *analytics*. We can see how players engage with the game, how long their playing sessions are, how they spend money, how long they play the game for, how they engage with other players, and at which point in the game they stop playing. All this information gives indications to the game designers and product owners about which parts of the game work and which ones need improvements. Combined with *qualitative player feedback* that a gaming studio receives through Player Support and players forums, designers can get a solid idea of what kind of changes players would like to see in the game.

Our *business goal* as game developers is primarily to keep players playing a game for as long as possible. This is called *"player retention."* Even if it sounds contradictory, it is even more important to keep a player in a game than entice them to spend money. There is a strong psychological reason for it. Players who play our game for a long time get committed to it. They invest time and often money too, and it becomes harder for them to leave. They form communities and relationships in our game. Sometimes, it's even harder to leave the *game community* than the game itself. This makes long-term players more loyal and more likely to spend money, and it also promotes the game to other potential players. We call this the *K factor*.

> **What is the K factor?**
>
> The *K* factor is a number indicating how much "word of mouth" potential our game has. For example, if our existing player tells five of their friends to download the game or sends the invite through social media, *K* expresses how many new players we will get into the game. We call players obtained in this way "organic." The *K* factor is expressed as a number. A *K* factor of 1 means that an existing player will attract another player into the game.

Why is this important for QA? In live ops, QA is almost always *embedded* in the team. The more QA understands the nature of the gaming business model, product goals, and players' behavioral preferences, the easier it is to prioritize tasks and champion for the player within the game team.

Of course, every game, regardless of the business model or target platform, has a **development phase** before entering live ops. In gaming studios that are already experienced with F2P games and live ops, they usually start with preparations for live ops while a game is still in development. That means that QA will be embedded in the team relatively early in the production phase. However, there are major differences between the development phase for traditional games and modern F2P games, particularly on *mobile*.

Premium games are designed as a closed system – they have a beginning and an end. As such, there is no live ops phase in traditional development for premium games; that means that games have to be of very high quality, with finalized content and minimum bugs on launch already. On the other hand, in the development phase of free-to-play games, we focus on creating a **minimum viable product (MVP)** that will have a limited geographical release (**soft launch**) to gather initial player data (**game KPIs**), before the future course of game development is decided. On many occasions, if KPIs are really poor, a game might even be canceled.

In traditional development, the period just before launch is the busiest time for QA, and most of the work is focused there. For QA in F2P games, while there is also an increased testing effort, it's not as overwhelming as for premium games. As premium games have finite content and no live ops phase, they have to be thoroughly tested before release from all aspects, including full platform compliance, game balancing, complete playthrough, all achievements, and basically, everything else!

Before *soft launch* in modern games testing, we want to make sure that a game works well enough to be enjoyed by players, but things such as fine-tuning and balancing are usually left to be modified, depending on game KPIs. QA will focus on testing the following:

- Early gameplay
- **First-time user experience** (FTUE)
- Building internal processes to handle live ops

For QA, that means optimizing *bug flow*, which can accommodate not only bugs that come from production but also ones that come from the live game.

While there are many commonalities in game development, we can see that there are also some significant differences. Next, we will take a deep dive into how to test new features in live ops.

How to test new features

We already covered briefly testing new code in *Chapter 10, Eat, Sleep, Test, Repeat: Test Methodology*.

Here, we will look at it exclusively from a live ops perspective. In live ops, we generally have four development tracks, as shown in *Figure 11.3*.

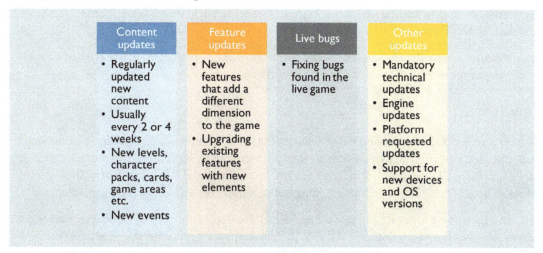

Figure 11.3 – The different types of game updates in live ops

Testing new content

The first development track is about **content production**. Every successful game in live ops has regular content updates. This provides players with new levels or areas of a game to play. Content usually comes out in cadence, and players learn to expect it at regular intervals. By adding new content, we keep our most loyal players engaged, and the game feels fresh and fun to play. Mature development teams have very well-organized content pipelines that are planned a couple of months ahead. The QA team's job here is to make sure that new content works as it should and can easily be integrated into existing gameplay, without any difficulties for the player. However, there are a couple of things we need to take into account when we test content.

Depending on our game architecture and content pipeline, it can be pushed out through a **submissions process** or through something we call *"backend push."* That means that content can be pushed directly to a live game from our own servers without the need for platform submissions. While this is an amazing benefit for the team and allows us to quickly control content flow, it also comes with its own challenges. We will talk about them in more detail later in this chapter.

The most important thing we test with *new content* is continuity. Does it fit as it should be with the content already in the game? Does it meet player expectations in quality and quantity (i.e., is there enough content for players to play until a new content drop is available)? Does the new content break something already existing in the game? When we work with more mature live games, we should also start to look into how a content update affects game performance and game size. Usually, well-prepared game architecture allows for more efficient use of resources and code optimization, but over time, even the best games might start to experience "bloat," which might affect game performance and slow down the frame rate.

The third development track is about dealing with **live game bugs**. We will talk about this in more detail later in this chapter.

Next, let's have a more detailed look into why new features are so important in live ops and how we handle testing them.

New features

We have now learned how to handle new content, but do we handle *new features* in the same way? Even with great new content, every game gets tired after some time. There are games out there, such as *Candy Crush* and *Clash of Clans*, that have been live for a decade and still going strong! These games last for so long because developers keep adding not only new content but also new game features.

To make a game more engaging and interesting, we can also develop *new features*. There are numerous reasons why we need to develop new features. Besides keeping players entertained, we also use new features to optimize our *KPIs*. New feature development is mostly focused on features that would have a positive impact on the player. They will either improve monetization and player retention or decrease churn. The *games analytics* team regularly gathers game KPI, and the product manager, together with the team, analyzes those numbers and turns them into new features. We can see this feature flow in *Figure 11.4*.

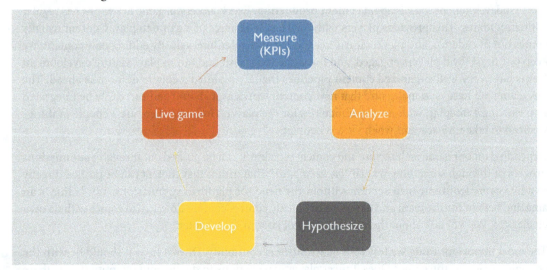

Figure 11.4 – Feature flow

How does this work in practice? Let's imagine that we have a mobile F2P game of the match 3 genre, and our retention on day 60 is lower than expected. The product manager, with the help of the team, will make a *hypothesis* about why is this happening. QA can also be helpful in these moments, as testers will have deep insight into all areas of the game and be very familiar with how players interact with the game. QA can also help to exclude hypotheses if KPIs are low because of a bug that we are not aware of. For example, if we presume that we have a bug where late levels often freeze when matching items explode, it might affect a player's retention if it happens frequently enough. However, we might test later levels and read players' comments to see that everything seems in order. Our next working hypothesis is that our current events are too repetitive, and players who are with us for around two months or more might find them boring. We call this phenomenon "**player fatigue.**" That means that our team will respond to those *hypotheses* by *developing* a new feature – a new type of event, which will be significantly different from the existing one and hopefully keep players engaged for longer.

In this example, we can see how much more versatile a role QA has in live ops. It's not only about testing content before it's pushed live; it's also about giving input about players' behavior, helping us figure out whether there are bugs or game issues that affect game KPIs, and doing regression testing to ensure that new features don't break anything in the old game.

Regression testing here goes even further. QA will have a chance to participate in the design process and give a pre-emptive warning if some new feature will not work out with already existing ones. In live ops, regression testing doesn't only mean we will check that a new feature doesn't affect the existing code. We also need to check it from a player's point of view – will the new feature make an existing feature obsolete? This can be particularly dangerous when we work on the game with multiple in-game currencies, for example.

Introducing new currency later in a game might make some of the old in-game currencies obsolete or decrease their value. That might resonate very poorly with the players, especially if they invested time (*content grind*) to earn that currency or made an **in-app purchase**. Instead of making the game more interesting and enticing for the player, we might instead anger our player base and cause them to leave the game. Of course, game designers usually take into account this type of thing when they decide on new major items in the game. But for games that have been live for a long time and with a multitude of features and events, along with millions of players in different parts of the game, it's sometimes difficult to fully model players' behavior and predict all the changes in gameplay. This is where QA support and insight become priceless. QA acts as a representative of the player, and as testers spend so much time with the game, they usually have very detailed knowledge of all parts of the game.

Another thing that can help us at this stage is feedback from the **player support**. Their role is not only to receive complaints from players and respond to them. They communicate directly with the players and are very aware of players' likes, dislikes, and other game preferences. **Players** also like to suggest new features and content themselves. Getting this information to the development team can help us design a game that players will truly love and relate to.

Unfortunately, in many teams, player support is kept separated from the development team, and lots of *player insights* never reach the game team. That's why it's important to find a way in development processes to include player support in development work. During my time at Next Games, we had one member of the player support group join our daily stand-up and feature planning meeting. That helped us not only to get timely player feedback but also helped player support to understand the development process. They could give back to players much more precise and reliable information, and that helped grow a positive community around our game.

When developing new features in live ops, we almost always work with a **minimum viable feature (MVF)**. What does that mean? As we have learned so far, while we get lots of data and information about player behavior that helps us form a solid hypothesis about how our features will be received by players, we can't really know for sure. It's a huge *risk* to develop a new feature and spend months of development time to polish it to the smallest detail, just to learn that our hypothesis wasn't exactly right and players didn't respond as we expected. Dedicating so much time to one feature that might or might not work can be also dangerous for a team's moral. A team can get attached to a feature and might feel disappointed or let down if it doesn't work as expected. They feel that their efforts were wasted.

After already significant opportunity loss and potential financial loss from working in development for so long, we will also deal with a team that is dissatisfied and less motivated. That's why all our hypotheses are tested on minimum viable features that are created in the shortest possible period, but with a quality that is still acceptable for a player. This is the time for QA to really shine, and rather than following strict checklists and focusing on ticking boxes, we need to use our own heads and critical thinking. It is crucial for QA to be embedded in the team in orderto be able to do this job well.

QA needs to have a good *understanding* of why we implement a feature and what its goal is. How is it supposed to affect a player? Is it supposed to encourage the player to spend a bit more money on a specific pain point or obtain a highly desirable item? Or is it supposed to increase player engagement by having more branching narratives or new social features? When they understand the goal of the feature, QA should put themselves in the player's position and think about how the feature at hand affects our target player.

Next, QA needs to understand that MVF is not a full or perfectly polished feature but, rather, a *first iteration* of it. QA needs to develop tests that will be good enough to find key bugs that can affect the performance of the new feature but not too rigid to report bugs that are not relevant yet. For example, a new feature should not crash or freeze a game, and that is definitively a bug that needs to be fixed before a new feature is pushed to live. However, changes in the strength balancing of existing characters by the introduction of a new ones should not be taken necessarily as a bug or problem, unless a change is really drastic, or it would make existing premium characters (ones that are bought or very hard to obtain) useless. We should ask ourselves the following questions when testing:

- Is this feature *stable* enough to be easily playable on a wide range of devices?

- Is this feature going to affect *players' behavior* in a desirable way?

- Will this feature be able to validate our working *hypotheses*?

- Is this feature going to introduce *new risks* to the existing game?

- Is this feature going to introduce risks to *future updates*?

- Is the feature *polished enough* that it looks sufficiently like the existing parts of the game?

In this stage, it's *not helpful* to test and report bugs that would be considered minor, good to fix, or that feature is lacking something that we already know about. Remember, this is "only" MVF. If the initial reception of the feature is positive, a team will continue working on iterations of it and add more polish and elements to it in the future. Right now, the game team doesn't need a reminder that the feature is still not perfect or complete.

We also need to keep in mind that *development cycles* in live ops are short, between one and three weeks at most. Generally, even simplified features will take more than one sprint to develop, unless your sprints are exceptionally long (which is never recommended!). A tester should start testing the feature before it's proclaimed "ready." The best approach is to use iterative testing as well – test a feature as it's getting ready and give meaningful, useful feedback back to the team. Look for key problematic issues early on – flaws in the game logic, integration risks, and any inherited technical risks.

Working together with your teammates and discussing openly will help the tester to focus on the right thing at the right time. We can sometimes even do early tests in the development environment, as long as it's done in collaboration with developers, and we are sure that we are *testing the right build*.

Before moving to the next part, let's briefly discuss what it means to be on the right build. During development, especially in the live ops phase, we might deal with *multiple game builds* at the same time. You will have multiple daily builds in development environments where developers commit a range of builds for their own testing and integration purposes. You will have builds in the testing environment, also sometimes several per day. Lastly, you will have a live game build. On top of all the game builds, we also deal with multiple **releases**. All of these come with some type of numerical indicator. While game build numbers are controlled by the development team and are automatic, let's investigate what we mean by *release*.

What is release?

All planned updates to the game are called releases. We usually assign numerical values to them to be able to differentiate between them. They are generally ascending – for example, 1.1, 1.2, 1.3, and so on. The release naming format is usually agreed upon among the team, and they are used in product road maps, content planning, and other documentation. Release numbers will also be communicated to other departments to ensure that everyone understands which content and time period we are talking about. Releases can be the same as build numbers, but they don't have to be. Having specific releases helps us in the long-term planning of game development.

It is fairly easy to mix up builds, but it's much harder to mix up releases. There is usually at least a few weeks' difference between the current release and the next one.

It is of utmost importance that we are always **on the right build** and that it was forwarded for testing to any outsourced testing partners. If we move to test a different build, we should inform the outsourced QA company immediately.

We should always confirm with the development team that this is the build on which we want to test the agreed items. If you want to test something that *is out of the agreed scope*, make sure that you spoke with developers about it first. Especially early in development, you might work on a branch that has only limited features or bug fixes ready for testing, and reporting bugs outside of the scope will be useless, as these areas were not ready to be tested to start with. Testing on the wrong build or focusing on testing things that are not ready yet can cause strain on the team relationship and waste lots of precious time. With clear and precise communication, we can make sure that these mistakes don't happen. It's always better to ask twice, "Is this the correct build for testing?" than spend hours on something that is useless and potentially disruptive for the team.

With this type of *collaborative, joint effort*, QA will be able to identify any critical issues early enough in the development cycle and decrease the risk of a new feature being a failure. It will also decrease heavy pressure on a team just before the release. If we did our job well, testing the final update should not discover any major unknown bugs.

We have now learned how to approach testing of new features in live ops. Next, we will talk about one of the staples of live ops that is still practically unknown outside of the game teams – game build submissions in live ops.

Dealing with submissions

We mentioned *submissions* a couple of times throughout this book. They are an incredibly important part of game development in which QA can play a *key role*. Before we go further, let's confirm what we mean by game submissions.

What are game submissions?

After the development and testing process is finalized, each game and game update needs to go through the process of submission to the target platform in order to be published to the stores and become available to the players. Under submissions, we consider the complete process before and after the actual act of submission to the platform, and it requires collaboration between multiple disciplines, including QA, any specialized submission teams, producers, the marketing team, and player support. The submission consists of numerous steps and activities that need to be executed before it can be considered done.

If we don't fulfill all platform requirements correctly or make omissions in our submission steps, our game build might fail platform submission. That means that the platform rejected this particular game build, and a new update will not be available to the players. Depending on the target platform, the timeline from submission to being published can be short as a couple of hours or can take even weeks.

We can see in *Figure 11.5*, further down in this chapter, an example of a **submissions readiness checklist**. This process is detailed and can be demanding, as we need to combine not only the execution of the steps but also timely and correct communication with other stakeholders. We can also see in more detail how different disciplines participate in the submission process and that communication between different stakeholders is crucial for success.

QA can play various roles in this process. As a minimum, QA will need to test the game build we submit to the platform and give some indication of its *submission readiness*. In many gaming studios, this process is called **"greenlighting."** It means that QA needs to give a "green light," just like we have in traffic lights, to indicate that QA is happy with the game build readiness. If a team is using this type of signaling, we will use "yellow light," which will indicate "proceed carefully – some concerns," and "red light," which means "do not continue with the submission process – there are critical issues." Of course, there are other types of readiness indicators. In some studios, the process can be *more casual*, and QA can give only a verbal report or short email describing their recommendations about the game build.

For an inexperienced tester, this process can be daunting. We already know that live ops are fast-paced, with frequent updates. It might feel that there is never enough time for the full regression round and in-depth testing. That might make the tester hesitant to give a thumbs-up to game builds, as they might feel that they missed something important.

It is important for testers who work in embedded teams and in live ops to have the right *mindset* for this type of work. *Testers who work in live ops* will benefit from following characteristics:

- Curious

- Enjoy collaborative working styles

- Feel confident to ask questions and raise concerns if needed

- Be open-minded and willing to consider different points of view

- Enjoy fast-paced work with little routine

- Be interested in the bigger picture and understand business requirements, industry trends, and at least the basics of free-to-play game design

- Be interested in the player's perspective and passionate about providing the best possible playing experience

While these skills will help testers in many other situations as well, they are prerequisites to be able to really thrive *working in live ops*. Being part of the development team, the tester will be included in or at least promptly informed about all the major decisions concerning the game and be able to adjust their testing plans and focus accordingly. That should help QA be better prepared for the submissions period and rarely face last-minute surprises.

When we talk about submissions in live ops, we need to keep in mind that there are some tests that are done *specifically* during this phase, especially on mobile platforms. Besides running a **Basic Acceptance Test** (**BAT**) and at least some regression, we need to run tests that are particular to mobile game updates. Those include the following:

- The build size (packed and unpacked).

- The build installation, with Wi-Fi and a mobile network.

- Updating the previous build.

- Updating on older builds (if your game updates are not always mandatory, you want to make sure that players can still update the game with the most recent update).

- Uninstalling – the player should be able to have a "clean" uninstall of the game, without any leftover files.

- Reinstalling – after the game has been deleted, the player is able to reinstall it without any issues.

- Game save – making sure that player progress is saved and that new update doesn't erase game progress or previous purchases.

- Localization testing for any new localized content.

- Any platform requirements (make sure that you check regularly with the platforms, as this changes frequently).

- Game compatibility with any new flagship devices that might have been released.

- Keeping an eye on battery consumption – as the game becomes bigger, it can start causing a high energy drain. This can seriously affect players.

Testers need to keep in mind that games in live ops are *fast to adjust*, and if our game architecture is properly optimized for live ops, lots of balancing and fine-tuning can be done through backend pushes. Live games are dynamic systems that can be influenced and modified "on the go" to respond better to players' behavior. That means that QA doesn't have to go through detailed balancing and playthrough tests as we should when we test premium games. The exception to this rule is if those kinds of changes are a crucial part of this particular release. In those cases, in agreement with game designers, we will include more thorough balancing tests as a part of the release testing.

Balancing tests could be about testing the balance of game difficulty, character balancing, level balancing, items drop frequency, or something else that is relevant to the particular game we are testing. All of these should help testers to feel confident in their decision about validating the target release ready for submission.

Of course, sometimes, we encounter circumstances that are out of our control, and we are in situations where we won't feel fully confident that the release candidate is as ready as we would like. In most game teams, we would have a *"cut off"* or *"code freeze"* time, when no new changes can be made to the build, besides agreed bug fixes (we will talk more about handling live bugs later in this chapter).

However, sometimes, we might get a late requirement from management or even from the platform and have to make those last-minute changes. Those situations can affect QA plans, and even if we work with a fluid schedule and understand that the only constant is change, we might simply not have enough time or resources to *confidently validate* a release candidate. If so, QA will generally cautiously recommend going forward, unless critical or blocker bugs have been found. In situations like this, it is particularly important to do testing on a live game as soon as the update is live, allowing you to be able to react quickly if there are any major issues with the game.

In some gaming studios, QA would have additional duties in the submission process and can take care of submissions themselves. In order to submit a release candidate to the platform, the checklist from *Figure 11.5* would need to be completed, all stakeholders informed about the imminent release, and all required items for submission will need to be delivered to QA (who takes care of submission in this scenario).

ACTIVITY	WHO	READINESS STATUS
Release candidate	Development	
Localization QA	Producer	
Release date confirmed	Producer	
UA scheduled	Marketing	
SoMe campaign	SoMe team	
Player support informed	QA	
RC testing	QA	
RC approval	Executive producer	
Appstore text	Copywriter	
Keywords	Marketing	
Game icon	Marketing artist	
New screenshots	Marketing artist	
Submission form	QA	

Figure 11.5 – Submissions checklist

We are primarily talking about submissions to mobile platforms, and to be able to have successful submission, you would need at least the following:

- A game name

- A properly packaged game build

- Platform-specified marketing materials (game icon, screenshots, and app store text)

- A list of devices that we want to blacklist (for Google Play) or operating systems versions we don't support (the App Store)

Submission to platforms requires some experience, as there is more detailed information that would need to be filled in order for submission to be successful. That's why in a big studio, submissions are usually handled by *specialized teams*.

Now that we have learned more about submissions to the platform, let's have a more thorough look at direct updates to the game – so-called "backend pushes."

Backend pushes

Game teams that are experienced with F2P games and live ops will usually design their technology stack to be able to update significant portions of the game without submissions to the platform. This is an exceptionally useful feature, as it allows us to release content faster, adjust things quickly, and even commit quick bug fixes. However, being able to do so doesn't mean that these changes shouldn't go through at least some QA.

As we don't go through the platforms, direct pushes to the game are much faster, but we still need to stick to the same rules. The game should still work as intended, new content needs to fit with the existing content without breaking anything, and the player should not experience any crashes, freezes, or significant lag. With backend pushes, QA is in a peculiar situation: we still need to test and validate the release, but if we take too long or a process is highly bureaucratic, we will lose all the advantage of being able to do fast changes.

What is the best setup to handle content pushes? This will depend a lot on your game architecture and team structure, but generally, good rules are as follows:

- Have a *dedicated server environment* that is a realistic copy of the live one. Make sure that you test all the changes you do here first. It is usually called "staging."

- *Develop a process* for the backend push to the live game. It doesn't need to be as detailed or strict as the one for the platform submissions, but make sure that it's well defined and that everyone on the team is familiar with it.

- Implement *live game testing practices*. As soon as the game is in a live environment, spend some time testing it. Running a quick BAT and checking how new content looks are recommended focused areas.

- The **QA process** for backend pushes should be much lighter, especially for non-scheduled, ad hoc changes. If our game architecture allows for new content or event pushes through the backend, QA should schedule testing for those updates in the testing environment as soon as possible and take time to test it properly. As content updates are scheduled to go live regularly, QA can adjust their time to follow the content update cadence in a timely manner.

A bigger challenge is *ad hoc changes*, such as smaller tweaks and adjustments to the game. It can easily happen that the game designer or product manager decides to make a change on their own, but as it's considered small, they don't involve QA, and they commit the change directly to the live game.

This is a very dangerous practice that can create lots of issues for the team. Let's presume that the game designer decided that a new character we recently introduced to our game is not strong enough, and they increase the character strength to 20% in the game management system. They are happy with how numbers look and push the change directly to the game, believing that this will make a new character become more desirable to the player, and hence, it will increase monetization. A couple of hours after that, the player support starts to receive messages from the players, complaining about balancing and broken UI. When QA checks the live game, they can see that the new character is too overpowered and made some other premium characters obsolete. Players who spent money on those characters are now very angry. To make things worse, it seems like increasing strength points to the character added another character to a UI field, and now UI field looks messy and is overflowing outside of the boundaries of the box. We can see, in this example, how one small, well-conceived, and perceived innocent change can cause havoc to a game very quickly.

For that reason, it is important to have a *quick validation system* for any change made to the game. QA should be reasonable and not demand in-depth tests for every change. The ideal process should be that changes are committed to the test environment first, QA is informed about what was changed (and potentially how it could affect other areas of the game), and the urgency with which this adjustment needs to go live. QA focuses on testing only the area affected by that change and signs off the update as soon as possible. Remember that these changes are supposed to be relatively small and quick. If QA holds on to them without action for too long, it is going to become tempting to the rest of the team to just skip QA altogether as "it takes too long."

Another thing we should keep in mind is whether we do have a proper, reliable *rollback procedure* for backend pushes as well. We should be able to quickly restore the game back to the previous stage and with minimum disturbance to the players. This is generally easier to do with backend pushes because it won't require submission to the platform. However, we need to build technical capacity in our systems to do so in the first place and make sure that the rollback process itself is determined. We will talk in more detail about that process a bit later in this chapter.

Now that we have learned more about how to do updates and release submissions in live ops, we will next look into how we handle bugs from live games.

Working with live bugs

Live bugs happen even to the best of QA teams. The nature of work in live ops is so fast-paced that speed and critical thinking are much more important than thorough reviews and iron-clad testing practices. We also work with many different *game components* and *various stakeholders*. It is normal that, occasionally, something unpredictable will happen, and we will encounter a bug in a live game.

Bugs in live games are most often reported by *players* themselves. Unfortunately, not enough game studios take live game testing seriously, although it might save up lots of time and money if we find the bug in the live game first. Besides players, live bugs are also found by game teams and QA, other people in the company, and people who are related to the game studio in some way – vendors, consultants, investors, partners, and so on.

Firstly, let's address live bugs that come from *player support*, as we will encounter those the most.

There are many things to take into consideration here. We should analyze the relationship between player support and the game team first. Player support can be the following:

- **Internal**: Player support is part of the company and the same people work in it on a regular basis
- **Outsourced**: Player support is outsourced to a professional company, and it's handled in a separate location
- **Partially outsourced**: For example, when we have a new major release coming out, we might want to add more seats to player support quickly and temporarily, or when we provide player support in different languages, that part of the support might be outsourced

In a studio organizational setting, player support usually falls under the jurisdiction of **marketing**, while QA is a part of the game development team. Player support will not be by default included in the game development team, as their role becomes important only in live ops. For that reason, it is really important to update the team setting for live ops and design ways to work efficiently with player support. The optimal way to work with player support is to include them in key game team activities and train them to do at least some basic QA. That way, player support can validate issues reported by the player themselves and escalate them appropriately. Unfortunately, we are not always in a position to do so, but one thing that is definitely key to handling live bugs quickly is to have open channels of communication with player support. That can be either chat channel, such as Slack or Discord, email, or something more automated. There are *player support tools* that can be linked to bug databases, and player support tickets can automatically show up as a bug report in your team's *JIRA* or other bug management tool.

When we get information about the bug from player support, we need to ask them the following questions to really understand its impact:

- How many people reported this bug?
- Does it seem like the amount of player reports is escalating?

- On which platform does it happen?

- Does it happen on multiple devices?

Answering yes to most of the preceding questions will tell us that we face a serious issue that needs to be addressed immediately. On the other hand, if we have one player complaining very loudly, it might just be an inconvenience and not indicate a major problem.

In *Figure 11.6*, we can see a typical live bug flow in live ops and how QA and player support work together to bring issues to the development team.

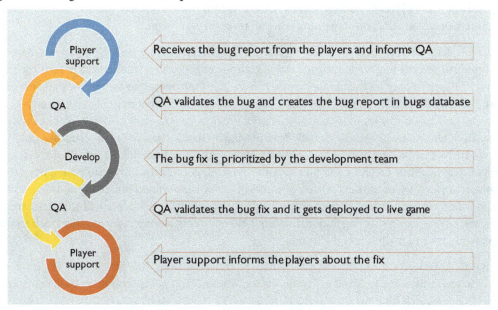

Figure 11.6 – A high-level live bug flow

When dealing with live bugs, we must keep in mind a sense of *urgency*. These bugs already affect our players, and consequently, they might affect game retention and monetization, which will ultimately hurt the studio's bottom line. That's why we need to take live bugs seriously and address them as soon as possible. It is also QA's role to represent the player in the team and convince the team that bug fixes need to take priority. In some studios, there are even small "bug teams" within the team that focus primarily on handling live bugs. This type of setting allows the team to handle bugs without delay but also without affecting the content and feature production pipeline.

Live bugs, just like any other bug we encounter, can have different *root causes*. Sometimes, they don't necessarily happen because of an error in code, but they might be related to server issues or possibly game engine issues. For some bugs, it might take time to find the root cause, and it might require investigation and exploration by several people. In cases like this, it is important to understand the complexity of the task and make sure that information flows between different stakeholders.

When a developer informs us that this issue needs to be investigated first and might take a couple of days before we can get a first attempt at a fix, it is crucial to *inform* player support and the marketing team about it, especially when we deal with a serious bug that affects a big portion of our players. They will develop a joint strategy on how to handle player expectations.

Not all live bugs are made equal. While we need to make sure that we checked quickly how widespread and impactful a bug is, we might come to the realization that some bugs are *not necessarily worth fixing*. How do we decide about that? Math can help – if it costs more to fix the bug than the damage the bug is causing, we are better off focusing on more impactful issues at hand. While this might sound tough and not really player-friendly, conversely, making tough decisions like this will free the team's hands and make them focus on something that can serve players better.

For example, let's presume that player support reported a frequent crash bug. Upon QA validation, we can confirm that the bug really happens with a high frequency, which would make it a critical bug. However, it happens only on the oldest supported version of the operating system. After discussing the issue with developers, it's agreed that this will be a quite tricky fix that might take up to a week to implement, and it might work only temporarily until the next new release. In situations like this, we need to check how many players we actually have playing on that version of OS. It seems like only 3% of players are on this OS, and from them, only 0.5% are buyers. After team discussion, it is decided that instead of spending time on fixing this bug, we will cut off support for the lowest supported operating system moving forward in the next release. We inform player support and marketing about it so that they can do timely actions to communicate with players about this. While we will still upset some players, the cost of fixing this bug and maintaining old operating system compatibility has become too labor-intensive to maintain in the future.

Now that we have learned a bit more about how we handle live bugs, let's have a look at a possible **worst-case scenario**, when we need to handle situations when bugs are exceptionally destructive and a bug fix is not a quick solution.

While these situations don't happen often, when they do, they cause immense damage to the games business and can lead to serious problems for the whole studio. Even with the best QA efforts, there could be unpredictable server bugs that were out of the scope of manual QA, or some forgotten legacy code could trigger serious issues. It could even happen that it was completely beyond QA control, as the wrong build was submitted by mistake. What can we do in situations like this?

To address this type of *urgency situations*, studios develop a *"rollback"* procedure. This is an internal studio procedure that triggers after it is decided that the current live build is unplayable or too damaging for the game, and it needs to be reverted to the previous, stable state. While this sounds relatively simple, it's not always so. Before we develop the technical ability to do rollback, we need to decide the following:

- Under which circumstances we will do a rollback
- Which person in the team makes the final call

- Who we need to inform about the rollback (you should always inform player support!)

- How we will communicate with the players

- How will we prioritize rollback and issues

An efficient rollback procedure should include some kind of *"alarm"* system that will also include automatic triggers. If we have issues, let's say, with server capacity, a bug might not occur immediately after a new release but only when a sufficient number of players start to download and play the game. If most of our players are in different time zones, we might experience a situation where a game stops working for players outside our core working hours. Having an automated system informing the designated person in the team can save us precious hours.

Another rule of thumb is that we *never do submissions* on a Friday unless we have a core team working weekends. If something happens with the new build, it might be much harder to get a team together outside of working hours.

Lastly, we want to make sure that we have a rollback procedure for platform submission as well as for backend pushes. QA's role in this situation is to help validate that rollback changes will work and not cause additional issues. Due to the urgency of the situation, any testing has to be very quick, and it is expected that the rollback version is an older version that we have confidence in. After every situation like this, it is a great practice to have a **"post-mortem"** meeting and analyze the root cause of this situation. These meetings should focus on practices on how to avoid this situation in the future, not on pointing fingers and finding who was to blame in the team.

Summary

In this chapter, we learned the ins and outs of live ops QA as well as some of the practices that are specific for this game phase. We learned how it differentiates from game development, how to handle continuous flow of new content and features, how submissions and releases work in live ops, and lastly, strategies on how to handle live bugs. We now know how to approach live ops testing, handle testing of different types of updates, and have skills to handle releases green-lighting process. We are now skilled in recognizing who is best to work in live ops, and we know how to handle emergencies in a live game.

In the next chapter, we will learn more about test management, what the purpose of a test plan is, and how to organize and lead QA teams.

12

Beyond Testing – Introduction to Test Management

It is impossible to have testing without **test management**. The discipline of test management goes deeper than just managing the testing team. Working in this role, you will get the opportunity to build a robust and supportive working environment for the testing team, which will help your team not only do an excellent job but also feel content and accomplished in their work. You will get the chance to advocate for QA as a discipline, but also support your team and advocate for bugs and testability. In this chapter, you will learn from practical examples how you can leverage various test reports in order to do so. We will also learn about test planning and methods in depth that can support us in our work with testing estimations.

In this chapter, we will cover the following in detail:

- A test management role
- A test plan
- Methods to help you estimate testing efforts
- Test planning and execution coverage

By the end of this chapter, you will have a good idea of everything that goes into test management and how it relates to testing activities. You will learn more about test planning and arguably the most difficult part of it, which is testing estimations. But first, let's take a deep dive into what the test management role is.

The test management role

While the focus of this book is primarily on games testing activities, it is important to mention test management as well. Test management is an important part of testing and it affects everything we do as testers. Furthermore, it sets up the testing framework and decides on the key points of how QA is done.

> **What is test management?**
>
> Test management is the process of planning and managing the overall testing efforts. Test management decides on the approach, strategy, tools, and execution processes that are utilized in testing activities. Furthermore, test management also includes people management: leading teams of testers, reviewing performance, and hiring and training new testers.

When we look at the definition of test management, we can clearly see how the deep impact it can have on QA activities. Unfortunately, if our test management is poor, even if you have the best testers on your team, the results will be sub-optimal. While test management is usually decided and run by QA managers, it also affects the work of everyone on the QA team. We will talk in more depth about QA careers in the next chapter, *Chapter 13, There Are No BUGS Without U – QA and the Game Team*, where we will go into more detail on what the structure of a QA team can look like and how QA roles relate to each other.

Another thing that test management takes ownership of is representing QA as a discipline to the rest of the company. Unfortunately, not all gaming studio leaders have the same level of understanding of the importance and intricacies of QA. It would be test management's job to ensure that key stakeholders understand the high-level QA principles and their importance and needs. Only then can QA as a discipline get sufficient support and consideration to be able to do its job well.

Although all aspects of test management are equally important, the biggest part of the test management's time will be dedicated to **test planning** and **test management**.

When we talk about test planning, we are talking beyond immediate testing activity planning, such as creating test cases and planning what to test next. Here we talk about more high-level planning: looking into tools that can serve us better in the future, making staffing plans, planning long-term testing resources, selecting outsourced partners, and making other long-term estimations. For this type of planning, we will need to have a different vantage point and use different tools than when we plan for our daily or weekly activities. We will cover those later in this chapter.

Another major part of test management is *managing the testing efforts*. This process includes creating reporting practices, supervising the workflow and performance, as well as troubleshooting. In every QA team, we should have some type of reporting practice. For example, when I used to run my own testing company, we always prepared a default daily *testing report*, which we sent to all our clients, even if they didn't specifically ask for it. You can see an example of that report in *Figure 12.1*:

Testing hours total:	30
Android testers:	2
iOS testers:	2

Model	Platform	Version
iPhone X	iOS	11.1
Galaxy S7	Android	7.0
Oukitel K10000	Android	6.0

Bugs Found

Priority	Amount
Highest	1
High	2
Medium	3
Low	4
Lowest	5

Build(s)	
Android	1.33.7
iOS	1.33.7

Figure 12.1 – An example of a daily testing report

This report had a high-level breakdown of testing activities, platforms, testers, and the number of bugs, with their severity levels. This daily report provided an overall snapshot of the testing activity to the customer, and they got confidence that testers had done their job and found valuable insights.

Of course, there are other type of reports as well. If you use some of the more sophisticated *testing tools*, you can get great insights into overall testing efficiency as well as the possibility to recognize testing bottlenecks early. During my work at Rovio as a QA manager, I often used **Jira**-generated reports, which helped me recognize issues with outsourced testers. In one of these reports, I could see that we had a very high percentage of bugs that were in invalid status; it was over 6%. Upon checking up on those bugs, I realized that bugs were difficult to understand. Some of the language was convoluted and many bugs were missing attached screenshots of issues. By enforcing an obligatory screenshot policy and asking testers to use simpler, more straightforward sentences, the number of invalid bugs soon decreased to under 2%.

Similarly, these types of reports helped me prove my QA point when I was speaking to people outside my immediate team. For example, one of our projects had over 10,000 active bugs and it was obvious that we wouldn't be able to meet the release deadline and have the game quality that we were looking for. I managed to get my request for extended testing rounds approved by using the testing report to support it.

Supervising the workflow is an activity that can take very little time in more independent teams that have worked together for a long time. In those teams, everyone is familiar with the processes, teams already work efficiently together, and there is little need to get involved or fix anything. On the other hand, when we are working with new teams or teams with a high staff rotation, there might be much more work with fixing and updating the workflow. If there are constant interruptions in a workflow and team members are struggling to keep up, it's a good time to have a look at your processes and see whether they are serving the team in the best possible way. Even the best-thought-out process can grow old, especially if there are lots of changes in team dynamics or the tools and methods that we are using. Rather than forcefully implement processes in the team, it's a much better and long-lasting strategy to look at the process itself first and see whether it still serves the team in the best way.

Troubleshooting is one of those work practices that can be challenging to exactly define. Even with the best planned and optimally staffed teams, there will always be some challenges. It falls under test management to troubleshoot anything QA-related. Usually, those challenges are either one of the following:

- Personnel-related (unplanned sicknesses, resignations, conflict, a new employee not working out, etc.)

- Tool-related (a tool breaks, becomes unavailable, or is insufficient for the workload)

- Product-related (previously unknown co-dependencies, significant scope changes, etc.)

- Schedule-related (dates are moved and the timeline is much shorter)

- Extraordinary circumstances (natural disasters, partner bankruptcy, etc.)

Even if we think that those challenges are pretty rare, they do occur surprisingly often. Once we had the whole testing round canceled as our testing partner in Poland was affected by floods. Another time, there was a military coup in Thailand and it prevented our development partners from getting into the office for a few days. With good risk planning and mitigation plan, we can prepare ourselves for at least some of these occurrences.

Now that we have learned what test management is and what it entitles, we will look next into the test plan, one of the main tools in test planning.

A test plan

A test plan is one of the *key components* of test planning and test management. While a test plan as a document is precisely described in official testing documentation, in ISTQB material, and by testing standards, in games, the test plan is often very different.

> **What is a test plan?**
>
> A test plan is a document that outlines all the aspects of the testing and it's prepared before testing activities start. The test plan, at minimum, includes information about who is doing the testing, what is being tested, how is it going to be tested, when is going to be tested, and where it is going to be tested.

We can see that a test plan can be quite an intricate document with lots of detailed information. In more traditional development, it used to be like that – a long document with lots of details. But, when we work with agile game development and a short development cycle, having exceptionally detailed documents that extend far into the future is counterproductive. Things change almost daily in modern games, especially on mobile. The test plan we need is the one that is useful to the team, contains the information we need, and can be easily updated as required

Traditionally, test plans were aimed at management. They could see everything that was planned and then the plan was either rejected or accepted and implemented. But, in modern game testing, test plans are primarily aimed at QA team members. They give us the important information that we require to do our job and help new team members as well as outsourced partners to onboard onto our project much faster. As the target audience of the test plan has changed, the format has changed as well. In modern games teams, the test plan is a living, collaborative document that contains the following:

- **Project intro** – The game name, target platform, and any history or "good to know" stuff should be listed here.

- **Testing tools** – Here, we will list all the tools we are using, ideally with links to bugs, databases, test case repositories, reporting tools, build distribution tools, and any other tools we might use.

- **Test environment** – Are we using any specific environment for testing and how do we access it, any specific hardware, network configurations, and so on?

- **Testing schedule** – Depending on the project, this is usually a high-level estimate, especially early in the project. As game development is going forward, we can give a more precise testing schedule. In live ops, this will highly depend on the cadence of updates.

- **Test deliverables** – Here we list all the reports that QA is going to provide throughout the testing period, spanning test coverage reports, daily testing reports, bug reports, and anything else that QA will provide.

You might have noticed that I didn't list *test cases* here. There has been some debate on whether test cases should be part of the test plan. As modern game testing is an everchanging activity, listing all of the test cases in a test plan would make it an unnecessarily long document. Instead, we can add links to our test case repository under the *Testing tools* section. That way, test cases will be easy to find for any testers, and if anyone from management is interested in more details, they can follow the link and always find the most updated list. At the same time, the only time when we need to update the test plan is if we actually change the link to the test case repository, which is much less work than keeping track of all changes in yet another document.

In what *format* you should keep your test plan? There are no strict rules about it. It can be anything from a document, spreadsheet, presentation, or even a wiki page. Whatever will work best for your team and for the test plan's intended purpose. However, please keep in mind that the test plan is a living document, especially in *live ops*, and it's recommended to put it in a format that is easy to update, share, and collaborate on with others.

Lastly, I would like to mention the length of the test plan as a document. I have seen traditional test plans that were over fifty pages long. In modern game testing, our test plan can be only one page long if that's sufficient to meet the testing team's needs. We should ensure that document scalability and practicability are your guiding thoughts: create a document that can develop and grow together with the team and that is easy to keep relevant.

Now that we have learned more about the test plan, next, we will focus on one of the more demanding aspects of test planning, which is testing work/effort estimations.

Methods to help you estimate testing efforts

Test effort estimation is one of the more demanding parts of test management, especially when we are dealing with a new game and we don't have much information about it. Getting to know where to even start can be daunting, and to top this off, there are also numerous different ways and methods of how to estimate your testing efforts. The estimation methods will depend on the following:

- The perceived risk
- The methodology your QA team is using
- The testing team
- The game stage
- The testing focus
- The complexity of game under test
- Code codependencies
- Studio, team, and QA processes
- Budgets

Let's start with one *simple example.* One tester works 40 h per week. The average amount of uninterrupted testing per day is 3 intervals of about 90 minutes. The rest of the time goes to setup, reporting, communication, and interruption. That means we have the actual time spent on testing in a week, 15 x 90 minutes, which is about 22.5 h. That's the real testing time you have available per tester.

Next, look at the game under test. Using your experience and skills, roughly estimate how many hours of testing you require (we will cover some helpful methods later in this chapter).

Lastly, look at the game release deadline. When you take into account all of this information, you will have an estimate of how many testers you will need in order to QA the game on time. Of course, there are many unknowns here: if you are at the beginning of a new game, nobody can tell with any certainty when all of the planned features will be ready to test. Nobody can even confirm with absolute certainty that all features will make it to the game at all!

The earlier in the project we make an estimate, the more likely we are going to be off. That's why the healthiest way to approach estimation is to go broad with your estimations early on, and as the project progresses, re-evaluate your estimation to be more precise.

The Delphi technique

One of my favorite techniques to start making estimates for a new project is the **Delphi technique**. With this technique, we run multiple rounds of interviews and surveys with team members and gather information that is further refined in each round. The success of this process will very much depend on who you are interviewing. Here, you should go broad: talk to the whole team that works on the game but also with other experts, who can give you valuable insights. After each round of information-gathering, consolidate the feedback you got and analyze it. Find the areas where you see the most *disputes or discrepancies* and focus on them next. In this way, you will find out where is the root cause of disagreement and eventually come to a consensus.

The Delphi technique is a great tool for gathering valuable information early in the project and making estimates that are informed and well thought out. It can be used not only to help estimate testing efforts but also to gain valuable insight into any complex issue.

Work Breakdown Structure (WBS)

In games, we often work with complex features with many different facets. Estimating big tasks or the whole game can be extremely difficult, as we don't really have an insight into all of the small components that make up the whole. That means we can easily miss something or underestimate its importance. A methodology such as WBS is extremely helpful in these cases. Using WBS, we break down a big structure into smaller sub-modules, which will be divided further into smaller functions. One way to control the granularity of WBS is to break it down into tasks that can be completed during one sprint, for example.

When we use WBS, it is important to review the final result and make sure that we haven't missed some co-dependency or functionality. After that, we can move forward with estimations. The idea behind this method is that it's much easier to estimate the effort for smaller, individual components than estimate an overall game in one shot. WBS can be also used to estimate budgets and personnel as it gives us a much more detailed picture of the work at hand.

One negative side of WBS is that when we are in the process of breaking down tasks, we come to the smallest allocation we use that makes sense. That can be something like 1 person hour or even smaller. But, in reality, there are lots of smaller tasks that often take less than our minimum allocation. Due to that, WBS sometimes has overly generous time allocation, especially if we do it at a very detailed level.

3-point estimation

This method shares lots of *similarities with WBS*, as we also start by splitting work into smaller, more manageable parts. After that, we will make not one but three different work estimations for each part. The idea behind doing this is that by taking possible different scenarios into account statistically, we will get the most probable estimation value. How do we do those estimates?

Firstly, we will do something we call an "*optimistic estimate*." This is the estimate in which everything will go exactly as planned, there will be no major distractions or challenges in the project, and all conditions will be optimal. *Let's call this estimate A.*

After that, we will do the *"most likely"* estimate. We will acknowledge that some things could go wrong, but most of the things will happen as planned. *This is an estimate M.*

Lastly, we will make the most "*pessimistic estimate*." Here, we consider that everything goes wrong, and all risks materialize. *We will call this estimate B.*

The formula to get a 3-point estimate is $E = A + (4*M) + B / 6$. We give more weight to the most likely estimate as it is more probable that it will happen. Using this method, we will get a fairly precise estimate that takes into account different types of scenarios.

A functional point measure

Unlike other methods we have previously discussed, a **functional point measure** is focused on the player's point of view. This method is based primarily on available documentation, such as a **Game Design Document** (**GDD**), features list, product backlog, or any other available form of documentation about the game we aim to test. Somewhat similar to WBS, we will also give estimates for each function of the feature that goes into the game, rather than the whole game in one go.

Each function of the feature will be put in one of the three categories: simple, average, or complex, depending on the complexity of the feature. We can see in an example in *Figure 12.2* what this type of categorization looks like.

FUNCTION	POINT	SIMPLE 1	AVERAGE 3	COMPLEX 5	TOTAL POINTS
CHAT	5	X	3	X	15
GUILDS	10	X	X	5	50
FUNCTION TOTAL	X	X	X	X	**65**
ESTIMATE DEFINED BY POINT (IN HOURS)					2.25h
TOTAL EFFORT (PERSON HOURS)					**146.25h**

Figure 12.2 – Functional point measure example

To each category, we will assign a specific *"weight"*. The more important the function is, the higher weight it will get.

Besides weight, we will add a *function point* to each feature. The more complex and difficult to implement a feature is, the higher the function point will be. There are usually set rules on how to decide a function point, to avoid project discrepancies and misunderstandings. It should be some sort of standard way to recognize the complexity of the feature (such as the number of interfaces it requires, frequency of user interactions, etc.), and numerical values will need to be on a set scale. The scale will be set based on similar projects and studio standards, but each point should equal a specific number of person hours. When we multiply the weight by the function point, we will get the *total functional point*.

As we see in our example, each functional point corresponds to 2.25 person hours. When we multiply the total number of points by 2.25 h, we will get the number of hours required to test this feature.

This method is particularly useful when we are just starting with the project and we don't have much development ready yet, but we do have ample documentation. It will give us a good long-term estimate of the efforts, but also help us think more analytically about the features we are looking to develop. Another benefit of the functional point measure is that if we realize that the hours allocated to functional points are wrong, we just need to change it once to automatically update all of our estimations, which saves us lots of time and effort.

Now that we have learned several useful methods on how to estimate working efforts, let's investigate test planning and execution coverage next.

Test planning and execution coverage

When we talk about test planning in this context, rather than thinking about what the optimal way to approach testing a particular feature or update is, we think from a much higher perspective. We make decisions on how we will approach testing of the game as a whole and set the *optimal working framework* for the testing team.

It is important not to get too granular in the test planning. This type of high-level planning is done early in the game life cycle, and throughout development, we will encounter many unknowns, and as a consequence, numerous changes. Creating detailed, rigid plans not only prevents testers from using their skills and initiative to the full but will also fail to meet the requirements of ever-changing development. At the same time, we do want to have high-level decisions made early on, as they will allow testers to focus on testing, rather than being boggled by administrative and managerial tasks that are not in their domain. Not only would they occupy a large part of the testing time, but they also might make testers feel stressed as they don't necessarily have the skills and experience needed to make those types of decisions.

So, what type of test planning we will do as a part of test management? We already spoke at length about the test plan document, which will contain most of the high-level test planning information that testers need. But how does the process of making those decisions go? This will depend on several things:

- The studio's policies and ways of working
- The available budgets and resources
- The perceived importance of the game we are working on
- Existing contracts and other contractual dependencies
- Development methodology
- The game's complexity and genre
- The perceived importance of QA in the team

Let's briefly look into each of them and how they can affect our plans.

Studio policies and ways of working

Each studio has its own unique processes, working culture, and accepted practices. QA as a discipline is not excluded from this and this will affect your test planning immensely. This will include lines of *communication* (who needs to know what and when), *reporting* practices, and overall *responsibilities*. Does QA as a discipline fall under operations or product? To whom would the QA director report and how? Does that person take an active interest in QA and have strong input or just need to be "in the know"? These are some of the things that we don't necessarily think about when we go about daily testing tasks, but they can leave a big mark on how things are done as well as on the overall atmosphere within the team.

The available budgets and resources

This one is easy to understand. Every project has a set *budget* and that's a set of *restraints* we need to work with. That means that the tools we use and the number of people we can have on the project will also be restricted by the amount of money that is given to the team. In some circumstances, the QA director can dispute those budgets with company management if they can confirm that they are not sufficient for QA to do its job effectively, but those decisions are never made lightly.

The perceived importance of the game we are working on

This is very specific to the gaming industry. Almost any medium-sized or large studio usually works on several games at a time. Depending on the internal setup and game studio strategy, some games will always be considered "*more important*" than others. There could be multiple reasons for this. For example, the game might be based on significant **intellectual property** (IP), be part two of an already successful gaming franchise, belong to a "current" genre, be the brainchild of senior team members with notable previous successes, be highly believed in by investors, and so on.

When we work with a game that is considered important, there will be always more *attention* put on that game, which will affect all activities that relate to this game, including QA. That means that we might get bigger budgets, but also more strict reporting, deadlines, and communication guidelines.

Existing contracts and other contractual dependencies

If we are working in an established studio, when we start working on a new game, previous games will have come before us. That means that the studio has already bought *licenses* for specific tools and rendered services from *QA suppliers*. There might be pressure to use existing tools and providers, especially if the signed contracts are for long-term usage.

It is also considered *more efficient* to use the same tools between teams as it makes people transition between teams much easier. For example, if you want to "borrow" a tester from another game team during a quiet period, if you use a different test repository and bug reporting tools, it might take several days, if not weeks, for that team member to become proficient at working with the new tools.

Usually, unless there are some valid reasons (such as making the game on a different platform, the game being significantly technically different, or an existing QA service provider not having bandwidth), we will probably stick with pre-existing tools and contracts.

The development methodology

There are big differences in how we will do QA depending on whether we use waterfall or agile methodologies. We covered those in detail throughout this book. As it makes such a significant difference in how games are done, it will definitely affect QA as well.

The game's complexity and genre

Not all games are made alike. When we talk about mobile games, there are huge differences in how we make *hyper-casual* versus *4X strategy* games or *RPGs*. A hyper-casual game can be made by literally a handful of people within a couple of weeks. 4X strategy games or RPGs will take a year to make and take dozens of people. We must take this into account when we are planning testing.

The perceived importance of QA in the team

QA is by no doubt an exceptionally important part of any game development, but there are still studios where it's not given enough credit for the meaningful and hard work it does. Doing test management and planning in those circumstances might be more challenging and will require lots of advocating to the company leadership, in order to get enough budget and resources to do optimal work.

Now that we have learned about high-level test planning, let's have a look at how we could *plan test coverage*.

How to plan test coverage

As before, here we are talking primarily about high-level coverage planning, which will be different from granular, daily-work planning. Firstly, we want to set a framework for *how we will measure coverage*. Is it going to be measured solely by test case execution? And as such, how will test cases be planned? An alternative way to monitor test coverage is to monitor the execution of use cases or requirements. That is a particularly good strategy if our team does not necessarily use test cases.

Test coverage's primary importance is that it gives us an insight into **product readiness**. But, especially in more complex games, just having information about how many test cases have been executed or which requirements have been tested with them might not give us the sufficient information that we need to get an idea of how ready the game really is. There is a very useful method we can use to improve the visibility of game readiness, which is called **level-3 testing** (not to be confused with integration testing, which is also sometimes called the same thing). Level-3 testing means that we will classify our tests into three different categories:

- *Category 1*: The game can be installed and the key game functions (the game core loop) work

- *Category 2*: The major and minor functions work well together in a variety of scenarios and the UX is not broken

- *Category 3*: The game consists of long-term reliability, wide coverage, and good performance, error handling, and recovery

Separating tests into those three categories allows us to have a better insight into what is working and what is still unknown. This information can be particularly useful when we are planning a *soft launch*, for example. While it's a must to have all tests in Category 1 executed and passed, we can probably live with some unclarity in Categories 2 and 3. When moving on to a *global launch* though, we will want tests from all three groups to be covered. Even if we can live with some ambiguity about Category 3 tests, if not addressed, they can cause us lots of problems in the long term and make the *live ops phase* exceptionally challenging.

Summary

In this chapter, we learned more about test management work and challenges and how it fits into overall studio operations. We learned about how to create a test plan and became familiar with several different methods that help us make test estimations. We also learned more in depth about test coverage. In the next chapter, we are coming to the end of our journey together into the world of modern game testing. We will learn more about the organization and structure of QA teams and the overall future of QA in games.

13

There Are No BUGS Without U – QA and the Game Team

We have reached the final chapter of this book, thank you for reading so far! For the end, I left some of the most interesting and up-and-coming things in game QA.

In continuation of *Chapter 12, Beyond Testing – Introduction to Test Management,* we will first talk about how to build great QA teams. While QA management has a major role in this, depending on your studio structure, almost everyone in QA will have an influence and their own role in the team-building process. We will learn more about different types of QA team organizations, why we would choose one over another, and how to work within them.

Outsourced QA is a norm in today's testing, but it's not necessarily as easy and straightforward as it might seem. To be able to really make the best of the collaboration between gaming studios and outsourced partners, and avoid downtime and expensive mistakes, we will learn in depth how to set up our joint work, how to monitor it, and troubleshoot it as well.

Before this chapter, we talked about all the different aspects of QA, but we didn't properly touch upon *game QA as a career*. Here we will learn more about what roles we have in QA, what type of career trajectory we can potentially have, and even some tips on how to excel in *job interviews* for game QA testing positions.

Test automation has been around for a while and it's getting more sophisticated by the day. While this book is solely focused on manual testing, it wouldn't seem fair not to at least mention the significant role testing automation has and explain high-level guidelines on how to perform it.

We will wrap up this chapter and this book with a look into the future. We will learn about trends and advancements in technology that affect existing QA practices, but they are expected to exponentially grow. In this chapter, we have the following topics:

- Building QA teams
- Working with remote QA teams
- A career in game QA
- Automated testing
- The future of game testing

Next, let's start by taking a deep dive into learning how to build great QA teams.

Building QA teams

In small and even medium-sized gaming studios (sized up to fifty people), it's not uncommon to have only one dedicated QA employee. But when a studio starts to work on multiple games or a game goes to live ops and becomes very successful, the QA department usually starts to grow. There are several different *ways to plan your QA team*. Let's have a closer look at them:

- *Adding more embedded QA to the game development teams*. A QA team is usually hired to work specifically on this game, and it will have its own structure within the team, with one of the QA team members acting as the QA lead. Each game team will have its own QA team that will work primarily within the game team rather than with the QA teammates from different games. This approach is great in teams and companies that favor flat organizational structures and collaborative working practices. QA can get really deep insight into the product and participate in decision-making about the games.

- *Increasing embedded QA in teams and building QA as a disciplinary structure*. With this approach, we hire people to work in specific teams, but they will report to a QA structure outside of their own game. That means that the company will have a QA director or QA manager who will work across game teams and will have the responsibility to lead and support QA efforts in all of the teams. In this type of QA organization, testers can be moved between teams.

- *Building QA as a stand-alone organization within the company*. This is the most traditional way to build a QA team, where we build QA as a department within the company rather than as part of each game team. In this type of organization, testers are rarely embedded into the team, and most of the time, they are assigned to the game in a specific phase for a specific task, almost acting as an outsourced QA team.

Every gaming studio is different and there are other ways to organize the **QA team structure**. For example, one of the most efficient QA teams I have seen is presented in *Figure 13.1*:

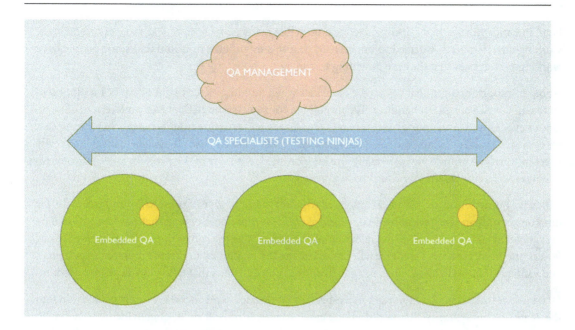

Figure 13.1 – QA team structure example

Here we can see that QA is embedded into the teams and has its own independence. The studio also had *QA management*, which mostly made QA-related decisions that influenced all teams: tools, partnership contracts, representing QA at the highest company level, QA budgeting, and supporting recruitment efforts. But this studio also had an *independent QA unit* that wasn't permanently assigned to any team. Its members were considered top-level testing experts and had lots of unique specializations, among other things. They acted as "testing ninjas" – they would be assigned to any project that needed extra help, specialized services, or encountered problems.

This example shows how by combining different approaches to team building, we might find the optimal solution. Of course, this type of approach worked as the studio was large, with multiple high-profile games in production and live ops. In smaller studios with only one or two active game projects, this structure might be too heavy and inefficient.

How do we start *building QA teams*? Depending on the type of organization, the first QA team members will either be the game testers who will work on the particular game or the QA manager, who will take charge of building QA as a discipline across the whole company, eventually assigning people to the game teams.

When we are *hiring* people to work in QA, we need to consider what kind of structure we have already, as this will affect what type of people we want to hire. For example, if you hire a highly skilled tester who is used to working in a **flat team structure**, even if they have exceptional skills, they will not thrive in a highly hierarchical organization. The same goes for testers who used to work in hierarchical organizations. They might struggle to deal with the levels of independence and decision-making that go hand in hand with work in self-organized teams. While many people can re-learn to work in different working environments, we need to understand that this might take time and that some people have working preferences that they are unwilling to change.

Another important point that we need to consider when building effective QA teams is a **willingness to learn**. Games are ever-changing. Technology is constantly updated, player preferences change, genres evolve, and even your own company's organizational structure might change. Something that we consider a fact today might become obsolete only a few months down the road. To be able to really excel in this type of industry, especially working on the front lines of the product as a QA does, we will need to have a passion for *continuous learning*.

When we build QA teams, it's more important to select the right type of personality and soft skills for our company, than what are considered "hard skills." But that doesn't mean that our team should be very uniform and all of the team members should be alike. Quite the contrary, the more **diverse** are our testers, the more efficient a team we will build. Having the possibility to include different experiences and vantage points will allow for making better-informed decisions that take more facts into account.

Of course, **testing skills** are important too, especially if you need someone who can jump hands-on into the game QA immediately. But hard skills are easier to learn than soft skills, or convincing someone to change their approach to work. For that reason, it is important that during job interviews, we don't test only for QA skills but also ask insightful questions about preferred ways of working, communication styles, and other values that are important in our organization.

Now that we have learned the basics of how to build efficient internal QA teams, let's have a more thorough look into how to effectively include outsourced QA in our teams.

Working with remote QA teams

Remote QA teams have been part of game testing for a very long time. When we talk about remote QA teams, we can consider them as follows:

- Outsourced professional QA companies
- Freelancers and collaborators (outsourced QA professionals)
- Internal employees working from home

In this chapter, we will focus on the first type and how to work with *outsourced professional QA companies*.

Almost all gaming studios will at some stage use *outsourced QA*. For example, localization QA is almost always done by outsourced, specialized QA companies. Sometimes, we also use them for other specialized kinds of testing, such as compliance testing. We already spoke about this in *Chapter 3, A Deeper Look – Types of Testing in Games*. Besides those, we also often use outsourced QA to support daily testing tasks.

While it is generally accepted that you don't need any specific skills to work with remote, outsourced teams, that's not the case. In order to have a good working relationship and get the most out of the outsourced testers, we need to learn how to do so. When we are starting to work with outsourced QA, we should first ask the following:

- What is the agreed quantity of outsourced testing? Is it 1 tester per day or more? For how long? Can we increase or extend testing resources?

- What is the agreed way of booking resources? Are they prebooked for your project already? Do you have to make a request to someone to get resource allocation?

- How will you deliver your game builds to the testers? Are there any security protocols? Does your outsourced partner need builds delivered at certain times?

- What are the partners' working hours? Are they in the same time zone?

- To whom you can escalate any issues that might arise?

With this basic information, you will gain a backbone for organizing your high-level work with outsourced partners. Next, you can start planning how to organize daily operations with your testing partners.

As a first step, you should specify *what part of the testing* you want the outsourced team to cover. If you don't give them specific guidelines, they will test what they think is the right thing to test. Keep in mind that outsourced testers only have the information that you provide them with. They don't participate in your team meetings, they can't overhear discussions between coders and designers, and they will not see emails where the producer is explaining why priorities have shifted for this release. Outsourced testers know only what you tell them and can only access the information you send them. While they can be very skilled testers, they could easily focus on the wrong thing simply because they don't have sufficient information.

Another problem that can arise from this situation is that you duplicate work. If you have internal testers and outsourced testers working simultaneously on the same build and if you don't give them guidelines, they might all end up testing the same things, while some areas of the game won't be covered at all.

In order to get the most out of your outsourced teams, before the testing round starts, you should prepare the following information for them:

- *Test scenarios* or test cases that you expect them to cover during the testing period.

- Confirm the *priority* for this testing round, as it changes depending on the phase of the game or the content of the update. This could be something such as confirming a new feature is working, or regression due to several complex bug fixes.

- Specify the *testing order* priority – which test cases must be run first.

- Any known project *risks*, dependencies, and deadlines.

In my experience, it has been shown to be the best practice to have a **kickoff meeting** prior to the start of testing. In the kickoff meeting, there should be not only test managers but also the testers who will mostly work on the game during this project round. If we work with a large group of testers, we can instead invite only the test leads or senior testers to the call. During this meeting, we have the opportunity to present all the intricacies of our game that are relevant to QA, and outsourced partners have the chance to ask direct questions and ask for the support they need. Doing this before testing starts can resolve lots of potential problems in later stages.

Test outsourcing process

Besides *testing instructions*, we also need to make sure that we have set common *processes* for the outsourced testers, so they can seamlessly work with our team. Our processes should include the following:

- **Communication**: What channels we are using and how. Chat programs such as **Slack** and **Discord** are good for resolving any ad hoc issues, but we want to have email communication for any major changes. We also need to specify who needs to be informed about what, who speaks up for the team, and who has access to the communication channels.

- **Schedule**: What is the overall testing (or testing project) schedule (when testing starts and when it ends) and the lead time to increase or decrease testing efforts and what are the daily working hours, expected delivery times, expected build delivery times, and so on?

- **Hardware**: What devices are we using for this testing round and in which priority?

- **Software**: What bug reporting tool is used, who is setting up the bug flow, how do we assign bug severity levels, and how do we handle bugs from external QA?

- **Deliveries**: What reports are expected from the testers, as well as any other documentation or deliveries?

- **Task management**: How do we deliver builds, what information needs to accompany builds, and how do we request changes in testing?

- **Troubleshooting practices**: How to escalate any potential issues.

While it might take some time to set all of these up, especially when working for the first time with an outsourced partner, it is a necessity for *smooth collaboration*. If these parameters are not set early on, each side is going to presume that their approach will work, but that might not be the case. Then, we encounter situations where outsourced testers are on the wrong builds, key people don't get reports, reports don't include the information we need, developers don't see crucial bugs on time, as well as a slew of other potential problems. Not only might we waste lots of money and effort but we also jeopardize our relationship with our testing partner. Spending a couple of days ahead of the project to organize it properly can save us weeks of wasted efforts and mutual frustrations.

After we set up common ways of working, it is always advisable to give clear guidelines to outsourced testers on how to *report bugs*. There is a big chance that they work also for other gaming studios, but each one of them has slightly different preferences. If you would like an outsourced team to report bugs according to your own internal standards, you should give them clear instructions. You should specify exactly what you want bug reports to look like. The easiest way to do that is to have a *sample bug report*, which your partner can use as an easy guideline. But besides the format, it's crucial to have an understanding of how bugs will be handled.

Sometimes, QA partners will have their own internal control and one senior person will review all bugs before they are sent to a client. While this approach assures a standard quality of bug reports, it requires additional resources and time. There is also the issue of timing: receiving all the bugs at the end of the day means that a developer won't have a chance to look at them before the next day unless they stay overtime.

Another approach is that someone internally reviews all the bugs from an outsourced partner. We are not only looking for quality of reporting but also for potential duplicates, missing information, or wrong priority or severity level. It might be harder for outsourced testers to get these aspects right, especially early in the project. While this approach ensures that we get excellent bug reports that will be taken seriously, it might require lots of internal resources to handle the load, especially when there is a significant volume of bugs.

Lastly, we can just allow external bug reports to be assigned directly to developers. This is a good approach after we have worked with the partner for some time, but early on, there might be quite a few irrelevant bugs. Developers will start ignoring them and then we can get into a situation in which there is an actual blocker bug that is ignored, as the general quality of bugs coming from the outsourced partners hasn't been great.

As we can see, each approach has its own benefits and risks. It's up to the internal **test lead** or **game producer** to decide which approach is the best for our team and our game.

Even with the best planning and organization, there is always the chance for something to go wrong. *Misunderstandings and mistakes* easily happen when we work with ever-changing products and environments and limited resources. What do we do in those cases?

Outsourced QA companies want you to be happy with their work. If you are happy with their performance, there is a good chance that you will hire them again and that means more business. While they try to do their best, sometimes, we do encounter problems. In these cases, it is important to understand first what happened and stop any actions that are either damaging or wrong. For example, if testers are on the wrong build or focusing on testing the wrong feature, we should stop testing immediately. After that, we should provide them with the correct build or instructions as soon as possible. In the meantime, it's important to understand why this happened. Was it a lack of communication? Or was it because a certain tool was broken? Our course-correcting action will depend on finding the root cause of the problem that occurred.

Occasionally, we encounter different types of problems. We are all people, and it might happen that our ways of working and communicating just clash. Sometimes, problems that occur might be of a more *personal* nature. In those cases, it's important to escalate the issue to your supervisor and not get involved in conflict. Be factual (take notes or screenshots of the conversation) and explain to your supervisor how this affected you and your work. In situations such as these, sometimes, a simple apology and clearing out communication will help, but in some rare cases, differences are just too much, and a working relationship simply doesn't work. In those cases, the outsourced tester will be removed from the project.

Measuring outsourcing effectiveness

Before we wrap up this part of the chapter, it is important to talk about different ways *to measure outsourced testers' effectiveness*. Very often, this is approached in a very simplified manner, where we only look at the speed of test execution and the number of bugs. Those metrics on their own though won't give us a complete picture of the quality of our outsourced testing partner. While these are important indicators of how work is done, there are other parameters we should consider when we work with outsourced testers:

- **Responsiveness** – Changes happen and sometimes we need to ask our partners to stop what they are doing and focus on something else instead. In those cases, the responsiveness of outsourced partners will be very important. The same goes for other crucial communication – if we need quick confirmation or answers to an inquiry, it should not take hours to get an answer. Waiting too long to respond makes the client feel insecure about testing partner work. Because when we look at these situations from the outsourced QA company view, your gaming studio client has no visibility in your work. They presume that you are doing your job, but the longer they don't hear from you, the more doubtful and concerned they'll become. Responsiveness is also an indicator that we have a relationship where outsourced partners listen to our requests and are less likely to make mistakes.

- **Troubleshooting** – We all make mistakes, but how we handle them makes a huge difference. If our testing partner owns their mistakes and doesn't try to hide them, but instead analyzes them and uses them as an opportunity to learn, this is a much better approach than hiding them and hoping they won't be noticed. An even worse scenario is that when a mistake is noticed, they try to shift the blame and avoid responsibility. If we notice a pattern of problematic behavior around any issues that arise, we are better off not working with that provider, as they become a liability to our project.

- **Skills** – Are the testers skilled enough to do their job with minimum guidance and without unnecessary mistakes? Are they familiar with the testing methodology and testing approaches? Do they understand the platform ecosystem and how comparable games in this genre work? Having reliable, professional, and experienced testers will make a big difference in how fast testing can be done with confidence.

- **Ease of working** – Even if we work with the most skilled people, if they are difficult to work with, it might not be the right match. Difficult to work means different things for different teams. In general, if your partner is not willing to adapt to your way of handling testing, bugs, and communication, it will be quite hard to work with them long-term. It might also require additional internal resources just to correct and adjust outsourced testing. In those cases, it will make more sense to focus only on internal testing and drop outsourced help, or alternatively, look for another partner.

We have learned how to organize outsourced testing and how to ensure that we work effectively with our outsourced partners. Next, it's time to learn more about careers in game QA and where they can take us.

A career in game QA

For a long time, QA was considered an *entry position* in the gaming industry. It was presumed that people starting in QA used it only as a stepping stone to move toward game design or production. That is still true in many cases. It is considered a "natural" transition to move from QA to production and then possibly further up the management path.

But with more modern ways of working and independent teams with flat hierarchies, the need to move up the ladder is not necessarily there. Embedded QA in a games team often has a range of responsibilities and duties that far exceed traditional QA. It often gets involved with game design and product management, and depending on the individual skills, with coding or art. That makes QA as a job far more exciting, and it can lead to better salaries and work appreciation.

But let's look at the traditional breakdown of QA roles. We can see it in *Figure 12.2*.

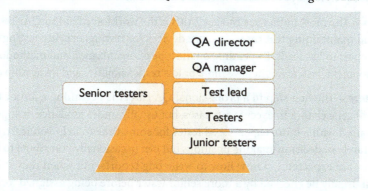

Figure 13.2 – Overview of traditional QA roles

We can see that in this type of hierarchy, we have the QA director at the top and then junior testers several steps below. Please note that not all gaming studios use the same nomenclatures. I've seen testers being called test analysts and test leads being called coordinators and many other titles. To better understand what job responds to which level, let's have a better look into what each title entails:

- **QA director** – The ultimate authority in the QA department. They usually work with the company's top management, own the QA budget, represent QA as a discipline at the highest level, and participate in strategy sessions and recruitment plans.

- **QA manager** – Usually leads either a particular section of QA (such as localization or automation, for example) or acts on a more operational level than the QA director. For example, they decide on testing tools; oversee QA processes; approve hires; approve QA discipline training plans, hardware purchases, and software purchases; participate in the decision-making process for testing partners; have HR responsibilities for test leads; and own the recruitment process.

- **Test leads** – Test leads have the responsibility of running QA for a specific game. They will own internal QA processes, advocate for the game team's needs, request tools and resources, troubleshoot issues, organize and distribute work, review internal and external testers' work, and may participate in the recruitment processes.

- **Senior testers** – These are on the same hierarchy level as test leads, but they don't have the same responsibilities. While test leads are primarily managers who sometimes test as well, senior testers are skilled experts with lots of experience, that focus mostly on improving and optimizing testing practices. They act as mentors and coaches for other team members, and they might have HR responsibilities as well. Sometimes, they also participate in the recruitment process, but always advise on it, as well as on other practical aspects of QA. They are usually highly respected team members, not only in QA, and their word and recommendation hold a lot of weight, even if they are not decision-makers themselves.

- **QA/Testers** – The most numerous category, this is the workforce behind QA. Testers focus on creating and maintaining test cases, prepare devices for testing, execute testing tasks, report bugs, and report to test leads. Depending on the type of organization and methodology used for game development, testers might have more or less responsibilities and ownership of their work.

- **Junior testers** – The first step in a professional QA career is becoming a junior tester. In this role, you will get a chance to execute test cases, but usually under guidance or supervision. You might be paired with a more experienced tester for some time to help you learn faster. Junior testers are rarely in decision-making positions but can occasionally contribute to test planning efforts. They are expected to know how to write bug reports, but when they start, their first reports will usually be checked by a more senior tester before being assigned for fixes.

In some larger studios, testing teams can also be organized by specialty. You might encounter jobs such as validation tester, functional tester, development tester, and others.

A career in QA can also lead to a career in other disciplines or careers in game management. Most often, a QA career in games will lead into production, as you can see in *Figure 12.3*:

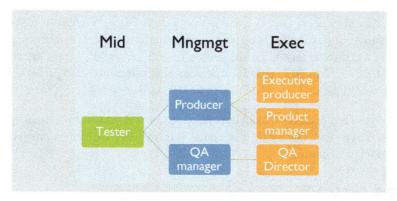

Figure 14.3 – Possible career trajectory in QA

In *Figure 12.3*, we can see that after starting your career in QA, besides going the QA management route, you can also have a path through production, which can potentially lead to studio management. It is considered a somewhat "natural" transition to production, as game producers' job is to oversee the overall development of the game. Working in QA, you become very familiar with all aspects of game development, product risks, and scheduling. That gives you a great foundation to continue working in production, and if interested, in product management.

We spoke at length about the possibilities and career pathways in QA, but how difficult is it to get a *job in QA teams* in the gaming industry? Usually, it's somewhat easier to get your first chance in the gaming industry through QA than through other disciplines. On average, there are more junior QA openings than those for associate producers, for example. The gaming industry is well known for preferring employing people with previous gaming experience, so making your first step can be challenging. Here are some of the things that might help you get your job in game QA:

- Any *previous testing experience*. If you don't have a background in QA, try joining beta testing groups, playtests, and so on. Even if it's not considered professional experience, it will help you get an insight into the world of professional QA and it will work to your benefit when applying for jobs.

- Attending *gaming conferences* and events. While some gaming conferences are for professionals only, there are many events that are friendly to people who are not in the industry yet. It's worth checking if you have a local **IGDA** chapter, as they might have open local events and open learning sources. Lots of jobs in the gaming industry are not advertised, and building your own network of industry contacts can help you.

- *Student groups* and work placement programs help. In some countries where the gaming industry is particularly strong, such as the UK and Finland, there are programs that help you get internships or work placements in gaming studios. Check locally whether such schemes exist in your area.

- Learn about games and *play games*. While it's not necessarily a pre-requisite for the job, it will help showcase your passion for the product, and your learning curve once you get a job will be shorter. I was literally asked to name my five favorite games when I was interviewed in the gaming industry first time! Even if I was already a very accomplished professional in QA, I probably wouldn't get that job if I couldn't name any games.

We have learned what kind of career we can have in game QA and got some practical tips on how to go about getting a job in game QA for the first time. Next, we will look into automated testing and how it affects manual game testing.

Automated testing

We can't finish this book without touching upon **automated testing**. This is a huge topic, and as such, it's not the focus of this book. It is important to mention it though and explain how it affects manual testing in game teams.

When we talk about testing automation in games, we split it into two different groups.

The first is **load testing** on our game's backend. Here, testing automation is a must, as we will simulate different types of player load on the backend. For example, we will test how our backend behaves when we have a sudden surge in downloads, an increased number of calls to the server, and similar scenarios. We are not only looking to find bugs or performance issues with servers. We are also looking for *breaking points*: under which load, our backend starts to break. Having this information helps us understand when we need to start to plan to enhance our backend capacity. For example, if we are planning to do a huge marketing campaign for our next update, which includes guild systems and three weekly events, you definitely want to know whether your servers are up for the test. Not only that we can expect more players than usual but they will also put more pressure on the servers due to the new features, which are very backend-dependent.

This type of testing is usually done by development teams themselves and QA doesn't participate in the process.

The second group is *client-side testing automation*. This type of testing is done by specialized automated testers. Here we test the functionality of the game; its UI, UX, and performance; and other player-facing parts of the game. In order to execute testing automation properly, we need to do the following steps:

1. Just like with manual testing, we would need to determine the *scope of testing*. What are we planning to test by using automation?

2. After that, *develop test scenarios* that will cover your targeted scope.

3. The next step is to write a **test automation script** based on the test scenarios. When we run the script, it will emulate player behavior.

4. When the test automation script is ready, we will need to *execute* it on a predetermined set of different devices and operating systems. Test automation scripts are executed mostly automatically, and we need minimum human involvement.

5. *Analyze* the results and assign bugs that need to be fixed.

6. *Verify* bug fixes and run regression tests.

As we can see, the process of testing very much follows similar steps that we would do when we do *manual testing*. The major difference here is that to prepare test automation scripts, the tester will need to have at least some coding skills. We use specialized **test automation tools** to run our test automation scripts, and depending on the tool, we will need to have scripting skills to be able to create automation scripts from test scenarios. Some of the most popular tools are **Appium**, **Unity Test Runner**, **Selenium**, and **Robot Framework**, but there are others too. Some studios who take automation as a crucial part of their QA efforts even develop their own proprietary automation tools.

One of the main challenges of test automation is the *maintenance* of the test scripts. Every time we change something in the game, we need to change the script accordingly; otherwise, we will get fake fails. It is important to prepare robust and well-thought-out scripts the first time around to ensure that they are easily maintained in the future.

We can see that in automation testing, we don't really need a human executing test cases. Does this mean that automation will replace human testers? The answer is no. We should not be afraid of automation taking away testing jobs or making testing positions obsolete. There are several reasons for that:

- *Time* – To do test automation effectively, it takes time to set up operations, hire the right profile of people, and put automation tools to use. It takes much more time to put automation to use compared to manual QA, which we can start much quicker. Also, test scripts need to be regularly updated to reflect changes made in the game.

- *Price* – To be able to start using test automation, the game studio needs to frontload most of the cost before testing can even start. Furthermore, test engineers who work with the automation tool usually have higher pay grades than manual game testers. That can make automation testing seem pricier than manual testing.

- *Maintenance* – Testing scripts need to be regularly maintained and not only does that take more time than maintaining manual test cases, but it can also be done only by test engineers.

- *Out-of-the-box thinking* – Even the best scripts are just that: scripts. They can't change their approach if they see something unusual or awkward. Scripts can never fully replace the heuristic approach of seasoned QA professionals.

- *Some things can only be tested by humans* – Is a new feature fun? How will a player feel when encountering a specific problem or story? Does the new IAP feel like a good value when we look at the gameplay? Those questions can only be answered by humans.

- Automation testing is a great tool that can replace humans doing very *repetitive* and dull tasks or tasks that would simply require *too many resources* to be executed efficiently. It also opens a whole new branch of QA at the intersection of testing and coding, which can provide exciting career opportunities.

Test automation can be a reliable ally in testing efforts, and I hope we will see it more in game QA in the future. This brings us to the last part of this book, where we will talk exactly about that: the future of game testing.

The future of game testing

We have arrived at the last part of this book. There is no better way to end this story than by providing the seeds for future ones. We will investigate the latest trends in technology, team organization, and the gaming industry in general, and analyze how they will affect the future of game testing.

These days, it looks like everyone is talking about **AI**. We can already use it for game art, marketing texts, game narration, and even coding. In the near future, we will probably see games out on the market that have been almost completely created by AI. With the growth of AI technology and the wide adoption of AI tools, we can expect that this is going to have a strong effect on *test automation* as well. The test automation of the future will become more sophisticated and be able to execute some of the tasks that right now, only humans can do. AI will be able to learn from testing experiences on its own and continuously improve its performance. With the advancements in AI tech, we might look into the future where test scripts will be fully developed by tools such as **ChatGPT**.

Will we be able to use AI in *manual testing* too? Probably yes. One obvious task would be writing the *test cases*. While humans would still need to prepare the test focus, with adequate prompts for AI, we will be able to create a wide range of tests very quickly.

Another interesting technology that is a big part of the gaming industry is **AR and VR**. Every year, both the hardware and software are getting better and providing more and more immersive, realistic experiences to gamers and other audiences. While we have seen the adoption of this technology among players already, especially with AR games where we have a couple of great successes such as the **Pokemon Go** game, VR hasn't reached as much popularity yet. Enthusiasts and early adopters have been excited about the possibilities of VR for some time, but we haven't seen large-scale adoption among players.

Testing VR has its own *challenges* – whether a limited pace of testing due to the time that a person can spend wearing a VR set without side effects, the physical space requirements for testing VR, or specific VR game mechanics that are experienced differently due to full immersion (teleporting, falling, bouncing, etc.). Due to the relatively small amount of released VR games compared to the games on traditional platforms, VR testing is still in its infancy. With wider adoption of the hardware among players, we can expect an increase in creative content too. That would also affect demand for *VR testing* and we will probably encounter it more frequently in the future.

Besides only technical advancements, we can also see that the *methodology* behind how we make games is changing. Traditional game development with huge teams, narrow specialization, and rigidly defined milestones is becoming rarer. Many European mobile gaming studios, especially in Scandinavia, utilize agile or hybrid agile methodology and base their work on relatively small game teams. Those teams have significant independence in how they run operations. That makes the decision-making process fast and more adaptive. This type of approach works great in live ops and gives a competitive advantage to the companies who utilize it: they can react much faster to the demands of players and iterate with less pressure and higher speed. Gaming studios from Scandinavia have been exceptionally successful using this approach. If you look at the companies such as King, Supercell, Small Giant Games, Mojang Studio, and Rovio, they have been incredibly successful. I believe that we will see more changes toward flat hierarchies and increased team independence in other parts of the world as well. Not only do we have proof of success that it works but it also goes hand in hand with working in live ops for years, even decades to come. This of course also affects how QA is done. We will see QA growing to become a more multidisciplinary role, where testers will actively participate in product and process-making decisions.

We will also see *live ops* becoming an even more predominant phase of work. The F2P business model is spreading on PC and consoles, and there is a demand for people who are familiar with live ops and its way of working. We spoke about testing in live ops at length in *Chapter 11 – Are You on the Right Version? Live Ops and QA*. As we have already seen several games in live ops for over a decade and counting, we can confidently predict that live ops will become a dominant phase of work.

With the post-pandemic adoption of a *working from home* model, we will also see changes in how we work internally and with external partners. As more and more game teams are now 100% remote by design, communication and way of working are adapting to accommodate remote setups. This brings a better understanding of the requirements of distant work that will spill over into working with external QA partners as well. We will be able to work more efficiently, with better mutual understanding and with already established, smooth lines of communication.

Working from home will also affect how we hire people. We will be able to hire talent from anywhere in the world, without worrying about the cost of relocation, the adaptation time, or whether an international employee will feel welcome enough in a new country. In return, this will make our teams more diverse and therefore more successful.

Working with remote employees from other countries comes with its own challenges. Even if our employee doesn't need to physically move, they need to get adjusted to different cultural norms, ways of working, and communicating. That can sometimes be more challenging to do only online. It can also be harder to form new friendships and find mentors and champions at work. It will be up to company management to take these new realities into account when making operative and strategic decisions, to ensure that they are building robust, *supportive, equitable, and inclusive* working environments.

Working from home brings another challenge as well – working with *devices*. Unfortunately, testing on consoles is practically impossible to do at home, and testers who work primarily on that platform will be required to spend at least some time in the office. Mobile testing brings another challenge, which is that we might want to test on several different devices and we can't expect that each tester has their own, large hardware portfolio. This will require occasional trips to the office to exchange your devices, but it doesn't require the tester to be there full-time. Studios will need to organize a very sturdy and reliable HW management system that provides instant visibility into devices' availability and traceability. We learned about the importance of testing hardware in *Chapter 5, It Must Be Hardware: Testing Hardware in Modern Game QA*.

The future might hold another type of solution for this problem though and that is **virtualization**. We already have some great results using **cloud-based** tools that simulate testing environments, including a range of devices, operating systems, and configurations. Using fully *virtual testing environments*, combined with advances in test automation, will allow us to do testing more efficiently and reliably than ever.

Summary

In this final chapter, my goal was to give you an overview of the parts of QA that, while already important, might become even more significant in the future of game development. First, we learned about *QA team* structures. We learned how to organize them and how to build them into a reliable, efficient, and indispensable part of game development. Next, we learned about how to work with *outsourced QA companies* as an extended part of our own testing teams. We investigated how QA is organized and what type of *QA career* trajectory you might have. We touched down on *testing automation*, an important part of QA, the significance of which is going to increase tremendously in the future. And lastly, we spoke about the *future of game QA* and trends that might shape our industry in the future.

I sincerely hope that you find this book insightful and that it helps you in your work. It has been an amazing experience putting decades of my QA experience into one concise and organized guide, which will hopefully serve you well for years to come.

Index

F

G

`Packtpub.com`

Subscribe to our online digital library for full access to over 7,000 books and videos, as well as industry leading tools to help you plan your personal development and advance your career. For more information, please visit our website.

Why subscribe?

- Spend less time learning and more time coding with practical eBooks and Videos from over 4,000 industry professionals

- Improve your learning with Skill Plans built especially for you

- Get a free eBook or video every month

- Fully searchable for easy access to vital information

- Copy and paste, print, and bookmark content

Did you know that Packt offers eBook versions of every book published, with PDF and ePub files available? You can upgrade to the eBook version at `packtpub.com` and as a print book customer, you are entitled to a discount on the eBook copy. Get in touch with us at `customercare@packtpub.com` for more details.

At `www.packtpub.com`, you can also read a collection of free technical articles, sign up for a range of free newsletters, and receive exclusive discounts and offers on Packt books and eBooks.

Other Books You May Enjoy

If you enjoyed this book, you may be interested in these other books by Packt:

API Testing and Development with Postman

Dave Westerveld

ISBN: 9781800569201

- Find out what is involved in effective API testing
- Use data-driven testing in Postman to create scalable API tests
- Understand what a well-designed API looks like
- Become well-versed with API terminology, including the different types of APIs
- Get to grips with performing functional and non-functional testing of an API
- Discover how to use industry standards such as OpenAPI and mocking in Postman

Software Test Design

Simon Amey

ISBN: 9781804612569

- Understand how to investigate new features using exploratory testing
- Discover how to write clear, detailed feature specifications
- Explore systematic test techniques such as equivalence partitioning
- Understand the strengths and weaknesses of black- and white-box testing
- Recognize the importance of security, usability, and maintainability testing
- Verify application resilience by running destructive tests
- Run load and stress tests to measure system performance

Packt is searching for authors like you

If you're interested in becoming an author for Packt, please visit authors.packtpub.com and apply today. We have worked with thousands of developers and tech professionals, just like you, to help them share their insight with the global tech community. You can make a general application, apply for a specific hot topic that we are recruiting an author for, or submit your own idea.

Hi!

I Nikolina Finska, author of *Modern Game Testing*, really hope you enjoyed reading this book and found it useful for increasing your productivity and efficiency in games QA.

If you found this book valuable, it would really help us (and other potential readers!) if you could leave an honest review on Amazon sharing your thoughts. Go to the link below to leave your review:

Go to the link below or scan the QR code to leave your review:

`https://packt.link/r/1803244402`

Your review will help me to understand what's worked well in this book, and what could be improved upon for future editions, so it really is appreciated.

Best Wishes,

Nikolina Finska

Download a free PDF copy of this book

Thanks for purchasing this book!

Do you like to read on the go but are unable to carry your print books everywhere?

Is your eBook purchase not compatible with the device of your choice?

Don't worry, now with every Packt book you get a DRM-free PDF version of that book at no cost.

Read anywhere, any place, on any device. Search, copy, and paste code from your favorite technical books directly into your application.

The perks don't stop there, you can get exclusive access to discounts, newsletters, and great free content in your inbox daily

Follow these simple steps to get the benefits:

1. Scan the QR code or visit the link below

https://packt.link/free-ebook/9781803244402

2. Submit your proof of purchase
3. That's it! We'll send your free PDF and other benefits to your email directly

www.ingramcontent.com/pod-product-compliance
Lightning Source LLC
Chambersburg PA
CBHW060549060326

40690CB00017B/3654